James Johonnot

A natural History reader for School and Home

James Johonnot

A natural History reader for School and Home

ISBN/EAN: 9783337025038

Printed in Europe, USA, Canada, Australia, Japan

Cover: Foto ©Paul-Georg Meister /pixelio.de

More available books at **www.hansebooks.com**

"The groves were God's first temples."

A

NATURAL HISTORY READER

FOR SCHOOL AND HOME.

COMPILED AND ARRANGED BY
JAMES JOHONNOT,
AUTHOR OF
"PRINCIPLES AND PRACTICE OF TEACHING," "A GEOGRAPHICAL READER,"
"COUNTRY SCHOOL-HOUSES," ETC.

NEW YORK:
D. APPLETON AND COMPANY,
1, 3, AND 5 BOND STREET.
1883.

PREFACE.

The philosophy which underlies the art of reading may be briefly stated. In the process of mental development objects are observed, and the perceptive faculties are thereby cultivated. In this way the mind comes in possession of the bundles of related ideas which we term thoughts. These thoughts seek expression, and in the endeavor to express, speech is cultivated. The form of speech is a matter of imitation. A thought is expressed by a sentence, and the child, in learning to speak, uses either fragmentary or complete sentences. When sentences are written, the process of obtaining and expressing the contained thought is reading.

Under the old system, which, happily, is now rapidly becoming obsolete, the mechanical pronunciation of the words of a sentence in their proper order was called reading; but most improperly so, as the apprehension and rendition of the thought, which constitute the very essence of reading, formed no part of the process. The means were mistaken for the end, and the true end was not reached. In consequence of this mistaken notion, reading exercises, in the schools where it prevailed, were dull, distasteful, and unprofitable to the pupil, and monotonous and unpleasant to the hearer.

The means employed in these schools were as vicious as the theory adopted. The pupil was required to pronounce words which he did not understand, a process not only negatively barren and wasteful, but positively evil, as it engendered the habit of regarding words as disassociated from ideas. Again, he was required to attempt to read that which was quite beyond his mental grasp, or which was so foreign to his experience that, understanding being hopeless, he ceased to try to understand, each successive lesson more widely separating language and thought. The diet of husks, unfortunately, was not confined to the prodigal who had wasted his substance in riotous living.

Under the later system, the truth is recognized that the object of all school exercises is to promote mental growth, to which end ideas and thoughts are indispensable. Words, like bank-notes, are regarded, not for their intrinsic, but for their representative value. In so far as they clearly reveal the gold of thought, they may be taken for genuine coin, but, failing in this, they are worthless counterfeits. The kinds of ideas and thoughts are also a matter of serious moment. In each stage of the mind's growth those only should be used that will command the attention by the interest excited, that will stimulate the reflective activities of the mind, and that will incite to further observation and investigation.

With these objects kept clearly in view, reading, and the general acquisition of language, become secondary, and not primary processes. They are incident to the general objects of instruction. Reading matter is selected upon the same principles as studies—that which will interest, stimulate, and incite. At every stage of growth it is such as will best serve the present purposes of the mind, and, at the same time, promote the next step in advance. The pupil reads because he is anxious to know. His progress is rapid because he is interested. His manner of reading is correct, because he understands the thought, and thought controls the expression.

PREFACE.

The present work has been prepared as a companion to the Geographical Reader, to furnish reading matter of this desirable kind. Natural History, whether considered in its relations to mental development or as furnishing the mind with useful knowledge, can scarcely be overestimated. It deals with life in all its varied forms, and from concrete facts it rises to a consideration of those principles upon which human existence depends. Its common facts are such as come under the cognizance of every pupil, giving a basis of personal observation which makes the treatment of every department intelligible and of the greatest interest.

In selecting the articles, an endeavor has been made to secure the interest which comes from variety. Care has been taken also that the statements shall be scientifically correct, though mere scientific abstracts have been avoided. The poetry and general literature of natural history have also received due consideration. In many of the articles it will be found that the statements are clear and precise, answering the demands of science, but at the same time are crisp and sparkling, stimulating the imagination, and giving that nameless charm which appeals to the sense of beauty and arouses the finer emotions and sentiments. In beauty of literary form, and in variety of literary expression, the work will be found fully equal to the reading books that have an unlimited scope of subjects.

Another point has been kept in view. The old primal animal instinct in man to hunt and kill; necessary in savage life, still persists, and is sufficiently strong without special cultivation. At present the lower animals need no longer be regarded as enemies to be destroyed, but rather as friends to be cultivated, or as curious objects to be studied. Most of the articles selected, it will be seen, are pervaded by a strong humanitarian sentiment, which is felt as an underlying principle, and is all the more effective from not being formally expressed. The tenderness and finer emotions which come from the study and care of creatures inferior to ourselves are elements essential to the highest character.

It will be seen that the general subjects follow each other in an ascending series, conforming in the main to scientific treatment. In each branch the topics relating to home life are first presented, to the end that instruction may be based upon experience, that greater interest may be excited, and that the pupils may be led to make careful and accurate observations—a most necessary step in true mental development. These details of life about home are followed by a series of sketches, which, while exciting present interest, have a tendency to produce a hunger that only large reading and reflection will satisfy.

PRINCETON, N. J., *March 3, 1883.*

INTRODUCTORY.

To TEACHERS.—Mechanical and unintelligent reading is the great reproach of our schools at the present time. In the process of instruction, whenever the attention is almost exclusively directed to words, such reading inevitably results. The cause of the evil at once suggests the remedy: make thought the primary object of attention, and regard words as important only as containing the thought. When the subject is intelligible and interesting, it takes full possession of the mind, compelling the proper delivery. Productive effort on the part of teachers will therefore be directed to the end that the pupils clearly understand what they read.

When pernicious habits are once formed, the task of the teacher is a difficult one. He must not only teach the right way, but he must eradicate the false notions, and correct the consequent false practice. Of one thing, however, he may be sure: one factor indispensable to his success is the use of reading matter which will interest the pupils and thereby arouse mental activity. The greater the interest, the more quickly will the best results be obtained.

The tones of reading usually should be those of common conversation. The general law in regard to reading is that it should be like speech under similar circumstances. When the pupil reads a sentence which he has used in expressing a thought, the delivery will conform to speech with great exactness. When reading the thoughts of others, this conformity will be in the exact ratio of the conformity of the thought and form of expression to the mental habits of the reader. In impassioned reading, the intense emotions need be indicated rather than acted, the reading becoming speech moderated. Giving full weight to all these modifying and exceptional circumstances, the statement that "reading is speaking from the book" is true.

In using this book, something more than mere reading should be accomplished. It can be made instrumental in development and training in many different ways.

First.—At the close of each lesson the subject-matter should be familiarly discussed in class, for the purpose of ascertaining whether all the points are understood, and of exciting a greater interest. Obscure points should be cleared up by the teacher.

Second.—If there are literary allusions, they should be briefly noticed and explained, just enough to awaken curiosity, but not enough to satisfy it. A great mistake may be made by dwelling too much upon mere accessories and side-issues: the perspective is destroyed, the attention is diverted from the main topic and dissipated on irrelevant details, and continuity of thought is broken up.

Third.—Immediately after the lesson, or the next day, the pupils may be called upon to state orally the main points. Care should be taken that thoughts, not language, are reproduced. In this way accuracy and fluency in speech are cultivated, and a test is made of both understanding and memory.

Fourth.—Each topic and sub-topic may be made the basis of a composition exercise. In the effort to reproduce, the use of capitals, punctuation, and all the mechanics of construction are mastered, and the practice tends to clearness and precision in expression. By both the oral and the written exercises another good results : the pupil incidentally and unconsciously learns the art of arrangement in thought. This art may afterward be supplemented by the science which gives the reason for the order.

Fifth.—When the topics relating to familiar things are read, let the pupil describe some similar thing, or relate some incident bearing upon the subject, which has come under his own observation or has been told him. Such an exercise associates the school-lesson with personal experience, and produces that functional activity of the mind which is one of the principal ends of education.

Sixth.—Special topics suggested by the lesson may be given out which will require careful observation, and sometimes investigation extending over considerable time. Notes of results may be made, and the whole topic finally presented in the form of a report. This trains the perception, and calls into active exercise all the higher faculties of the mind.

Seventh.—Attention may next be called to the literature of the subject, and books may be searched for further information upon this and kindred topics. Items in newspapers that touch upon the points under consideration may be clipped and preserved, and magazines laid under contribution. When the mind is awake and alert, it is surprising how much valuable matter may be found that would otherwise have escaped notice.

As resultants of such a course as is here pointed out, pupils will become eager to pursue studies of which they have obtained a smattering and in which they have taken so much interest, and education will be rescued from the reproach of being a mere process of cramming words, or unrelated facts, and will become in fact what it is in name—the means by which all the functions of the mind are aroused into healthful activity.

ACKNOWLEDGMENTS.—In many cases, for the purposes of this work, it has been found necessary to abridge articles as they originally appeared. Whenever the language of the author has been preserved throughout, or when slight changes, rendered necessary by the abridgment, only have been made, the author's name has been appended to the article. Where both language and arrangement have been changed to a considerable extent, or when the facts from different authorities have been made into a kind of mosaic, no names in justice could be given.

It will be seen that several of the articles are credited to the magazines from which they were selected; in these cases the names of the authors were not given. It must not be thought, however, that our indebtedness to the magazines is confined to the few selections directly ascribed to them. A large majority of the articles in the book first made their appearance in some one of the English or American periodicals. Some of these have been collected into books, forming an important part of the literature of the subject, and some of them still remain waifs and estrays. In this country the "Atlantic Monthly," "Harper's Magazine," and the "Century" have been the mediums through which much of the best literature of natural history has been given to the public.

Through the magazines, John Burroughs, at once scientific observer and poet, first became known; and we are sure that the few beautiful extracts which we have made from his essays will lead to a desire for a more general perusal of the volumes which he has published; and we are equally sure that taste thus developed will be in the direction of purity and refinement, both of thought and diction. The faculty of understanding the language of birds, which Oriental fancy in the Arabian tales ascribed to magical art, seems to have been inborn with Mr. Burroughs, and he, more than any other writer of the present day, may be considered the accredited interpreter of the feathered creation.

We are most largely indebted, however, to the "Popular Science Monthly" for the material used. Many of the articles credited to different authors first appeared in its pages, and the most valuable productions from the English magazines were given to the American public through its mediumship. That its articles are not confined to dry statements of scientific facts is sufficiently attested by the admirable sketches from the pen of Rev. Samuel Lockwood. This amateur observer has a poetic insight and a sense of humor which invests every subject with which he deals with a peculiar human interest.

While thus expressing our obligations, we would say that in return we have endeavored to put good matter to the best of uses—that of instructing and inspiring the young.

CONTENTS.

PART I.
HOME PLANTS AND THEIR WAYS.

	PAGE
Prelude to the Forest Hymn................................*Bryant.*	1
The Pride of New England.....................*Atlantic Monthly.*	2
How Plants Travel........................*M. Schele De Vere.*	6
Twining Plants..............................*Francis Darwin.*	11
Hook-Climbers..............................*Francis Darwin.*	15
The Hospitality of Plants...................*M. Schele De Vere.*	25
The Rhodora...................................*Emerson.*	30

PART II.
STRANGE PLANTS AND THEIR WAYS.

The Builder's Tree of China....................*World of Wonders.*	31
The Scholar's Plant of Egypt..................*World of Wonders.*	32
A Migratory Rose..........................*Chambers's Journal.*	35
Refreshment-Trees..	39
The Monarch of African Forests...................*Figuier.*	42
The Sacred Tree of India......................................	45
The Eucalyptus..	48
The Sensitive-Plant ....*Shelley.*	52

PART III.
LOW LIFE IN THE SEA.

Animated Jellies........................*World of Wonders.*	54
Flowers of the Sea....................*Rev. Samuel Lockwood.*	57

	PAGE
Stars of the Sea...	62
Builders in the Ocean..	66
Corals, and How they are Studied..........*Mrs. Elizabeth C. Agassiz.*	70
The Coral Grove.....................................*Percival.*	76
Crabs and their Ways..........................*Rev. Samuel Lockwood.*	78
Fiddlers upon the Shore........................*Rev. Samuel Lockwood.*	81
Sea-Hermits and their Homes....................*Rev. Samuel Lockwood.*	83

PART IV.
HIGHER LIFE IN WATERS.

The Devil-Fish and his Kin......................................	86
Shooting and Angling Fishes.........................*Francis Francis.*	91
Hunting-Fishes....................................*Francis Francis.*	94
Fishes Armed with Lightning......................................	97

PART V.
PIGMY WORKERS AND BUILDERS.

Ants: their Homes and Habits....................................	101
The Aphides and their Keepers....................*Rev. J. G. Wood.*	105
Spinners of the Mulberry-Trees...................................	109
Honey-Gatherers...	113
The Humblebee...*Emerson.*	119

PART VI.
QUEER LITTLE FOLKS.

The Pit-Digger and its Victims....................*T. W. Higginson.*	122
How Mosquitoes Manage..................................*Réaumur.*	123
Plant-Eating and Omnivorous Ants.................................	128
Carnivorous and Agricultural Ants.................................	132
The Praying Mantis..............................*Science Monthly.*	137
The Katydid...*Holmes.*	140

PART VII.
CURIOUS DWELLERS OF SWAMP AND FOREST.

The Monarch of the Swamp..	142
Capture of a Cayman.............................*Charles Waterton.*	148

CONTENTS.

		PAGE
Tussle with a Constrictor	*Charles Waterton.*	152
Chameleons; their Habits and Color-Changes	*Science Monthly.*	157
The Chameleon	*Merrick.*	162

PART VIII.
OUR FOREST CHORISTERS.

Songsters of the Garden	*James Russell Lowell.*	164
The Song of Birds	*J. Elliot Cabot.*	172
Life and Song in the Woods	*John Burroughs.*	177
Bird Life and Motion	*Atlantic Monthly.*	183
Birds in Autumn	*Atlantic Monthly.*	188
Robert of Lincoln	*Bryant.*	190
The Mocking-Bird	*Alexander Wilson.*	194
The Persevering Songster	*Boston Traveler, 1851.*	199
Bird-Notes	*White's Selborne.*	201
Ode to the Sky-lark	*Shelley.*	204

PART IX.
OTHER NEIGHBORS IN THE TREES.

Homes in the Woods	*John Burroughs.*	207
Humming-Birds	*James H. Partridge.*	211
My Aërial Visitor	*Atlantic Monthly.*	215
Rare and Beautiful Nests	*John Burroughs.*	218
Bird-Ways	*Atlantic Monthly.*	220
The Bank-Swallow	*Ernest Ingersoll.*	225
Jays and their Mission	*Jared P. Kirtland.*	229
Summary Justice	*Chambers's Journal.*	233
The Bird of Night	*Rev. Samuel Lockwood.*	236
The Owl-Critic	*James T. Fields.*	240

PART X.
STRANGE BIRDS AND THEIR WAYS.

The Flamingo		244
Birds-of-Paradise	*James H. Partridge.*	247
Talking Birds and their Ways	*N. S. Dodge.*	252
The Apteryx		257

CONTENTS.

		PAGE
The Stork	Hermann Masius.	260
Three Views of the Eagle		265

PART XI.

OUR FOUR-FOOTED COMPANIONS.

The Pet of the Household	J. W. De Forest.	271
Our Canine Servants	Chambers's Journal.	275
Conscience in Animals	G. J. Romanes.	283
Puss with a Mission	J. W. De Forest.	288
Canine Justice	Chambers's Journal.	289
Helping a Friend	Chambers's Journal.	292
Pierrot the Faithful	Arsene Houssaye.	293
Emotional Expression	Charles Darwin.	298
To Flush, my Dog	Mrs. Browning.	303

PART XII.

OUR FOUR-FOOTED NEIGHBORS.

How Rats Manage	T. W. Higginson.	306
The Chipmunk at Home	Charles C. Abbott.	310
An Excavator	John Burroughs.	314
Forest Engineers	T. W. Higginson.	316
Elephants, and how they are Caught	T. W. Higginson.	321
The Force of Instinct	Miss Cooper.	327
Curious Friendships	Chambers's Journal.	330
The Lion and the Spaniel	Henry Brooke.	336
Home Life of Scottish Deer	Charles Edward Stuart.	338
Deer-Stalking in the Scottish Highlands	Charles Edward Stuart.	343

PART XIII.

STRANGE ANIMALS AND THEIR WAYS.

Musical Mice	Rev. Samuel Lockwood.	352
Bats and their Habits	Prof. Burt G. Wilder.	355
The Lemming and its Migrations	Temple Bar.	358
The Coati Mondi	Rev. Samuel Lockwood.	362
Jemmy	Frank Buckland.	369

CONTENTS.

The Aard-vark..................*From the French of Oustalet.*	374
The Ornithorhynchus...	377
Grizzly ....*Bret Harte.*	380

PART XIV.
FOUR-HANDED FOLKS.

House-Pets in Trinidad......................*Charles Kingsley.*	381
The Living Bridge ....*Adventures in the Tropics.*	384
Jacko ....*Frank Buckland.*	387

PART XV.
ADVENTURES AND INCIDENTS.

Our Hunting-Lodge and Neighbors.........*Charles Edward Stuart.*	394
The Sloth..................................*Charles Waterton.*	401
Illustrative Stories....	407

LIST OF ILLUSTRATIONS.

	PAGE
"The Groves were God's first Temples." (*Frontispiece.*)	
Clasping Leaves	17
Tendril Hooks	18
Tendril Coil	21
Coil and Disk	22
The Papyrus	34
The Rose of Jericho	36
The Traveler's Tree	40
The Baobab-Tree	43
The Banyan-Tree	46
The Medusa	55
Sea-Anemones	59
Upper and Under View of Star-Fish	63
Serpent Star-Fish	65
Coral Madrepore	67
An Atoll	69
Coral Porite	73
Edible Crab	79
Fiddler-Crab	82
Hermit-Crab	84
The Octopus	87
Octopus Running	88
The Angler-Fish	92
The Torpedo	99

LIST OF ILLUSTRATIONS.

	PAGE
The Silk-Worm	111
Mosquitoes	125
Warrior Termites	130
The Praying Mantis	138
Alligators in Florida Swamp	144
The Nile Crocodile	146
The Chameleon	158
A Forest Warbler	179
Bobolink	192
Humming-Birds	216
Bank-Swallows and their Nests	226
A Group of Owls	238
Flamingo and Nest	245
Bird of Paradise	249
The Apteryx	258
The Stork	261
The Eagle	266
Pierrot the Faithful	295
A Fierce Dog	299
An Affectionate Dog	300
A Cat, Savage, and ready to Fight	302
An Affectionate Cat	303
American Chipmunk	311
Beaver Dam	317
The Stag	349
The Lemming, or Norway Rat	359
Coati-Mondi	364
Coati-Mondi Asleep	365
The Suricate (Jemmy)	370
The Aard-Vark	376
The Ornithorhynchus	378

NATURAL HISTORY READER.

PART I.

HOME PLANTS AND THEIR WAYS.

PRELUDE TO "A FOREST HYMN."

1. THE groves were God's first temples. Ere man learned
To hew the shaft, and lay the architrave,
And spread the roof above them,—ere he framed
The lofty vault, to gather and roll back
The sound of anthems; in the darkling wood,
Amid the cool and silence, he knelt down,
And offered to the Mightiest solemn thanks
And supplication.

2.   For his simple heart
Might not resist the sacred influences
Which, from the stilly twilight of the place,
And from the gray old trunks that high in heaven
Mingled their mossy boughs, and from the sound
Of the invisible breath that swayed at once
All their green tops, stole over him, and bowed
His spirit with the thought of boundless power
And inaccessible majesty.

3.   Ah, why
Should we, in the world's riper years, neglect
God's ancient sanctuaries, and adore
Only among the crowd, and under roofs
That our frail hands have raised ?   Let me, at least,
Here, in the shadow of this aged wood,
Offer one hymn—thrice happy, if it find
Acceptance in His ear.

Bryant.

THE PRIDE OF NEW ENGLAND.

1. ABOVE all the trees of the New World, the elm deserves to be considered the sovereign tree of New England. It is abundant both in field and forest, and forms the most remarkable feature in our cleared and cultivated grounds. Though the elm is found in almost all parts of the country, in no other is it so conspicuous as in the Northeastern States, where, from the earliest settlement of the country, it has been planted as a shade-tree, and has been valued as an ornament above the proudest importations from a foreign clime. It is the most remarkable of the drooping trees except the willow, which it surpasses in stateliness and in the variety of its growth.

2. When I look upon a noble elm, though I feel no disposition to condemn the studies of those who examine its flowers and fruit with the scrutinizing eye of science, or the calculations of those who consider only its practical use, it is to me an object of pleasing veneration. I look upon it as the embodiment of some benign intention of Providence, who has adapted it in numerous ways to the wants of his creatures. While admiring its grace and majesty, I think of the great amount of human happiness and of comfort to the inferior animals of which it has been the blessed in-

strument. How many a happy assemblage of children and young persons has been, during the past century, repeatedly gathered under its shade in the sultry noons of summer! How many a young May-Queen has been crowned under its roof, when the greensward was just daisied with the early flowers of spring! And how many a weary traveler has rested from his journey in its benevolent shade, and, from a state of weariness and vexation, when o'erspent by heat and length of way, has subsided into one of quiet thankfulness and content!

3. Though the elm has never been consecrated by the Muse, or dignified by making a figure in the paintings of the old masters, the native inhabitant of New England associates its varied forms with all that is delightful in the scenery of his own land, or memorable in its history. He has beheld many a noble avenue formed of elms, when standing in rows in the village, or by the rustic road-side. He has seen them extending their broad and benevolent arms as a protection over many a spacious old farm-house and many an humble cottage, and equally harmonizing with all. They meet his sight in the public grounds of the city, with their ample shade and flowing spray, inviting him to linger under their pleasant umbrage in summer; and in winter he has beheld them among the rude hills and mountains, like spectral figures keeping sentry among their passes, and, on the waking of the year, suddenly transformed into towers of luxuriant verdure and beauty. Every year of his life has he seen the beautiful hang-bird weave his pensile habitation upon the long and flexible branches of the elm, secure from the reach of every living creature. From its vast dome of interwoven branches and foliage he has listened to the songs of the earliest and latest birds; and under its shelter he has witnessed many a merry-making assemblage of children, employed in the sportive games of summer.

4. To a native of New England, therefore, the elm has a value more nearly approaching that of sacredness than any other tree. Setting aside the pleasure derived from it as an object of visual beauty, it is intimately associated with the familiar scenes of home and the events of his early life. In my own mind it is pleasingly allied with those old dwelling-houses which were built in the early part of the last century, and form one of the marked features of New England home architecture during that period. They are known by their broad and ample, but low-studded rooms, their numerous windows with small panes, their single chimney in the center of the roof, that sloped down to the lower story in the back part, and, in their general unpretending appearance, reminding one vividly of that simplicity of life which characterized our people before the revolution. Their very homeliness is delightful, by leaving the imagination free to dwell upon their pleasing suggestions. Not many of these charming old houses are now extant; but whenever we see one, we are almost sure to find it accompanied by its elm, standing upon the green open space that slopes up to it in front, and waving its long branches in melancholy grandeur over the venerable habitation which it seems to have taken under its protection, while it droops with sorrow over the infirmities of its old companion of a century.

5. The elm is remarkable for the variety of forms which it assumes in different situations. Often it has a drooping spray only when it has attained a large size; but it almost invariably becomes subdivided into several equal branches, diverging from a common center, at a considerable elevation from the ground. One of these forms is that of a vase, the base being represented by the roots of the tree that project above the soil and join the trunk, the middle by the lower part of the principal branches, as they swell out with a graceful curve, then gradually di-

verge, until they bend downward and form the lip of the vase by their circle of terminal branches. Another of its forms is that of a vast dome, as represented by those trees that send up a single shaft to the height of twenty feet or more, and then extend their branches at a wide divergency, and to a great length. The elms which are remarkable for their drooping character are usually of this shape.

6. At other times the elm assumes the shape of a plume, presenting a singularly fantastical appearance. It rises upward, with an undivided shaft, to the height of fifty feet or more, without a limb, and bending over with a gradual curve from about the middle of its height to its summit, which is sometimes divided into two or three terminal branches. The whole is covered, from its roots to its summit, with a fringe of vine-like twigs, extremely slender, twisted, and irregular, and resembling a parasitic growth. Sometimes it is subdivided at the usual height into three or four long branches, which are wreathed in the same manner, and form a compound plume.

7. Unlike other trees that send up a single undivided shaft, the elm, when growing in the forest, as well as in the open plain, becomes subdivided into several slightly divergent branches, running up almost perpendicularly until they reach the level of the tree-tops, when they suddenly spread themselves out, and the tree exhibits the parasol shape more nearly even than the palm. When one of these forest elms is left by the woodman, and is seen standing alone in the clearing, it presents to our sight one of the most graceful and beautiful of all arborescent forms.

Atlantic Monthly.

HOW PLANTS TRAVEL.

1. Plants have both life and motion; we dare not as yet say whether it be the effect of a mere dream, of a mechanical pressure from without, or of instinctive life within. For what do we as yet know of the simplest functions of the inner life of plants? Who has not, however, observed how the pale sap courses through the colossal stems of gigantic trees and the delicate veins of a frail leaf, as rapidly and marvelously as through the body of man? Take a microscope, and you will see the plant full of life and motion. All its minute cells are filled with countless little currents, now rotary and now up and down, often even apparently lawless, but always distinctly marked by tiny grains which are seen to turn in them or to rise without ceasing.

2. But plants move not only where they stand, they travel also. They migrate from land to land, sometimes slowly, inch by inch, then again on the wings of the storm. Botanists tell us of actual migrations of plants, and a successive extension of the domain of particular floras, just as we speak of the migration of idioms and races. Individual plants, however, travel only as man ought to travel, when they are young. If they have once found a home, they settle quietly down, grow, blossom, and bear fruit. Therefore it is that plants travel only in the seed. For this purpose, seeds possess often special organs for a long journey through the air.

3. Sometimes they are put, like small bomb-shells, into little mortars, and fired off with great precision. Thus arise the well-known emerald rings on our greenswards, and on the vast prairies of the West, which some ascribe to electricity, while the poet loves to see in them traces of the moonlight revels of fairies. The truth is scarcely less po-

etical. A small circular fungus squats down on a nice bit of turf; it prospers, and fills with ripening seed; when it matures, it discharges the tiny balls already mentioned in a circle all around, and then sinks quietly in the ground and dies. Another season, and its place is marked by an abundance of luxuriant grass, feeding upon its remains, while around it a whole ring of young fungi have begun to flourish. They die in their turn, and so the circle goes on enlarging and enlarging, shifting rapidly, because the fungi exhaust the soil soon of all matter necessary for their growth, and closely followed by the rich grass that fills up their place and prevents them from ever retracing their steps.

4. A similar irritability enables other plants also to scatter their seeds far and near, by means of springs bent back, until a breath of wind, a falling leaf, or the wing of an insect, causes them to rebound, and thus to send the pollen with which they are loaded often to a great distance. The so-called touch-me-not balsam scatters its ripe seeds, by such a contrivance, in all directions, and the squirting cucumber is furnished, for the same purpose, with a complete fire-engine. Some of the geraniums, also, of our greenhouses have their fruit-vessels so curiously constructed that the mere contact with another object, and frequently the heat of the sun alone, suffices to detach the carpels, one by one, with a snapping sound, and so suddenly as to cause a considerable jerk, which sends the seeds far away.

5. Other fruit-vessels, again, have, as is well known, contrivances the most curious and ingenious by which they press every living thing that comes near them into their service, and make it convey them whithersoever they please. Everybody is familiar with the bearded varieties of wheat and other grain; they are provided with the little hooks which they cunningly insert into the wool or hair of grazing cattle, and thus they are carried about until they

find a pleasant place for their future home. Some, who do not like to obtain services thus by hook and crook, succeed by pretended friendship, sticking closely to their self-chosen companions. They cover their little seeds with a most adhesive glue, and when the busy bee comes to gather honey from their sweet blossoms, which they jauntily hang out to catch the unwary insect, the seeds adhere to its body, and travel thus on four fine wings through the wide, wide world. Bee-fanciers know very well the common disease of their sweet friends, when so much pollen adheres to their head that they can not fly, and most miserably perish, one by one, under the heavy burden which these innocent-looking plants have compelled them to carry.

6. We have but little knowledge as yet of the activity of life in the vegetable world, and of its momentous influence on the welfare of our own race. Few only know that the gall-fly of Asia Minor decides on the existence of ten thousands of human beings. As our clippers and steamers carry the produce of the land from continent to continent, so these tiny sailors of the air perform, under the direction of Divine Providence, the important duty of carrying pollen, or fertilizing dust, from fig-tree to fig-tree. Without pollen there come no figs; and, consequently, on their activity and number depend the productiveness of these trees; they therefore regulate, in fact, the extensive and profitable fig trade of Smyrna.

7. When neither quadruped nor insect can be coaxed or forced to transport the young seeds that wish to see the world, they sometimes launch forth on their own account, and trust to a gentle breeze or a light current of air rising from the heated surface of the earth. It is true, nature has given them wings to fly with, such as man never yet was skillful enough to devise for his own use. The maple —our maple, I mean—has genuine little wings with which it flies merrily about in its early days; others, like the dan-

delion and the anemone, have light downy appendages, or little feathery tufts and crowns, by which they are floated along on the lightest breath of air, and enjoy, to their hearts' content, long autumnal wanderings. These airy appendages are marvelously well adapted for the special purpose of each plant—some but just large enough to waft the tiny grain up the height of a mole-hill, others strong enough to carry the seed of the cedar from the low valley to the summit of Mount Lebanon.

8. The proudest princes of the vegetable kingdom often depend for their continuance on these little feathery tufts, which but few observers are apt to notice. A recent writer tells us that, a few years ago, the only palm-tree the city of Paris could then boast of suddenly bore fruit. Botanists were at a loss how to explain the apparent miracle, and skeptics began to sneer, and declared that the laws of nature had failed. An advertisement appeared in the papers, inquiring for the unknown mate of the solitary tree. And behold, in an obscure court-yard away off, there had lived, unknown and unnoticed, another small palm; it also had blossomed apparently alone, and in vain—but a gentle breeze had come, and carried its flower-dust to its distant companion, and the first palm-fruit ever seen in France was the result of this silent mediation.

9. Reckless wanderers, also, there are among the plants, who waste their substance, and wildly rove about the world. The rose of Jericho, and a club-moss of Peru, are such erratic idlers that wander from land to land. When they have blossomed and borne fruit, and when the dry season comes, they wither, fold their leaves together, and draw up their roots, so as to form a light, little ball. In this form they are driven hither and thither on the wings of the wind, rolling along the plains in spirit-like dance, now whirling in great circles about, now caught by an eddy and rising suddenly high into the air. It is not until they reach a moist

place that they care to rest awhile, but then they settle down at once, send down their roots, unfold their leaves, assume a bright green, and become quiet, useful citizens in their own great kingdom of plants.

10. Seeds that have not learned to fly with their own or other people's wings, it seems are taught to swim. Trees and bushes which bear nuts love low grounds and river-banks. Why? Because their fruit is shaped like a small boat, and the rivulet, playing with its tiny ripples over silver sands, as well as the broad wave of the Pacific, carry their seed alike, safely and swiftly, to new homes. Rivers float down the fruits of mountain regions into deep valleys and to far-off coasts, and the Gulf Stream of our Atlantic carries annually the rich products of the torrid zone of America to the distant shores of Iceland and Norway. Seeds of plants growing in Jamaica and Cuba have been gathered in the quiet coves of the Hebrides.

11. But we need not go to far-off countries to see plants wandering about in the world: our own gardens afford us, though on a smaller scale, many an instance of the recklessness of those very plants that are so much commiserated because they can not move about and choose their own home. Every casual observer even knows that many bulbs, like those of crocus, tulips, or narcissus, rise or sink by forming new bulbs above or below, until they have reached the proper depth of soil which best suits their constitution—or perhaps their fancy. Some orchids have a regular locomotion: the old root dies, the new one forms invariably in one and the same direction, and thus they proceed onward year after year, though at a very modest, stage-coach rate. Strawberries, on the contrary, put on seven-league boots, and often escape from the rich man's garden to refresh the weary traveler by the wayside. Raspberries, again, mine their way stealthily under ground by a subterranean, mole-like process; blind but not unguided, for

they are sure to turn up in the brightest, sunniest spot they could have chosen had their eyes been wide open and their proceedings above ground.

M. Schele de Vere.

TWINING PLANTS.

1. CLIMBING plants are, first of all, divided roughly into those which twine and those which do not twine; twiners are represented by the hop and the honeysuckle, and all those plants which climb up a stick by winding spirally round it. Those which are not twiners—that is, which do not wind spirally round a stick—are such as support themselves by seizing hold of any neighboring object with various kinds of grasping organs; these may be simple hooks, or adhering roots, or they may be elaborate and sensitive tendrils, which seize hold of a stick with a rapidity more like the action of an animal than of a plant. I wish now to insist on the importance of distinguishing between these two methods of climbing, in one of which the plant ascends a support by traveling spirally round it; in the other, fixes on to the support by seizing it at one place, and continuing to seize it higher and higher up as its stem increases in length.

2. I have heard the curator of a foreign botanic garden bitterly complain of his gardeners that they never could learn the difference between these two classes of climbing plants, and that they would only give a few bare sticks to some tendril-bearing plant, expecting it to twine up them like a hop, while the plant really wanted a twiggy branch, up which it might creep, seizing a twig with each of its delicate tendrils, as it climbed higher and higher. These two kinds of climbers—twiners and non-twiners—may be seen growing up their appropriate supports in any kitchen-

garden, where the scarlet-runners twine spirally up tall sticks, while the peas clamber up the bushy branches stuck in rows in the ground.

3. A hop-plant will supply a good example of the mode of growth of true twining plants. Let us imagine that we have a young hop-plant growing in a pot; we will suppose that it has no stick to twine up, and that its pot stands in some open place where there are no other plants to interfere with it. A long, thin shoot will grow out, and, not being strong enough to support itself in the upright position, will bend over to one side. So far we have not discovered anything remarkable about our hop; it has sent out a straggling shoot, which has behaved as might be expected, by falling over to one side. But now, if we watch the hop-plant closely, a very remarkable thing will be seen to take place.

4. Supposing that we have noticed the shoot, when it began to bend over, pointed toward the window—say a north window—and that, when we next look at it after some hours, it points into the room, that is to say, south, and again north after another interval, we shall have discovered the curious fact that the hop-plant has a certain power of movement by which its shoot may sometimes point in one direction, sometimes in another. But this is only half the phenomenon, and, if we examine closely, we shall find that the movement is *constant and regular*, the stem first pointing north, then east, then south, then west, in regular succession, so that its tip is constantly traveling round and round like the hand of a watch, making on an average, in warm August weather, one revolution in two hours. Here, then, is a most curious power possessed by the shoots of twining plants, which is worth inquiring further into, both as regards the way in which the movement is produced, and as to how it can be of any service to the plant.

5. Questions are often asked in gardening periodicals as to how hops or other climbing plants always manage to grow precisely in the direction in which they will find a support. This fact has surprised many observers, who have supposed that climbing plants have some occult sense by which they discover the whereabouts of the stick up which they subsequently climb. But there is in reality no kind of mystery in the matter: the growing shoot simply goes swinging round till it meets with a stick, and then it climbs up it. Now, a revolving shoot may be more than two feet long, so that it might be detained in its swinging-round movements by a stick fixed into the ground at a distance of nearly two feet. There would then be a straight bit of stem leading from the roots of the plant in a straight line to the stick up which it twines, so that an observer who knew nothing of the swinging-round movement might be pardoned for supposing that the plant had in some way perceived the stick and grown straight at it. This same power of swinging round slowly comes into play in the very act of climbing up a stick.

6. Suppose I take a rope and swing it round my head: that may be taken to represent the revolving of the young hop-shoot. If, now, I allow it to strike against a rod, the end of the rope which projects beyond the rod curls freely round it in a spiral. And this may be taken as a rough representation of what a climbing plant does when it meets a stick placed in its way. That is to say, the part of the shoot which projects beyond the stick continues to curl inward till it comes against the stick; and, as growth goes on, the piece of stem which is projecting is, of course, all the while getting longer and longer; and, as it is continually trying to keep up the swinging-round movement, it manages to curl round the stick. But there is a difference between the rope and the plant in this—that the rope curls round the stick at the same level as that at which it is

swung, so that, if it moves round in a horizontal plane at a uniform height above ground, it will curl round the stick at that level, and thus will not climb *up* the stick it strikes against. But the climbing plant, although it may swing round, when searching for a stick, at a fairly uniform level, yet, when it curls round a stick, does not retain a uniform distance from the ground, but by winding round like a corkscrew it gets higher and higher at each turn.

7. As plants have no muscles, all their movements are produced by unequal growth; that is, by one half of an organ growing in length quicker than the opposite half. Now, the difference between the growth of a twining plant which bends over to one side and an ordinary plant which grows straight up in the air lies in this, that in the upright shoot the growth is nearly equal on all sides at once, whereas the twining plant is always growing much quicker on one side than the other.

8. It may be shown by means of a simple model how unequal growth can be converted into revolving movement. The stem of a young hop is represented by a flexible rod, of which the lower end is fixed, the upper one being free to move. At first the rod is supposed to be growing vertically upward, but when it begins to twine one side begins to grow quicker than any of the others: suppose the right side to do so, the result will be that the rod will bend over toward the left side. Now, let the region of quickest growth change, and let the left side begin to grow quicker than all the others, then the rod will be forced to bend back over to the other side. Thus, by an alternation of growth, the rod will bend backward and forward from right to left.

9. But now imagine that the growth of the rod on the sides nearest to and farthest from us enters into the combination, and that, after the right side has been growing quickest for a time, the far side takes it up, then the rod will not bend straight back toward the right, as it did be-

fore, but will bend to the near side. Now the old movement, caused by the left side growing quickest, will come in again, to be followed by the near side growing quickest. Thus, by a regular succession of growth on all the sides, one after another, the swinging-round movement is produced, and by a continuation of this action, as I have explained, the twining movement is produced.

10. I have spoken as if the question of how plants twine were a completely solved problem, and in a certain sense it is so. I think that the explanation which I have given will remain as the fundamental statement of the case. But there is still much to be made out. We do not in the least know why every single hop-plant in a field twines like a left-handed screw, while every single plant in a row of beans twines the other way; nor why in some rare instances a species is divided, like the human race, into right- and left-handed individuals, some twining like a left-handed, others like a right-handed screw. Or, again, why some very few plants will twine half-way up a stick in one direction, and then reverse the spiral and wind the other way. Nor, though we know that in all these plants the twining is caused by the change in the region of quickest growth, have we any idea what causes this change of growth.

Francis Darwin.

HOOK-CLIMBERS.

1. THE common bramble climbs or scrambles up through thick underwood, being assisted by the recurved spines which allow the rapidly growing shoot to creep upward as it lengthens, but prevent it from slipping backward again; the common goose-grass (*Galium*) also climbs in this way, sticking like a burr to the side of a hedge-row up which it climbs. Most country boys will remember having taken

advantage of this burr-like quality of *Galium* in making sham birds' nests, the prickly stems adhering together in the desired form. Such plants as the bramble or *Galium* exhibit none of the swinging-round movement of climbers: they simply grow straight on, trusting to their hooks to retain the position gained.

2. In some species of clematis we find a mechanism which reminds one of a simple hook-climber, but is in reality a much better arrangement. The young leaves projecting outward and slightly backward from the stem may remind us of the hooked spines of a bramble, and, like them, easily catch on neighboring objects, and support the trailing stem. Or the leaf of a species of clematis may serve as an example of a leaf acting like a hook. The main stalk of the leaf is bent angularly downward at the points where each successive pair of leaflets is attached, and the leaflet at the end of the leaf is bent down at right angles, and thus forms a grappling apparatus.

3. The clematis does not, like the bramble, trust to mere growth to thrust itself among tangled bushes, but possesses the same powers of revolving in search of a support which simple or true twining plants possess. Indeed, many species of clematis are actually twining plants, and can wind spirally up a stick placed in their way. And the same revolving movement which enables them thus to wind spirally also helps them to search for some holding-place for their hook- or grapple-like leaves, and in many species the search is carried on by the leaves swinging round, quite independently of the revolving movement of the stem on which they are borne.

4. If a leaf of a clematis succeed by any means in hooking on to a neighboring object, the special characteristic of leaf-climbing plants comes into play. The stalk of the leaf curls strongly over toward the object touching it, and clasps it firmly. It is obvious how great is the advantage thus

gained over a mere hook. A leaf might be made to catch on to a neighboring twig by its bent stalk in such a way that, although it managed to stay where it was, it could

Clasping Leaves.

bear none of the weight of the plant, and would be liable to be displaced by a strong wind or other disturbance. But when the stalk of the leaf has curled round the twig, nothing could displace it, and it could take its share in the work of sustaining the plant.

5. The genus *Tropæolum*, whose cultivated species are often called nasturtiums, also consists of leaf-climbing plants, which climb like clematis by grasping neighboring objects with their leaf-stalks. In some species we find climbing organs developed, which can not logically be distinguished from tendrils; they consist of little filaments, not green like a leaf, but colored like the stem. Their tips are a little flattened and furrowed, but never develop into leaves; and these filaments are sensitive to a touch, and bend toward a touching object, which they clasp securely. Filaments of this kind are borne by the young plant, but it subsequently produces filaments with slightly

enlarged ends, then with rudimentary or dwarfed leaves, and finally with full-sized leaves; when these are developed they clasp with their leaf-stalks, and then the first-formed filaments wither and die off; thus the plant, which in its youth was a tendril-climber, gradually develops into a true leaf-climber. During the transition, every gradation between a leaf and a tendril may be seen on the same plant.

6. The family of the *Bignonias* is one of the most interesting of the class of tendril-climbers, on account of the variety of adaptation which is found among them. In one species the leaf bears a pair of leaflets, and ends in a tendril having three branches. The main tendril may be compared to a bird's leg with three toes, each bearing a small claw. And this comparison seems apt enough, for, when the tendril comes against a twig, the three toes curl round it like those of a perching bird. Besides the toes or tendrils, the leaf-stalk is sensitive, and acts like that of a regular leaf-climber, wrapping itself round a neighboring object.

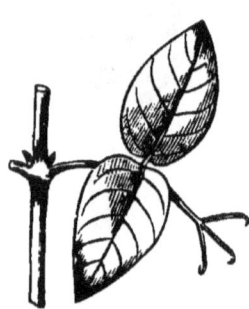

Tendril Hooks.

7. In some cases the young leaves have no tendrils at their tips, but clasp with their stalks, and this is a case exactly the reverse of *Tropæolum*—a tendril-climber whose young leaves have no tendrils, instead of a leaf-climber whose young climbing organs are not leaves. Thus the close relationship that exists between leaf- and tendril-climbers is again illustrated. This plant also combines the qualities of another class of climbers, namely, twiners, for it can wind spirally round a support as well as a hop or any other true twiner. Another species also helps to support itself by putting out roots from its stems, which adhere to the stick up which the plant is climbing. So that here are four different methods of climbing—twining, leaf, ten-

dril, and root-climbing—which are usually characteristic of different classes of climbers, combined in a single species.

8. The tendrils of the Virginia creeper may here be worth noticing. This plant can climb up a flat wall, and is not adapted to seize sticks or twigs; its tendrils do occasionally curl round a stick, but they often let go again. They, like bignonia tendrils, are sensitive to the light, and grow away from it, and thus easily find out where the wall lies up which they have to climb. A tendril which has come against the wall is often seen to rise and come down afresh, as if not satisfied with its first position. In a few days after a tendril has touched a wall the tip swells up, becomes red, and forms one of the little feet or sticky cushions by which the tendrils adhere. The adherence is caused by a resinous cement secreted by the cushions, and which forms a strong bond of union between the wall and the tendril. After the tendril has become attached it becomes woody, and is in this state remarkably durable, and may remain firmly attached and quite strong for as many as fifteen years.

9. Besides this sense of touch, by which a bignonia tendril distinguishes between the objects which it touches, there are other instances of much more perfect and incomprehensible sensibility. Thus, some tendrils, which are so sensitive that they curl up when a weight of one thirtieth or even one fiftieth of a grain is placed on them, do not take the least notice of a shower of rain whose falling drops must cause a much greater shock to the tendrils.

10. Again, some tendrils seem to have the power of distinguishing between objects which they wish to seize and their brother tendrils which they do not wish to catch. A tendril may be drawn repeatedly over another without causing the latter to contract.

11. The tendrils of another excellent climber (*Cobæa scandens*) possess some curious properties. The tendrils are

much divided, and end in delicate branchlets, as thin as bristles, and very flexible, each bearing a minute double hook at its tip. These are formed of a hard, woody substance, and are as sharp as needles; a single tendril may bear between ninety and a hundred of these beautiful little grappling-hooks. The flexibility of the tendrils is of service in allowing them to be blown about by a breath of wind, and they can thus be made to seize hold of objects which are out of reach of the ordinary revolving movements. Many tendrils can only seize a stick by curling round it, and this, even in the most sensitive tendril, must take a minute or two; but with *Cobæa* the sharp hooks catch hold of little irregularities on the bark the moment the tendril comes into contact with it, and afterward the tendril can curl round and make the attachment permanent.

12. The movement of the little hook-bearing branches is very remarkable in this species. If a tendril catches an object with one or two hooks, it is not contented, but tries to attach the rest of them in the same way. Now, many of the branches will chance to be so placed that their hooks do not naturally catch, either because they come laterally, or with their blunt backs against the wood, but after a short time, by a process of twisting and adjusting, each little hook becomes turned, so that its sharp point can get a hold on the wood.

13. The sharp hook on the tendrils of *Cobæa* is only a very perfect form of the bluntly curved tip which many tendrils possess, and which serves the same purpose of temporarily holding the object caught until the tendril can curve over and make it secure. There is a curious proof of the usefulness of even this blunt hook in the fact that the tendril is only sensitive to a touch on the inside of the hook. The tendril, when it comes against a twig, always slips up it till the hook catches on it, so that it would be of no use to be sensitive on the convex side. Some ten-

drils, on the other hand, have no hook at the end, and here the tendrils are sensitive to the touch on any side.

14. There is a remarkable movement which occurs in tendrils after they have caught an object, and which renders a tendril a better climbing organ than any sensitive leaf. This movement is called spiral contraction. When a tendril first seizes an object it is quite straight, with the exception of the extreme tip, which is firmly curled round the object seized. But in a day or two the tendril begins to contract, and ultimately assumes the corkscrew-like form represented in the figures. It is clear that in spirally contracting the tendril has become considerably shorter;

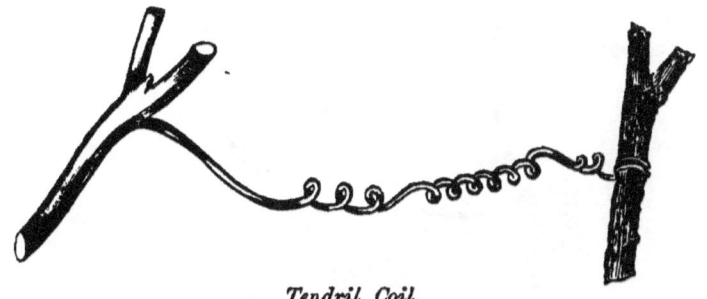

Tendril Coil.

and, since the end of the tendril is fixed to a branch, it is obvious that the stem must be dragged nearer to the object which its tendril has caught. Thus, if a shoot of bryony seizes a support above it, the contraction of the tendril will pull up the shoot in the right direction. So that in this respect the power of spiral contraction gives a tendril-climber an advantage over leaf-climbers which have no contracting power, and, therefore, no means of hauling themselves up to supporting objects.

15. But the spiral contraction of tendrils has another use, and this is probably the most important one. This use depends on the fact that a contracted tendril acts like a spiral spring, and is thus converted into a yielding instead

of an unyielding body. The spirally wound tendril yields like an elastic thread to a pull which would break the tendril in its original condition. The meaning of this arrange-

Coil and Disk.

ment is to enable the plant to weather a gale which would tear it from its support by snapping the tendrils, if they were not converted into spiral springs. After the tendril has taken hold of a support, spiral coils can be made in it only by the middle part of the tendril turning, and this will cause the coils to be turned one half in one direction and one half in the other.

16. As in the process of natural selection the hook-climbers appear to have grown out of the twiners, the question may occur, Why is hook-climbing a more perfect method of climbing than turning? Why, when a plant had become a twining plant, did it not rest satisfied? The fact that leaf- and tendril-climbers had been developed out of twiners, and not *vice versa*, is a proof that climbing by leaves or tendrils is a more advantageous habit than twining; but we do not see why it should be so. If we inquire why *any* plant has become a climber, we shall see the reason. Light is a necessity for all green plants; and a plant which can climb is enabled to escape from the shadow of other plants with a far less waste of material than a forest-tree, which only pushes its branches into the light by sheer growth. Thus, the weak, straggling stem of a climbing plant gets all the advantages gained by the solid, column-like tree-trunk. If we apply this test—which is the most economical plan of climbing, twining or leaf-climbing—we see at once that a plant which climbs by seizing wastes far less material than one which twines. Thus, a kidney-bean, which had climbed up a stick to a height of two feet, when unwound from its support was found to be three feet in length, whereas a pea which had climbed up two feet by its tendrils was hardly longer than the height reached. Thus, the bean had wasted considerably more material by its method of climbing by twining round a stick, instead of going straight up, supported by its tendrils, like the pea.

17. There are several other ways in which climbing by tendrils is a much better plan than twining. It is a safer method, as any one may convince himself by comparing the security of a tendril-bearer in a heavy wind with the ease with which a twiner is partly blown from its support. Again, by looking at those leaf-climbing plants which still possess in addition the power of twining, it will be seen how incomparably better they grasp a stick than does a

simple twiner. And again, a twiner from being best fitted to climb bare stems often has to start in the shade, whereas a leaf- or tendril-climber can ramble for the whole extent of its growth up the sunny side of a bush.

18. To repeat once more the steps which it is believed have occurred in the evolution of climbing plants : It is probable that plants have become twiners by exaggerating a swinging-round or revolving movement, which occurred in a rudimentary form, and in a useless condition, in some of their ancestors. This movement has been utilized for twining, the stimulus which has driven the process of change in this direction having been the necessity for light.

19. The second stage has been the development of sensitive leaves by a twining plant. No doubt at first no leaf-climber depended entirely on its leaves—it was merely a twiner which helped itself by its leaves. Gradually the leaves became more perfect, and then the plant could leave off the wasteful plan of growing spirally up a stick, and adopt the more economical and more effective one of pure leaf-climbing.

20. Finally, from sensitive leaves were developed the marvelously perfect tendrils which can perceive one fiftieth of a grain, and can show distinct curvature within twenty-five seconds after being touched, tendrils with delicate, sticky ends, or endowed with the power of moving toward the dark, or of creeping into little cracks, or with that mysterious sense of touch by which a tendril can distinguish a brother tendril from an ordinary twig, and can distinguish the weight of a rain-drop hanging to it from that of a bit of thread—in short, all the delicate contrivances which place tendril-bearers so eminently at the head of the climbing plants.

Francis Darwin.

THE HOSPITALITY OF PLANTS.

1. As if in return for the manifold services which plants require and receive from their fellow-creatures, they show kindness of their own to animal life, and shelter and feed the most timid as well as the noblest of beings with the hospitality of their generous life. In early childhood already we are taught that even the smallest of seeds—the mustard-seed—grows up to be a tree, "in whose branches the fowls of the heavens have their habitation," that "both Judah and Israel dwelt safely, every man under his vine and under his fig-tree, all the days of Solomon," and that Deborah, the prophetess, "dwelt under a palm-tree." Modern science has furnished as numerous striking and detailed instances of the great variety of life which is thus intimately connected with the vegetable kingdom.

2. It is not only that the plaintive nightingale sings in the murmuring poplar, while the gay butterfly loves the sweet-scented rose, that the somber yew hides the owl's nest, and the dark northern pine harbors the fur-clad squirrel. Animals, invisible to the naked eye, have been found to float in the sap of trees, and even the smallest moss has its own tiny insect, which it boards and lodges. Aphides and gall-insects live, in every sense of the word, on the leaves of plants, flies and butterflies on their flowers, and ants and worms crowd upon them, after death, in countless multitudes. Every plant, moreover, is inhabited by some insect to which it affords an exclusive home. Many caterpillars are born and die with the leaf on which they live, while, on the other hand, the proud monarch—oak—alone supports seventy different kinds of insects, a swarm which sets all measurement at defiance, and, moreover, replaces by numbers and the enormous voracity with which they are endowed, what they want in bodily magnitude.

3. Plants have to support guests of every size and shape. The butterfly and its less gaudy relations drink with their long trunks sweet honey out of gorgeously colored flower-cups; four-winged bees carry away the precious dust of anthers in large spoons fastened to their thighs; gall-insects pierce with sharp daggers the tender leaf, drink its refreshing juice, and deposit their eggs in the delicate texture; beetles gnaw and saw with a hundred curiously shaped instruments through the hardest wood of noble trees; naked, helpless-looking worms make the very trunk their cover and their home, and with sharp augers often destroy whole forests. The ingenious ant of South America has its winter residence in the warm ground, and its cool summer-house on tall plants. For there grows on the banks of the Amazon River a gigantic reed, nearly thirty feet high, which is frequently crowned with a large ball of earth, like the golden globe on the utmost end of a lofty church-steeple. This is the comfortable home of myriads of ants, which retire to these safe dwellings, high and dry, at the time of rains, and during the period of inundation, rising and descending in the hollow of the reed, and living on what they find swimming on the surface of the water.

4. Another curious lodger of a South American plant is the famous cochineal-bug, well known from the precious red color that bears its name, and which it draws from a certain cactus until its body becomes impregnated with the brilliant scarlet. It is probably the most sedentary of all insects, making but one short journey in early life, and then settling down for ever upon one and the same spot. As soon, namely, as the young insect leaves its egg, it manifests great activity and a restless desire to travel. But, alas! it finds itself upon a prickly, thorny stem, hanging high in the air, and in contact with no other. But Nature soon comes to its aid, and sends a small spider to spin a silken thread from branch to branch. Upon this

slender, trembling bridge, the young cochineal wanders boldly out to a new world, seeks a promising spot, deliberately sinks its fragile trunk into the juicy leaf, and never draws it back again—drinking, drinking, like a toper as he is, through his whole existence.

5. Even larger inhabitants are often found on quite small plants. Thus, England produces a slight but well-supported thistle, which is frequently found to have little elaborate nests hanging down at an elevation of a few inches from the ground. These contain not insects, but mice, though of the smallest variety known, and are occasionally large enough to hold as many as nine young ones, carefully stowed away and well secured against all enemies and dangers.

6. Birds seem, of course, the most natural lodgers of plants; they find there abundance of nourishment, all the material for building their nests, and a well-protected home. The eagle gathers the knotted branches of oaks or pines, to bring up his fierce brood upon the hard, uncushioned couch; the thorn tears a handful of wool from the passing sheep for its tiny inhabitants; and the despised mullein covers its broad leaves with the softest of downs to line the bed of the delicate children of the humming-bird. There is probably no bush and no tree that has not its own particular bird; everywhere do the fowls of the air find a foliage, thicker or thinner, to shelter them against rain, heat, and cold; a hollow trunk affords safe and warm lodgings; soft moss carpets their dwellings, and insects and worms swarm around, to offer, at the same time, food in abundance. They give, in return, life and sound to the immovable plant. Song-birds of many kinds perch and sing their beautiful anthems on every spray; locusts trill their monotonous and yet pleasing note among a world of leaves through long summer noons, and the katydid utters its shrill cry during sultry nights. They all love their home,

making it their dwelling by night and by day, and many are the instances in which birds, that had long lived in certain trees, have died from homesickness when they were felled.

7. Nor has man himself neglected to avail himself of trees as a dwelling or a home. Already Lucinius Mutianus, an ex-consul of Lycia, took special pleasure in feasting twenty-one guests in a hollow plane-tree; and modern travelers tell us of a gigantic baobab in Senegambia, the interior of which is used as a public hall for national meetings, while its portals are ornamented with rude, quaint sculptures, cut out of the still living wood. The sacred fig-tree of India, which, as Milton says,

> "Branching so broad along, that in the ground
> The bending twigs take root, and daughters grow
> About the mother-tree a pillar's shade
> High overarched, with echoing walks between,"

is worshiped as sacred, and the lazy, helpless priest, the Bonze, builds himself a hut, not unlike a bird's cage, in its branches, where he spends his life dreaming, in contemplative indolence, under its cool, pleasant shade.

8. Nay, whole nations live in the branches of trees. There is a race of natives of South America, west of the mouth of the Orinoco, the Guaranis, who have never yet been completely subdued, thanks mainly to their curious habitations. The great Humboldt tells us that they twine most skillfully the leaf-stalks of the Mauritius palm into cords, and weave them with great care into mats. These they suspend high in the air from branch to branch, and cover them with clay; here they dwell, and in a dark night the amazed and bewildered traveler may see the fires of their dwellings high in the tops of lofty trees.

9. Thus it is that vegetable and animal life go hand in hand, showing that beautiful bond of love which pervades all nature, even in its minor parts. Where there is life, there

are plants, and on land and on water, on the loftiest mountain-top and in the very bowels of the earth—everywhere does man find a plant to minister to his support and enjoyment, everywhere he sees plants quietly and mysteriously perform their humble duty in the great household of nature. Plants alone—it would at first sight appear—have no home, for they seem to be at home everywhere. Turn up the soil where you will, to any depth, and such a rich abundance of vegetable life is mixed with the loam that almost instantaneously plants innumerable spring up from seeds, which may have lain slumbering for thousands of years in the warm bosom of our mother earth.

10. Man himself can not master this exuberance of vegetable life. He may change it by cultivation, it is true, but that also only for a time. And what is a generation or two in comparison with the eternal earth? Do not even in our day, and before our eyes, lofty trees raise their proud heads where our fathers cut the green turf with their sharp plow? In vain does man take the Alpine rose from the banks of its pure mountain brook and plant it in the lowly valley; in vain does he bring costly seeds from the Indies, and the warm climes of the tropics, even to the ice-clad coast of Norway. They live and pine and die. It is true he sometimes seeks to reverse Nature itself. He places bubbling fountains on the top of high hills, and plants lime-trees and poplars between great masses of rocks; vineyards must adorn his valleys, and meadows spread their soft velvet over mountain-sides. But the poet of old already has taught us that you may drive out Nature even with the pitchfork, and yet she will ever return.

11. A few years' neglect, and how quickly she resumes her sway! Artificial lakes become gloomy marshes, bowers are filled with countless briers, and stately avenues are overgrown with reckless profusion. The plants of the soil declare war against the intruders from abroad, and claim once

more their birthright to the land of their fathers. The fine, well-trimmed turf is smothered under a thousand coarser plants, rank grass and fat clover overspread the exotics; briers climb up with the aid of hooks and ladders, as if they were storming a fortress; nettles fill the urns of statues with their thick tufts, and unsightly mosses creep up the very faces of marble beauties. Wild cherry-trees and maples seize on every cornice and cleft of every stately mansion, hardy, invincible roots penetrate into the slightest opening, until at last victory is declared, and the trees of the forest wave their rich foliage over the high turrets, and raise triumphantly on spire and pinnacle the gorgeous banner of Nature.

M. Schele de Vere.

THE RHODORA.

1. IN May, when sea-winds pierced our solitudes,
I found the fresh rhodora in the woods,
Spreading its leafless blooms in a damp nook,
To please the desert and the sluggish brook.
The purple petals, fallen in the pool,
   Made the black waters with their beauty gay:
Here might the red-bird come his plumes to cool,
   And court the flower that cheapens his array.

2. Rhodora! if the sages ask thee why
This charm is wasted on the earth and sky,
Tell them, dear, that if eyes were made for seeing,
Then Beauty is its own excuse for being.
Why thou wert there, O rival of the rose!
   I never thought to ask, I never knew;
But in my simple ignorance suppose
   The self-same Power that brought me there brought you.

Emerson.

PART II.

STRANGE PLANTS AND THEIR WAYS.

THE BUILDER'S TREE OF CHINA.

1. A TREE of great importance in the uses of daily life to those who dwell in the localities of its growth is the bamboo. It is found in Asia and the West Indies, but it is in the eastern portion of the former continent that it enters most largely into the needs of the people. It has a hard texture, with hollow, jointed stems, and grows to a height of about fifty feet. Strictly speaking, the bamboo is a gigantic grass, but, as great numbers grow together to a lofty height, it has the aspect of a noble tree. It rarely attains to a thickness of more than ten inches, or a distance between the joints of more than five feet.

2. The Chinese have developed the art of bamboo culture, for with them it is the national plant to such a degree that they produce black as well as yellow bamboo, and the Emperor has an officer whose special duty it is to look after his bamboo gardens. It is said that a famine was prevented in India in 1812 by the sudden flowering of the bamboo-trees, and fifty thousand people were in the jungles gathering the seed for food. To reach the blossoming time takes thirty years, when the plant produces seed profusely and then dies.

3. The young and tender shoots of the bamboo are

cooked as vegetables, and made into delicious sweetmeats by the confectioners. But it is the application of the bamboo in the industrial arts which marks its highest importance. Houses, boats, the yards, cordage, and sails of vessels, telescopes, aqueduct-pipes, water-proof thatching and clothing, water-wheels, fences, chairs, tables, bookcases, boxes, hats, umbrellas, fans, cups, measures, shields, pikes and spears, paper, and pipes, are all made from this protean tree, which almost rivals the palm in its usefulness. The pith is used for lamp-wicks; and exquisite carvings, inlaid with gold and silver, and far more elegant than ivory-work, are cut from their hard stems. The wood, indeed, is so full of silex that thin slices serve the purpose of knives. By experiment, Mr. Edison has found that the carbonized fibers of the bamboo furnish the best material for the incandescent electric lamp, and are now used in his system of electric lighting. In some of the East Indian countries, as in Burmah and Siam, whole cities are built from the bamboo, houses being lashed together, and capable of being taken apart like a tent.

World of Wonders.

THE SCHOLAR'S PLANT OF EGYPT.

1. ONE of the most interesting plants of the Eastern Continent is the papyrus, from which is derived our word paper. It was called *papu* by the ancient Egyptians, whence the Greek word *papuros* and the English word *paper* come. The old historian Herodotus called it *bublos*, and from this the old Greeks derived their name for a book, *biblion*, which word we have perpetuated in our Bible.

2. The paper reed, or papyrus plant, belongs to the family of sedges, and it is found now on the marshy banks of rivers in Abyssinia, Syria, and Sicily. It is now rarely found in the Nile, though it is from its Egyptian associa-

tion that the historic interest of the papyrus plant began. During the long servitude of Egypt under the warlike races which overran it, and the loss of interest in literature, it is probable that the culture of the papyrus plant utterly ceased.

3. The part played by the papyrus plant in the early history of civilization was a very important one. With the exception of parchment, made from the skins of animals, it was the only material used by the most intellectual of the ancient nations—the Egyptians, the Greeks, and Romans—for the purpose of books. The papyrus, being far more easily obtained and easy to use than the parchment, thus became the indispensable fact in the preservation of ancient literature. Papyrus rolls are now frequently found wrapped around the mummies taken out of the catacombs on the Nile, and these have furnished a great insight into the manners and customs of the old Egyptians.

4. The stem of the papyrus is smooth, triangular in shape, and attains a height of from five to twenty-five feet. It bears long, grassy leaves springing from near the base, and its flowers form small, flattened spikes of from six to eight flowers each, clustered in great numbers in a component head from fifteen to twenty inches long, supported at its base by a many-leaved cup. The stalks are always half submerged in the marsh or water, and the whole appearance of the plant is very graceful. It is now cultivated occasionally as a hot-house plant, both as a curiosity and for decoration.

5. The right of growing and selling the papyrus was a government monopoly in Egypt, and was directly under the charge of the priests, who cultivated it in large quantities near their temples, which were generally located on the banks of the Nile. It was used for a great variety of purposes. Its graceful plumes crowned the statues of the gods

and decorated their temples; its pith was eaten as food; wickerwork boats, baskets, and boxes were woven of its stalk, and of its bark were made sails, cordage, mats, cloth, and sandals, for the priests; it was applied as medicine for the cure of ulcers; it furnished materials for torches and candles, and its roots were used for fuel and manufactured into utensils and furniture.

The Papyrus.

6. But it was in the manufacture of paper that it was put to its most important use. The mode of manufacture was as follows: The inner skin of the stalk was divided by means of a sharp needle into as many thin plates as the size would admit. These were placed on a table, and kept continually moistened by Nile water. Over these slips a transverse layer was placed, after which the whole was subjected to pressure, till the plates adhered closely together in a sheet. The sheets were then dried in the sun, beaten smooth and firm with a mallet, and polished with a piece of ivory or shell. The breadth of the sheet was limited by the length of the papyrus slips, but its length could be extended indefinitely.

7. When finished, the papyrus sheets were rolled on a wooden cylinder, the ends of which, projecting beyond the papyrus roll, were beautifully decorated by painting and carving. Such was the material on which the most important results of ancient thought were inscribed.

8. Papyrus was used for writing purposes at a very remote period in Egypt, and during the time of Herodotus it was an important article of commerce, which it continued to be for seven or eight centuries. The Romans, it is said, imported all their papyrus from Egypt, but improved the manufacture of it. It was believed that nowhere else than in Egypt did the plant grow in its full perfection and fineness of fiber. During the early days of the Roman empire a papyrus famine gave great alarm to learned men, and the senate was obliged to regulate its distribution by edict.

World of Wonders.

A MIGRATORY ROSE.

1. STRANGE as the heading of this paper may appear to the reader, the flower is nevertheless an entity—a thing that exists, and may be handled; a plant almost as regular as the swallow in its flittings to and fro; one that travels many miles annually; and, what is more, a fashionable one—resorting to the sea-side during the hottest season, to indulge in a swim among the cool billows of the Mediterranean. The name of this remarkable vegetable phenomenon is the *Rose of Jericho* with the unlearned. Very many superstitions are connected with this extraordinary plant in the minds of Bedouins and other Arab tribes. The ancients attributed miraculous virtues to it.

2. To behold this little rose, it is not necessary to tell you "to go to Jericho"; no such uncomplimentary journey is required. In the arid wastes of Egypt, by the bor-

ders of the Gaza desert, in Arabia's wilderness of sands, on the roofs of houses and among rubbish in Syria, abundant specimens are to be met with. But, like many other things of insignificant exterior, few pause to look upon or handle this wayside shrub, which nevertheless carries with it a lesson and a moral.

3. By the laws of *germination,* there are, we are told, these three things necessary for a plant—humidity, heat, and oxygenized air. The first of them is indispensable, inasmuch as without it the grain or seed would not swell, and, without swelling, could not burst its shell or skin; and heat, in union with water, brings various gases to young plants —especially oxygen—which are necessary for their existence.

The Rose of Jericho.
The dead plant and a leafy branch.

4. With these facts before us, and a knowledge that rain seldom falls in most places where the rose of Jericho thrives, how are we to account for the extraordinary circumstance of this plant being periodically abundant and flowering at precisely the same season year after year, when, by the acknowledged laws of germination, there has been that succor wanting which is indispensable to propagate vegetation? Now appears the most remarkable and most direct interposition of Nature for her offspring—an interposition little short

of miraculous, and, indeed, apparently so fabulous as to be unworthy of record. But the fact has been established beyond doubt that, for its own purposes, this little plant performs annual journeys over a large extent of country, and into the ocean, whence, at a stated period, it, or rather its offspring, returns to the original haunts, takes root, thrives, and blossoms.

5. In the height of spring, when Nature casts her brilliant vesture, set with flowers and flowerets of a hundred varied hues, over the fertile valleys and hills of Syria and part of Palestine; when every breeze is laden with rich incense from orange groves or honeysuckle dells—then, unheeded amid the rich profusion of vegetation, or isolated amid the desert sands, blossoms the tiny rose of Jericho. On house-tops, where the sun's fierce rays rend crevices; on dust-heaps, where half-starved, wretched curs prowl and dig for food or a resting-place; where multitudes throng the streets, and where neither foot of man nor beast has ever left imprint on the broiling sand—there sprouts this wonderful little plant.

6. When summer has fairly set in, and flowering shrubs have ceased to blossom—about the same season of the year that Mr. Bull and his family are meditating a month's trip to the sea-side for fresh breezes and sea-bathing, when the whole house is turned topsy-turvy in the pleasurable excitement of packing for the month's holiday—the rose of Jericho begins to show symptoms of a migratory disposition also. How astonished Mr. Brown would be if his gardener rushed in with the startling intelligence that some favorite rose-bush or other plant in the garden had evinced sudden signs of restlessness, and, after a few preliminary efforts, had quietly taken itself off for the season!

7. Hadji Ismail, the Bedouin camel-driver, who witnesses this phenomenon annually, encountering scores of roses while migrating, simply pauses to stroke his prolific

beard and fresh charge his pipe, while he pours into the eager ears of some untraveled novice legends about this wonderful rose — legends replete with fairy romance, in which almost invariably a certain unmentionable gentleman comes in for a volley of invectives, as being the instigator of this mysterious freak of nature.

8. The first symptom the rose of Jericho gives of an approaching tour is the shedding of all her leaves; the branches then collapse, apparently wither, and roll themselves firmly into the shape of a ball. Like the fairies that traveled in nut-shells, this plant ensconces itself in its own frame-work of a convenient shape, size, and weight for undertaking the necessary journey. Not long has the flower assumed this shape when strong land-breezes sweep over the land, blowing hot and fiercely toward the ocean. In their onward course, these land-winds uproot and carry with them the bulbs or frame-work of our rose; and, once uprooted, these are tossed and blown over many and many a dreary mile of desert sand, till they are finally whirled up into the air, and swept over the coast into the ocean.

9. Soon after the little plant comes into contact with the water, it unpacks again, unfolds itself, expands its branches, and expels its seeds from the seed-vessels. Then, I presume, the mother-plant finishes her career, or is stranded a wreck upon the sea-beach. However this may be, it seems evident that the seeds, after having been thoroughly saturated with water, are brought back by the waves, and cast high and dry upon the beach. When the westerly winds set in with violence from the sea they carry these seeds back with them, scattering them far and wide over the desert, and among inhabited lands; and so surely as the spring-time comes round will the desolate borders of the desert be enlivened by the tiny blossoms of the rose of Jericho.

Chambers's Journal.

REFRESHMENT-TREES.

1. ALEXANDER VON HUMBOLDT first made known to the civilized world, on his return from South America, the remarkable qualities of the cow-tree. Of the delicious sap produced by this tree for the thirsty traveler he thus writes: "We were assured that the negroes on the farm, who are in the habit of drinking large quantities of this vegetable milk, consider it is highly nutritious; an assertion which startled me the more as almost all lactescent vegetable fluids are acrid, bitter, and somewhat poisonous. Experience, however, proved to us during our residence at Barbula that the virtues of the cow-tree had not been exaggerated."

2. This strange tree is an evergreen which is found in the mountains of Venezuela. The sap flows freely when the bark is wounded, and it is safe to drink freely, for the fluid, which has the color and taste of milk, is not only cool and refreshing, but is full of nutriment. The natives of Venezuela all know this tree well, and find in its delicious sap a substitute for both food and water in time of need. Some attempt was made, indeed, at one time by the Venezuelan government to extend its growth in parts of the country where it was not natural, but, like all efforts of South Americans which exact watchfulness and trouble, it speedily died out without accomplishment.

3. The traveler's tree of Madagascar is another example of the kindly provision of nature for the requirements of the human kind. This tree is very abundant throughout the island, and rises from the ground with a thick, succulent stem like that of a plantain. Long, broad leaves grow from opposite sides of the stalk, so that the tree looks like a huge, green, open fan. "Many of the trees," says a traveler, "reach thirty feet from the ground to the lowest leaves. I frequently counted from twenty to twenty-four

leaves on a single tree, the stalk of each leaf being eight feet long, and the broad leaf itself being about six feet long.

The Traveler's Tree.

The whole of these twenty-four bright-green, gigantic leaves, spread out like a fern at the top of a trunk thirty feet high, presented a spectacle as impressive as it was rare and beautiful."

4. The chief distinction of the tree is that during the most arid season it contains a large quantity of pure, fresh

water, supplying to the traveler the place of wells in the desert. So abundant and pure is the water that the natives will not take the trouble to go to a spring or well, but draw off and drink the fluid of this tree. The Rev. William Ellis, in his account of a visit to Madagascar, says he was skeptical of these accounts, and resolved to test their truth. Passing a clump of the trees, one of his bearers thrust his spear-head several inches deep into the thick, firm end of the leaf-stalk, where it joined the trunk. Instantly a stream of water gushed forth, about a quart of which was caught in a pitcher. The water was found to be almost ice-cold, clear, and perfectly sweet.

5. "But," says Mr. Ellis, "in Madagascar this tree might with propriety be called the builder's instead of the traveler's tree. Its leaves form the thatch of all the houses on the eastern side of the island. The stems of the leaves form the partitions and oftentimes the sides of the houses, and the hard outside bark, having been beaten out flat, is laid for flooring. I have seen the entire floor of a long, well-built house covered with its bark, each piece being at least eighteen feet wide and twenty or thirty feet long. The leaves make water-proof wrappers, when green, and they also serve the purpose of table-cloths and plates at meals."

6. Charles Kingsley gives this description of a climbing plant valuable to travelers, which is found in the tropical forests of Trinidad: "You walk on and are suddenly stopped by a gray, lichen-covered bar as thick as your ankle. You follow it up with your eye, and find it entwine itself with three or four other bars, and roll over with them in great knots and festoons, and loops twenty feet high, and then go up with them into the green cloud over your head and vanish, as if a giant had thrown a ship's cable into the tree-tops.

7. "At one of the loops your companion, if you have a

forester with you, will spring joyfully. With a few blows with his cutlass he will sever it as high up as he can reach, and again below, some three feet down ; and, while you are wondering at this seemingly wanton destruction, he lifts the bar on high, throws his head back, and pours down his thirsty throat a pint or more of pure cold water. This hidden treasure is, strange as it may seem, the ascending sap, or rather the ascending pure rain-water which has been taken up by the roots, and is hurrying aloft to be elaborated into sap, and leaf, and flower, and fruit, and fresh tissue for the very stem which it originally climbed, and therefore it is that the woodman cuts the water-vine at the top of the piece which he wants first, and not at the bottom, for so rapid is the ascent of the sap that if he cut the stem below, the water would all have fled upward before he could have cut it off above."

THE MONARCH OF AFRICAN FORESTS.

1. IN the tropical forests of Africa, extending across the entire continent, one tree is found of such immense size and longevity as to be justly considered the monarch of the forests. This is the baobab, or, as it is called by the French settlers on the Senegal, the monkey-bread tree. The trunk of this tree usually does not exceed from fifteen to thirty feet in height, though it sometimes attains an elevation of sixty feet. In girth, however, it reaches the enormous size of forty to seventy-five feet. The branches are from fifty to seventy-five feet long, their extremities bending toward the ground and often touching it, so as to completely conceal the trunk. The leaves are large, compound, and star-shaped, being divided into five radiating leaflets. They are very abundant, and of a dark-green color, the entire foliage casting a dense shade.

2. At a little distance the baobab presents the appearance of a dome of verdure, covering an area of one hundred and sixty feet in diameter. Adanson, the first naturalist who studied and described this tree, estimated that some of

The Baobab-Tree.

the specimens that he observed were at least six thousand years old. This is now considered an exaggeration, though undoubtedly some of them have reached an immense age, rivaling in this particular the big trees of California and the eucalyptus of Australia. Livingston estimated that one of these trees which he examined was fourteen hundred years old.

3. In tenacity of life this tree is remarkable. Having once obtained a foothold in the soil, it retains its position with great persistence. When stripped of its bark, a new growth will appear; and when the entire inside of the trunk has decayed, or has been eaten out by insects, the thin outer section retains sufficient vitality to give nurture to the foliage above. Fire will not destroy it, and even after it has fallen it continues to grow in length, the roots retaining their vitality, and sending up new shoots.

4. Like the palm, the baobab is remarkable as furnishing a great variety of articles useful to man. The fruit, which grows in great abundance, is soft and pulpy, and is inclosed in a long, dark-green, woody pod about the size of a quart bottle. It is edible, of an agreeable flavor, but rather dry. It forms an important part of the food of the natives, and is transported across the desert, where it makes its appearance on the shores of the Mediterranean. The pulp between the seeds tastes like cream of tartar, and is used by the natives for its medicinal qualities in case of fevers. From the fibers of the bark a strong cord is manufactured, and to obtain this material the tree is frequently stripped of its entire bark, which, however, does not appear to disturb its growth, as a new bark directly makes its appearance.

5. The superstitions connected with this tree are of an entirely different character from those associated with the banyan by the natives of India. The musicians and poets who preside at all ceremonies performed at the tombs of the negro kings are called Guerrots. During their life, their talent gives them influence and a certain kind of respect; but they are regarded as sorcerers, and after death the respect is succeeded by a deep-seated horror for their

supposed connection with malignant powers. The people think that if one of these evil beings were to be buried in the earth, like the bodies of other men, celestial vengeance would descend upon all those who committed the sacrilege. So, to avert divine wrath, they select the trunk of some baobab-tree already partially hollowed out by insects or fungi, increase the cavity to a sufficient size, and in it suspend the body of the Guerrot, closing the entrance with a plank. The body here becomes perfectly dry, and is changed into a mummy without further preparation.

6. In ancient Egypt the body was regarded as sacred, and an endeavor was made to preserve it for all time. To this end the bodies of the great were embalmed, and deposited in tombs hewn out of the solid rock. In central Africa the body is preserved through detestation instead of reverence, the baobab-tree taking the place of the rocky sepulchre.

Figuier.

THE SACRED TREE OF INDIA.

1. THE majestic banyan-tree is lord of the forests of India, and is one of the marvels of the vegetable world. Its seeds are carried by the winds or dropped by the birds in crevices in the rocks, or even in buildings or on trees, and, when there is sufficient moisture, they germinate and send rootlets downward to the earth, where they secure a permanent foothold. If the long root reaches down from the top of a tree, it speedily enlarges, and in a short time destroys the original stalk which gave it life and nourishment.

2. The banyan rarely attains a great height, from sixty to a hundred feet being the maximum. During its first hundred years it behaves very much like other trees, developing a sturdy trunk, and an immense, dome-like head spreading far out on all sides. Its leaves are smooth and glossy,

and of a bright green. Its foliage is so dense as to afford a cooling shade and effectually prevent the growth of underbrush. It produces an abundance of mild, insipid, fig-like fruit, which is used both for food and for medicinal purposes.

3. At the end of the first century of its life the banyan begins to exhibit its eccentric propensities. Its arms have grown so long as to be no longer capable of supporting

The Banyan-Tree.

themselves, and they bend downward until their ends rest upon the earth. Now, the little twigs, which have hitherto been contented with producing leaves, send forth rootlets which find lodgment in the ground; the sap, changing its direction and flowing upward, converting the small stems into trunks, and affording an effectual support to the overweighted branches. The great horizontal masses are now supported at both extremities, as a bridge by its piers. The main limbs reach gigantic size, and send out lateral branches, which, in turn, take root and form new supports. These new trunks often rival or surpass the parent stem, and this process continues for ages, until the tree covers acres of ground, and presents the appearance of a marvelous colonnade of stems supporting numberless living rafters, and all covered with a dense canopy of perennial green.

4. There is a banyan in Ceylon which measures fifteen hundred feet around the branches—more than a quarter of a mile. Under the shade of a still larger tree on the banks of the Nerbuddah, in India, which measures a circuit of twenty-two hundred feet, whose large trunks number three hundred and fifty-four, whose small ones exceed three thousand, and whose foliage makes a home for thousands of birds and monkeys, the chief of Putnah used to encamp in magnificent style.

5. Here he would entertain his guests on his tiger-hunting expeditions. Separate tents were gorgeously fitted up as bed-chambers, and each guest having one had three servants at his command. Saloons, drawing-rooms, dining-rooms, smoking-rooms, kitchens—all were perfectly appointed. Including all the animals and servants, there were seven thousand individuals in the retinue, yet the great banyan easily sheltered them all. Here, when the glow and flush of the fierce sun had given way to the cool dews of evening, the guests of the Oriental prince sipped their sherbet or champagne, and watched the movements of the dancing girls, while the monkeys chattered and the night-birds sang in the leafage above, and the pale moonshine glinted down through the openings in the vast roof.

6. Such is the gigantic fig-tree of India, truly one of the wonders of the world, and not to be matched even in a country where a hot sun combines with a rich soil to pro-

duce the most striking and luxuriant forms of life. It may be safely asserted that some of these trees now standing were in existence when Porus drove his squadrons of elephants against the Macedonian phalanx of Alexander the Great, in the hope to save his kingdom from the dominion of the world's conqueror.

7. The Hindoos regard these trees as sacred, and under their shade perform many acts of religious significance. It is a singular fact that the banyan is frequently found sprouting up on the spot where the Hindoo widow has committed suttee—a fact which causes the ignorant native to regard it with tenfold superstitious reverence. The natural explanation of this phenomenon is, that the birds, attracted to the spot where the suttee is performed, in search of food, drop the seeds, which speedily spring up from the congenial soil.

THE EUCALYPTUS.

1. A FRENCH botanist, who accompanied an expedition in search of the lost navigator, La Perouse, about the year 1790, first described a hitherto unknown tree, which he found constituting the chief part of the forests around Botany Bay, Australia. From the fact that the flower-bud has on it a cover not unlike the lid of a tiny sugar-bowl, he called it the *Eucalyptus*—which means "well covered." The shape of the flower-bud above was very much like the globular brass buttons then in use, and hence he gave to the variety the specific name of *globulus;* so the bluegum-tree is known to-day in science as the *Eucalyptus globulus.*

2. As Australia and the adjacent islands became better known, it was found that a large part of the forests was

composed of this and similar trees, to which the general name of eucalypts has been applied. About one hundred and fifty varieties of these trees have been discovered and described. Most of them are evergreen, but the leaves vary greatly in form in the different varieties, some being grass-shaped, long, and narrow, while others are nearly as broad as long. The leaf of the *E. globulus* is of a bluish green, and hence it is popularly called the bluegum-tree. They have great tenacity of life, and grow to an immense size. The largest tree that is known is one in the province of Victoria, which measures four hundred and eighty feet in height, which is considerably higher than the tallest of the sequoias of California.

3. These trees all belong to the great order of myrtle-blooms, and are cousins to the pomegranate, pimento, and clove. They yield an abundance of a highly aromatic gum, which gives to them the universal common name of gum-tree. This gum, and the oils and resins obtained by distilling the bark and wood, have valuable medicinal properties. Diffused in the sick-room, they purify the air and germinate ozone.

4. The eucalypts are among the most rapid of growers. Bluegums have been known to reach the height of sixty-five feet, with a trunk more than three feet and a half in circumference, in seven years. But, with all this rapidity of growth, the young eucalypt seems doggedly resolved, for some years at least, to resemble its parent in no particular save in the aromatic odor of its leaves. The stem of the young tree is four-sided; the leaves have no appreciable petiole, half inclose the stalk, and are placed opposite each other. They are also set at right angles with the pairs above and below. The leaves are wide and heart-shaped, and the two sides are essentially different, the upper being exposed to the sun, and the lower kept in the shade and containing the breathing organs.

The leaves are thin, soft, and succulent, and of a bright grassy green.

5. The old tree seems to eschew all the indiscretions of its youth. The stalk becomes round, the leaves elongate, have a long petiole, and are placed alternate on the stalk. But a greater change takes place in the character of the leaf. It now becomes thick, leathery, dry, and of a bluish green; and it turns so that one edge is up, exposing both sides equally to the sunlight. To accomplish this change of position, the petiole actually twists itself as if it knew what it was about. The two sides of the leaf now become alike both in organs and function. The ribs and veins are alike prominent on each side, much as if the roof of a house should have beams and rafters inside and out. Breathing organs appear on both sides, and this is what gives to the eucalyptus one of its most peculiar characteristics. Both sides of the leaf work equally, and the tree becomes a double-cylinder pumping-engine, instead of a single one as in other trees.

6. The wood of the tree when freshly cut is soft; but the gum soon hardens, and it becomes well-nigh imperishable. The terrible ship-worm, which destroys most timber exposed to its ravages, lets it alone, making it invaluable for ship-timber, docks, and all marine structures. It is proof against that fearful scourge of tropical regions, the white ant; hence, in India it is used for the sleepers of railways and a multitude of other purposes. It furnishes valuable timber to the wheelwright, carpenter, and cabinet-maker. While the tree usually holds tenaciously to its leaves, it readily sheds its outer bark, and such immense pieces are sometimes detached that the natives make a rude hut from a single piece. It is specially valuable for shingles, as it does not easily burn, and the gum makes it lasting when exposed to the air. The bark of many species is serviceable for paper-making.

7. With all its utilities, the eucalyptus is most widely known for its sanitary qualities. From observation and experiment, it seems to deserve the name by which it is often known—the fever-tree. Its hygienic qualities have long been known in Australia, and this has led to extensive plantings in malarious regions where the climate will permit their growth. They are semi-tropical, and the ordinary varieties can not endure the cold. They flourish well in California, and in other like warm regions. A plantation in Algiers cleared a region of miasma where, previous to its introduction, the French garrison had to be changed every five days on account of malaria. Some of the most unhealthful parts of the Campagna near Rome have been rendered inhabitable by the eucalyptus groves.

8. The sanitary effects of the eucalyptus are twofold. From the peculiar structure of its leaves, as above shown, it has an enormous pumping power, it being estimated that a tree will eliminate from a swampy soil eight times its own weight in water every twenty-four hours. This moisture is delivered to the atmosphere in the condition of pure water, all deleterious substances being strained out by the tissues of the wood. In addition to this healthful drainage, the aroma of the leaves acts beneficially in two ways: first, by directly furnishing an invigorating tonic through the lungs, and, second, by creating ozone, and thus indirectly stimulating healthful action of the nerves and tissues.

9. The demonstrated value of the eucalyptus has made its spread very rapid, so that it now has become quite common in all civilized countries where the conditions are favorable to its growth. By care in cultivation, it will doubtless in time become acclimated to colder regions. But restricted as it now is, its value is so great that it may be considered as the great tree of the future.

THE SENSITIVE-PLANT.

1. A SENSITIVE-PLANT in a garden grew,
   And the young winds fed it with silver dew,
   And it opened its fan-like leaves to the light,
   And closed them beneath the kisses of night.

2. And the Spring arose on the garden fair,
   And the Spirit of Love fell everywhere;
   And each flower and herb on earth's dark breast
   Rose from the dreams of its wintry rest.

3. But none ever trembled and panted with bliss
   In the garden, the field, or the wilderness,
   Like a doe in the noontide with love's sweet want,
   As the companionless sensitive-plant.

4. The snowdrop, and then the violet,
   Arose from the ground with warm rain wet,
   And their breath was mixed with fresh odor sent
   From the turf, like the voice and the instrument.

5. Then the pied windflowers and tulip tall,
   And narcissi, the fairest among them all,
   Who gaze on their eyes in the stream's recess,
   Till they die of their own dear loveliness;

6. And the Naiad-like lily of the vale,
   Whom youth makes so fair and passion so pale,
   That the light of its tremulous bells is seen
   Through their pavilions of tender green;

7. And the hyacinth purple, and white, and blue,
   Which flung from its bells a sweet peal anew
   Of music so delicate, soft, and intense,
   It was felt like an odor within the sense;

8. And the rose like a nymph to the bath addressed,
   Which unveiled the depth of her glowing breast,
   Till, fold after fold, to the fainting air
   The soul of her beauty and love lay bare ;

9. And the wand-like lily, which lifted up,
   As a Mænad, its moonlight-colored cup,
   Till the fiery star, which is its eye,
   Gazed through the clear dew on the tender sky ;

10. And the jessamine faint, and the sweet tuberose,
    The sweetest flower for scent that blows ;
    And all rare blossoms from every clime
    Grew in that garden in perfect prime.
    Shelley.

PART III.

LOW LIFE IN THE SEA.

ANIMATED JELLIES.

1. THE visitor to the sea-shore will rarely fail to find among the growing sea-weeds little plant-like clusters, which at first appear to be vegetable, but they are really the curious little sea-animals called hydroids or jelly-fish. From each little plant there arise buds, which soon enlarge, float away, and become beautiful jelly-fish. There are other hydroids, in the shape of bells, and some which appear like miniature trees with all their foliage massed at the top, and from beneath which there depend bunches, as it were, of grapes or other fruit. These fruit-like clusters are jelly-fishes that stick fast, instead of detaching themselves and becoming free jelly-fishes, as in some other varieties.

2. The name *medusa* is applied to the most numerous, remarkable, and beautiful varieties of the jelly-fish. These graceful animals may be observed anywhere in our summer waters, generally not far from the shore. Seeming to the careless sight to be mere floating plants, a closer inspection discovers in them animal forms of the rarest beauty of form and color, that sail hither and thither, and apparently have even a certain power of controlling their movements against the set of wind and current.

3. The general name of the medusa was applied to this animal on account of the snake-like filaments which it possesses, highly suggestive of the serpent locks of the Greek Medusa, one of the Gorgons; perhaps, also, from

The Medusa.

the danger of contact which all too-curious observers incur. The property common to nearly all the jelly-fish—that of a most severe and painful sting—is in some of the medusæ a paralyzing power against which the strongest men stand no chance. It is believed by scientific men that many of the cases of the sudden drowning of experienced swimmers is owing in as large degree to the attack of these beautiful and inoffensive-looking sea-creatures as to cramp.

4. Floating on the bosom of the waters, the medusa resembles a bell, an umbrella, or, better still, a floating mushroom, the stalk of which has been separated into lobes more or less divergent, sinuous, twisted, shriveled, fringed, the edges of the cup being delicately cut, and provided with long thread-like appendages, which descend vertically into the water like the drooping branches of the weeping willow.

5. The gelatinous substance of which the body of the medusa is formed is sometimes as clear as crystal, sometimes opaline, and sometimes bright blue or pale rose-color. Indeed, almost every color of the solar spectrum is represented in these little creatures. The shining tissue, decked out in the finest tints, is so fragile that, when washed up on the beach, it disappears in the sun without leaving a trace behind. Yet these living soap-bubbles of the sea make long voyages, and in some parts of the ocean abound in such enormous quantity that they make the principal food of the greatest of sea-animals, the whale.

6. They swim by their long tentacles and by contraction and dilatation of their bodies; and the ancients, from this peculiar movement of the medusæ, named them *sea-lungs*. Wandering over the seas in immense battalions, if an obstacle arrests them or an enemy touches them, the umbrella contracts, the tentacles are folded up, and the timid animals sink into the depths of the ocean.

7. The medusæ are furnished with a mouth, placed habitually in the middle of the umbrella-like head; a mouth, too, which is rarely empty, for the animal is voracious in the extreme, devouring even shell-fish, and attacking suc-

cessfully fish four or five inches in length. In respect to size the medusæ vary immensely, some being very small, while others attain more than a yard in diameter.

8. They breathe through the skin, and the organs of digestion are very peculiar. The walls of the stomach are furnished with a great multitude of vibrating hairy appendages, which secrete a juice supposed to decompose the food and make it digestible. Scientists also assert that these creatures have a distinct circulation, organs of sense, and something like a nervous system. The medusæ, for the most part, reproduce themselves.* Few fishes are more marvelous in their construction, more beautiful and graceful in form, than the medusa, and there is none which can be more easily studied by the frequenter of the sea-side.

World of Wonders.

FLOWERS OF THE SEA.

1. OUR object now is to say something of one of these flower-like types of marine life, namely, the sea-anemone. It is significant, as showing the suggestiveness of these creatures, that, however diverse the nomenclature of science may be in regard to them, it is often almost poetical, and the words used are always expressive, and even possess pictorial significance. De Blainville named them *Zoantharia*, from which comes animal-flower. Dr. Johnson's term took a wider latitude, and, although quite formidable-looking, and not in the best taste, was very significant. He gave the name *Zoöphyte helianthoidea*, which is to say, the sunflower-like animal-plant.

2. In these terms the animal nature and the flower-like

---

* By simply detaching a portion of its body, each part becomes a perfect animal.

form are intended. The creature is really a polyp, a soft, almost pulpy, sac-like structure, with a fringe of tentacles, like a halo of rays, around the upper end; in the center of the circular fringe, the mouth, or oral aperture, being situated. Hence, it is often spoken of as an actinia, which really means possessing rays. The word is now worked into another word, *Actinozoa*, meaning rayed animals, that is to say, animals with rays around an oral disk. But the term is used to designate a class; hence, it includes all the polyps, those that construct coral, and the others. This class is again divided into several orders, one of which is named *Zoantharia*, or, as it is sometimes called, the Helianthoid polyps. It is in this order that the actinia proper is found; and, therefore, it is there that we must find our sea-anemone.

3. Taken in the hand, the sea-anemone imparts a slippery feeling, and it seems to have the consistency of leather. As the actinia erects itself, attached to a rock or stone, it looks like one of the purses formerly fashionable, if one such could be made to stand of itself erect, and have the frill around the upper end to project in a circle. But we must be more particular than this. The upright part, that which is called by naturalists the column, is hollow, like a sack. Its base is really a sucking surface, enabling it to adhere to any hard object. By this sucking base it can glide, or travel along, much like a snail.

4. And, as it thus moves, it can keep its flower spread out, and its many tentacles in constant play—in fact, fishing on the way. Their movement is, however, very slow. Indeed, a "snail-pace" would be alarmingly fast for an actinia. We have watched them attentively, and have found that an inch in an hour was a very satisfactory performance. At the top is an opening, called the oral cavity, which, in the *rosea*, is surrounded just inside with a beading of little dots. This opening may be called the mouth,

because the food is passed at this aperture into the stomach, which is a cylindrical sac, suspended below, and reaching about half-way down the great cavity of the column. Around the oral cavity, and external to it, is a plain sur-

Sea-Anemones.

face, which is technically known as the "disk." Around the disk, on its outer edge, is the fringe of tentacles. Each one of these is a little hollow cylinder, opening into the great cavity of the column immediately under the edge of the disk. In fact, these tentacles, or feelers, connect with the interior of the stem of the anemone, just as the fingers of a glove do with the interior of the same.

5. Let me invite you to a sight I have many times beheld. I have in captivity a hungry sea-flower. Knowing well what suits its palate, I take a delicate morsel like a pilule, and let it fall into the water. It descends upon the waving petals, or tentacula, on the point of one of which the pretty creature has caught it in an instant. How delicate the adjustment upon its more than fairy fingers! For a few moments it is balanced with the nicest poise on that dactylic petal. Ah! a voracious and unmannerly little bummer of a minnow sees the delicious morsel, and makes a rapid dash to snatch it from my pet. "Good! good! Well done, my bonnie!" I did not see the slightest motion of that indignant flower-creature; yet assuredly there was a movement, and an effective one, too: for the zoöphyte had shot one of its invisible shafts, and the ichthyic thief dashes off like one frantic with pain.

6. Is he hurt? Likely. His is an urticated experience. He is stung in the snout! See how he seems to shake his nose! He fairly seems to sneeze again, and actually conducts himself much like a puppy that, uninvited, has put his nose into a bowl of hot soup. Ah, ha! He is rubbing his fishy proboscis against a frond of sea-lettuce. Perhaps the salad may cool his burning pain. Mr. Fish soon recovers his equanimity of mind; and it is observable that his deference to Mrs. Actinia since that affair has been of a decidedly distant character.

7. Generally the sea-anemone will not spread her beautiful form in a bright light. Often, when all seemed sulky and there was a general collapse, we have restored the whole coterie to good-humor, simply by covering up the aquaria for an hour or two, and then uncovering, when the flowers will fully open. It was a great transformation to see, when

this change took place with our favorite—a fine, large, fawn-colored one, obtained from Newport. When in healthful expansion it was larger than a good-sized dahlia; and, although of a subdued neutral tint, yet in form and color we thought our marine flower the superior of its terrestrial rival.

8. Somewhere we read the lucubration of a philosopher that there was no humor in Nature, but all was serious. The observation struck us as very learned, but very silly. No humor in Nature? Nonsense! Come out from your candle-light cogitations unto some real observations in the sunny light of Nature's beaming face, and I can show you humor. Ay, fun, if you will—yes, even practical jokes. A large actinia took a notion to swallow a large scallop, which it had captured. After considerable stretching, it got the bivalve down into its stomach, and in due time the contained mollusk was digested. But what about the shell? Why, this—it could not get it up again! It was a double disaster—literally as to the scallop, and metaphorically as to the polyp: both were sadly taken in. Actinia now looked very serious—comically so—like one in an evil strait. Perhaps it felt as bad as a hen-pecked subject, for it had got itself around a pecten, and a *pecten maximus* at that. If a guest at tea should swallow the tea-saucer, matters would look alarming. And this bolted scallop was as big as a saucer.

9. The effect upon the actinia's looks was ludicrous, since there was a narrow, bulging, equatorial belt, strongly significant of an undue centrifugal force in activity at that place. Get rid of the saucer it could not; so it seemed, with a saucy air, to have made up its mind to resort to an expediency that should fairly checkmate the strange exigency. And this expediency was a change of base. In fact, it transformed its old base entirely. Tentacles grew out around it, an oval aperture appeared, and, in a word,

it became a double actinia, and the large scallop-shell was made a double base, and was accepted ever after as the demarkation of the two individualities. No fun in Nature? If this, despite a smack of sauciness, was not a practical joke of the first water, then bring out your specimen-brick, old Sober-sides!

Rev. Samuel Lockwood.

STARS OF THE SEA.

1. If the visitor to the sea-shore will go down among the big rocks left bare by the retiring tide, and will lift up the long sea-weeds which hang from their sides, he will find the curious "star-fishes," or "sea-stars," in some cases in great profusion, and clinging to the surface of the rock so firmly that they often leave some of their locomotive suckers attached when too quickly lifted from their places.

2. When seen out of water, the star-fish appears to have no power of motion. But such is not the case, as it moves along the bottom of the ocean with ease. The body so gradually merges into the arms or rays that one can hardly tell where the body ends and the arms begin. The rays are perforated by great numbers of membranous tubes, which issue from apertures. These are the feet of the animal, and consist of two parts—a bladder-like portion within the body, and the tubular part projecting outside and terminating in a disk-shaped sucker.

3. In progression the animal extends a few of its feet, attaches its suckers to the rocks or stones, and then, by retracting its feet, draws the body forward. The mode of movement is something like that of a ship dragging its anchor. The arms are usually kept on the same level, but the creature has the power of raising any of them to pass over an obstruction. The pace is slow, but, like that of the

LOW LIFE IN THE SEA. 63

tortoise, it is sure. The back or upper part of the star-fish is armed with spine-like projections, and is hard and rough,

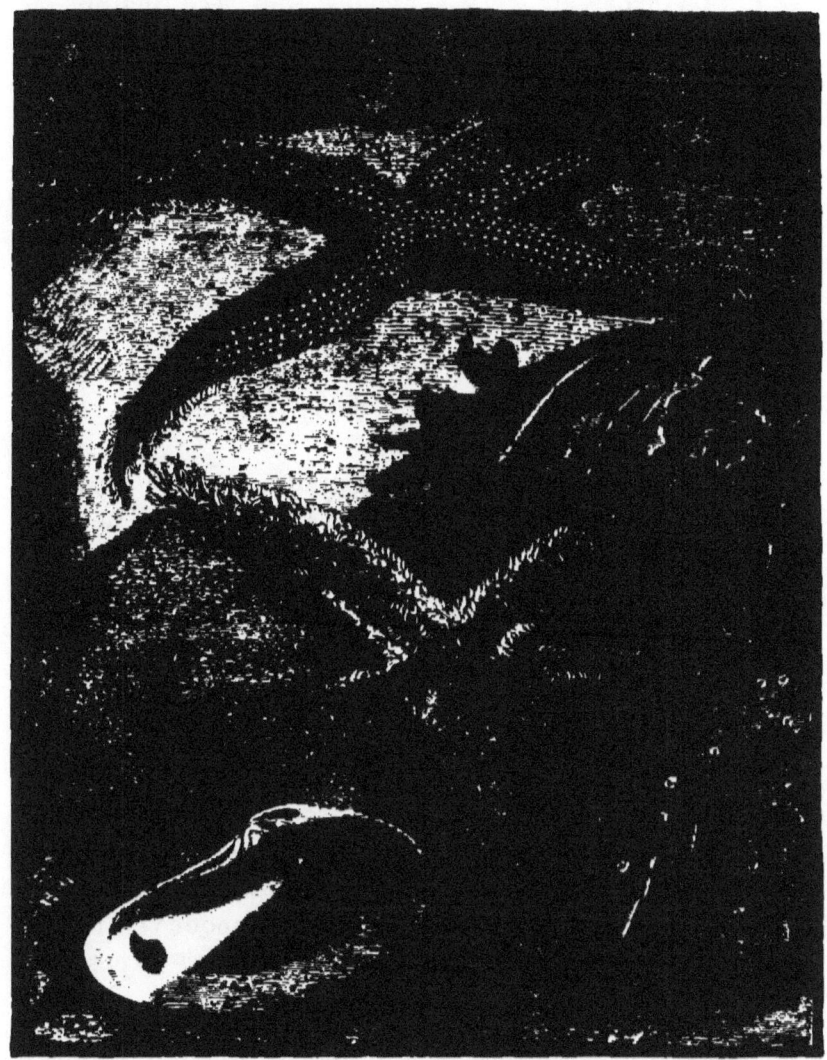

Upper and Under View of Star-Fish.

forming a kind of crusty shell, while the under side is soft, containing all the organs of life and movement. The mouth is in the center of the under side, and an eye is situated at the end of each of its five rays.

4. Star-fishes are very voracious, and feed mainly on mollusks. They are very destructive to oysters in many places, and thus come in direct competition with man for the possession of this delicious bivalve. Instead of swallowing their food as other animals do, they turn the stomach out of the mouth and over the animal which they wish to devour.

5. Star-fishes have a wonderful power of reproducing lost parts. If an arm is bitten off by a hungry fish, another grows in its place; and cases are known where all the arms but one have been detached, and the remaining arm and central portion of the body lived on and reproduced all the destroyed parts.

6. One of the most interesting traits about this low organized creature is its devotion to its young. The eggs are contained in little pouches at the base of the rays; and, when emitted, the mother star, instead of abandoning them, gathers them together and forms a kind of protecting arch over them, like a hen brooding her chickens. If the eggs are accidentally scattered, they are brought together again with great care.

7. In the same localities inhabited by these star-fishes we often find the "serpent stars," so called because their arms are long and slender, and curl at the end like a serpent's tail. They are also called "brittle stars," because they break so easily. One curious feature about the brittle stars is, that they break not only when they are exposed to some outside force, but they have the power to disjoint themselves, and they do so whenever they are in danger of capture or destruction. This ability and disposition to commit suicide is shared by no other animal with which we are acquainted. But as a compensation, and so that the species may not be destroyed, each part, in time, de-

velops into a perfect animal with all the parts complete; so that the self-destruction is but one step in the process of multiplication.

8. Professor Edward Forbes gives the following account of his efforts to capture a *Luidea*, one of the rarest species of brittle stars: "The first time that I took one of these creatures I succeeded in placing it entire in my boat. Not having seen one before, and being ignorant of its suicidal powers, I spread it out on a rowing-bench, the better to admire its form and colors. On attempting to remove it for preservation, to my surprise and disappointment I found only an assemblage of detached members.

Serpent Star-Fish.

My conservative endeavors were all neutralized by its destructive exertions; and the animal is now badly represented in my cabinet by a diskless arm and an armless disk.

9. "The next time I went to dredge I determined not to be cheated out of my specimen a second time. I carried with me a bucket of fresh water, for which the star-fishes evince a great antipathy. As I hoped, a *Luidea* came up in the dredge—a most gorgeous specimen. As the animal does not generally break up until it is raised to the surface of the sea, I carefully and anxiously plunged my bucket to a level with the dredge's mouth, and softly introduced the *Luidea* into the fresh water. Whether the cold was too much for it, or the sight of the bucket too terrific, I do not know; but in a moment it began to dissolve its corpora-

tion, and I saw its limbs escaping through every mesh of the dredge. In my despair, I seized the largest piece, and brought up the extremity of an arm and a terminal eye, the spinous eyelids of which opened and closed with something exceedingly like a wink of derision."

BUILDERS IN THE OCEAN.

1. IN the ocean within tropical regions are multitudes of little sea-animals resembling the sea-anemone in structure, known as coral polyps. They are made up of gelatinous matter, and consist of a sack-like body with a mouth at one extremity, surrounded by a row of radiating tentacles. These tentacles reach out and grasp the food necessary for the sustenance of the animal which the water brings. Unlike the sea-anemone, the coral polyp is attached at one extremity to the rock, and has no power of movement save the swaying of the body and the reach of the tentacles.

2. This animal takes from the water not only food, but it has the power of taking up the lime which is dissolved in the water, and of reconverting it into a solid substance. This lime is deposited in part at the bottom of its body next the rock to which it is attached, and in part between the tissues of the body itself. When the lime solidifies, the part of the animal which incloses the hard mass dies, so that coral is at once the framework and the tomb of the polyp.

3. Above the solid part the animal keeps alive, so that the coral is constantly growing upward and outward. A polyp with a single mouth multiplies itself by a kind of budding. A small bunch will appear upon the side of its body, which will soon develop into a perfect animal, with mouth and tentacles complete, as in the original animal.

Successive buds will appear upon both parent and child, until there is formed a community of polyps, each one perfect in itself, yet all united by the solid secretions, and by a common cavity in the softer parts.

4. This figure represents one of the immense variety of coral products, showing the work of the individual polyp,

Coral Madrepore.

the relations of one polyp with another, the branching of stems, and the general connections which form the community. The branch coral appears in hundreds of beautiful and fantastic forms; and, besides this, there are varieties which are hard and compact, like the ordinary rocks which we see on land. In every specimen of coral which we examine, we will find small cavities which mark the work of a single polyp, and which give to coral its characteristic appearance.

5. The coral-workers are found in all the tropical seas where the water is shallow enough for their operations. Although each one is tiny and insignificant, yet in the aggregate, from their vast numbers and ceaseless workings, they build up immense reefs in the ocean. Their building goes on in the water from the surface to a depth of one hundred and fifty feet, the hardier varieties building below, and the tender ones carrying on the work successively above. The necessary conditions in regard to depth of water are found only in the vicinity of the land, and hence the coral-workers are found near the coasts of continents and islands in tropical regions.

6. In many parts of the ocean, and especially in portions of the Pacific, long-continued investigation has shown that the land is gradually sinking. Among the islands, the low lands along the shore will first disappear, and it thus happens that the coral rock constructed next to the land is gradually changed to a reef at some distance from the land. The coral polyps meantime continue to build upward, keeping the coral rock nearly even with the surface, and this is changed to dry land above the surface by the dashing of the waves, which break off fragments and pile them upon the top of the undisturbed portion of the rock.

7. Some of the islands have only sunk a little way, leaving a reef partially or entirely inclosing it at a distance varying from half a mile to several miles from the land; some have sunk so that only the tops of the hills appear above the water, the coral-reef appearing now to surround several islands; and some of the islands have entirely disappeared, leaving a ring of coral-reef inclosing a lagoon, known as a lagoon-island, or atoll.

8. These circular reefs are found from one mile to

one hundred miles in diameter. The ring is usually from half a mile to one mile in width, with openings on the leeward side, through which vessels may pass. Seeds of plants

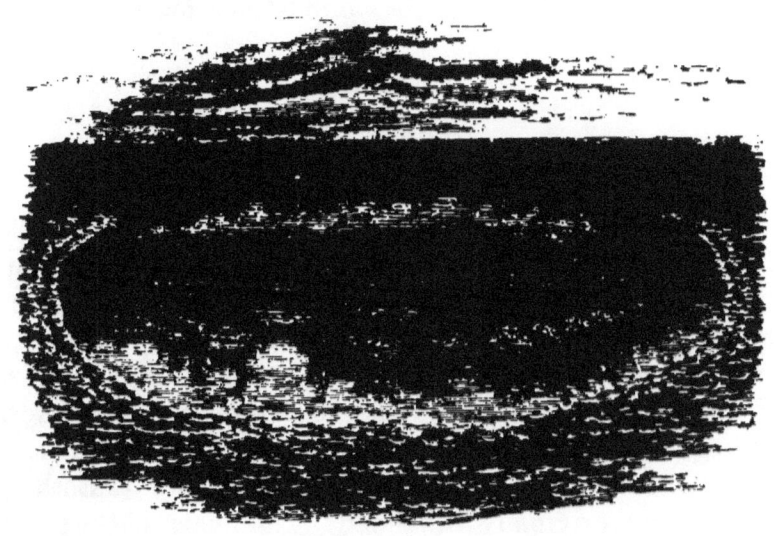

An Atoll.

are brought to these reefs by the waves and by birds, and there springs up a vegetation which covers the barren rocks and converts the reefs into lands suitable for human habitation. A coral-reef below the surface of the water, extending from the Caroline Islands toward Australia, is said to be continuous for five thousand miles, rivaling in extent the great mountain-ranges of the world. .

9. This bit of animal life, which is but little more than a speck of animated jelly, is thus seen to be a necessary link in the chain of causes which are slowly but surely changing the whole surface of the earth. The rains fall upon the land and form streams, which channel their way to the sea. The water, percolating through the soil, slowly dissolves the lime of the rocks, the solution forming one of the constituents of sea-water. Day by day the mountains

diminish, and the continents become less. As a compensation to these destructive forces, the coral-workers take up this solution and reconvert it into a solid form, constructing new lands and laying the foundations for new continents.

CORALS, AND HOW THEY ARE STUDIED.

1. Not very many years ago naturalists knew little about corals. The reef-building corals have their home in warm tropical seas, and they were chiefly known in Europe through the dried specimens brought home by seafaring men and given to their friends or stored in museums. These were either the solid, rocky masses called coral-heads, or fragments of the lighter branching kinds known as fan-corals and the like. There was a vague idea that these masses were originally inhabited by animals, but no one knew anything of their nature, their process of growth, or their appearance when alive. Even the red Mediterranean coral, so famous on account of the ornaments made from it, was more familiar to the fisherman who brought it up from the sea, and to the jeweler who wrought it into a thousand attractive forms, than to the naturalist. Indeed, there were few naturalists in those days living upon the sea-shore; their homes were chiefly in the central parts of Europe, in the large cities, where they found occupation as professors and teachers in the universities, and they depended chiefly upon museum collections for their knowledge of marine animals. The existence of the host of minute creatures living singly or in communities along every sea-shore was hardly known to science in those days.

2. A French physician residing at Montpelier, Peyssonel by name, first discovered the nature of these singular little beings. Having his home near the coast of the Mediter-

ranean, he could keep his specimens alive, and study them in their natural condition. He made his investigations upon corals, as well as upon what are called Hydroids. This name is given to a variety of small animals most of which live in communities. The facts discovered by Peyssonel were so interesting that naturalists began to feel, as they had never felt before, the importance of studying these seemingly insignificant creatures, and of studying them alive in their natural element. Since then a vast deal has been learned about them; and it was in the course of these researches that the corals were found to be allied with all the radiated animals, to have essentially the same structure as the sea-anemones, star-fishes, sea-urchins, and countless smaller animals belonging to the group of Hydroids.

3. In learning about the corals, we ought to know something about the men who have taught us the most about them. The first who studied the coral islands of the Pacific was Charles Darwin, the great English naturalist, and he wrote a charming and excellent book concerning them upon his return home from the exploring expedition in the ship Beagle around the world. Professor Dana, of Yale College, who accompanied the United States exploring expedition, made corals his especial study, and published an elaborate and valuable book concerning them, which is now considered an authority. And, lastly, Milne-Edwards, the French naturalist, though he has not had the living specimens before him, has taught us more than any one else of the hard parts of these animals—that is, of those portions of their structure which after their death are still preserved in the solid masses built by them.

4. Until he came to this country, Mr. Agassiz, like most European naturalists, had lived far from the sea-shore. It is true that in the heart of Switzerland he had gathered marine shells and corals, and had studied them; but they were the dead shells and corals of past ages, belonging to

a time when the countries which now shut Switzerland from the sea did not exist, and her western boundary was a sea-shore where corals built their reefs and shells lived on the beaches. When you learn something about the formation of mountains, you will see how such beaches may be raised from their natural level, so that the shells of animals which lived upon them are found at last among the mountains. On arriving in America, Mr. Agassiz began the study of the jelly-fishes, star-fishes, sea-anemones, and like objects living along our northern shore—animals which he had never before had the opportunity of watching alive. And, among other things, he became deeply interested in studying the structure of the little corals found about Martha's Vineyard Sound.

5. He procured living specimens, kept them alive in glass jars, changing the water frequently, and watched them during a whole summer, having drawings made from them to show the different parts of their body, their appearance when open or closed, and, in short, all the details of their structure. Thus it happened that he was quite familiar with these corals of our coast when he was invited by Professor Bache, then Superintendent of the Coast Survey, to make an examination of the coral-reef of Florida, in order to ascertain certain facts about it, the knowledge of which was important to the interests of navigation.

6. While making this survey he had, of course, the best opportunity for studying the animals themselves. He arranged a working-room, or laboratory, at Key West, and provided himself with a number of glass jars and large glass tubs, some of them so wide and deep that he could keep in them masses of living corals measuring two feet in diameter, completely immersed in water. This is a necessary condition. If you take a coral out of the water, he dies. There are some kinds so sensitive that, merely in order to take them from the sea and drop them into your jar, you

must place your jar under the water. The instant of transit while you lift the coral from his natural home would otherwise be sufficient to kill him.

7. Having arranged his working materials, Mr. Agassiz passed weeks in studying these minute creatures. He had microscopes, one or two assistants, and an artist, so that the work went on with a certain rapidity. But under the most favorable circumstances the progress is slow, because you must wait the moods of these capricious little creatures, who will hide themselves for hours, drawing in all their soft parts, and closing themselves against investigation. One day he sat watching a mass of living porites, which form the foundation of the reef. A specimen of this is shown in the figure. Every spot on the surface marks a separate individual, while the lines disposed about it like a star indicate the feelers. The animals are exceedingly small, scarcely larger than the head of a pin.

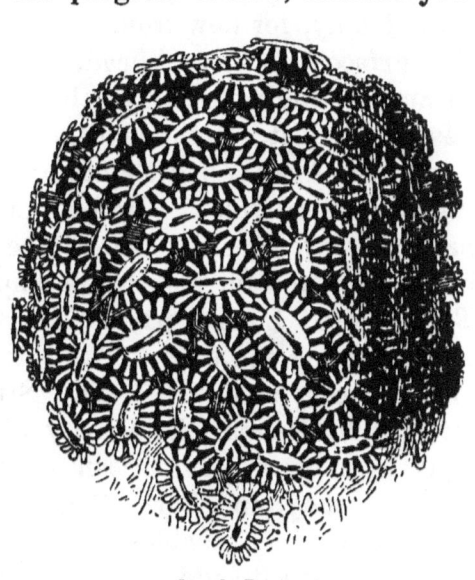

Coral Porite.

8. On this occasion Mr. Agassiz had been looking for a long time with a magnifying-glass at the minute creatures forming this singular community, when suddenly he saw a little, round, yellowish object—so small that it would scarcely have been noticed without the magnifier—protrude from the mouth of one of them. It was a new feature; he had never observed anything of the kind before, and he watched it with intense curiosity. It ad-

vanced more and more, creeping slowly out, and presently parted from the coral stock and floated free in the water, an independent being, oval in shape, a mere bubble for transparency and lightness, but evidently a living thing, since it moved about quite rapidly. He had seen the birth of a coral animal. While he followed its motions with wonder and interest, he perceived that the same process was going on over the whole mass. It was a birthday in this great family, for now from the countless mouths, crowding the surface of the coral-head, the same little objects began to appear, and were cast off like the first, till hundreds of new beings floated in the water around the parent community.

9. Mr. Agassiz had chanced upon the moment of breeding in a coral stock. He had never seen it, nor had any naturalist ever seen it before; he has never seen it since; he might watch for months, perhaps, and never see it again. This is what I mean when I say that these investigations are so baffling and slow. The patient waiting of years may give you only one such hour. Still, the time is not lost, for it is by intimate familiarity with the structure of animals, by constant comparison of one with another—by unwearied study, in short—that the observer acquires the knowledge which enables him to understand some entirely new fact when it suddenly presents itself.

10. Mr. Agassiz was unable to follow the history of his new brood beyond its first stages, because it was impossible to maintain the conditions necessary to rear them, and they soon died. But having ascertained that the young corals begin their existence as free, independent beings, and resemble the young of the soft-bodied radiates, so much is known of the latter, and of later stages in the life of the corals, that it was easy to put these facts together and make out the whole story.

11. Suppose such a being to be born into the sea—and no doubt they are cast in swarms from the coral stocks into

the water surrounding a reef. Independent and able to move about freely at first, it presently selects a suitable spot, and attaches itself to the rocks or to the sea-bottom by one end. This end flattens and adheres to the ground just as in the sea-anemone, fitting itself gradually to the surface on which it rests, while the upper end spreads and becomes a little depressed at the center. That depression marks where the mouth is presently to be, and it deepens until it becomes a hole, and feelers or tentacles gradually develop around it.

12. And now begins that phase in the life of a coral animal by which it differs from all the other radiates, and is enabled, notwithstanding its diminutive size, to play so important a part in the history of the world. There are hard particles of lime in its substance, and these accumulate, first, at the base of the body where it is attached to the ground, so that it becomes firm and immovable, afterward on the outside wall, and between the partitions. Now the whole has a solid frame, the only parts of the little coral which remain soft being the stomach within the body, the mouth, and feelers. These latter retain their flexible contractile character through life, and decompose when the animal dies.

13. There is one fact in the nature of the coral animals which affects their choice of a resting-place, and has a direct bearing on the strength and solidity of the structures they build. The more compact kinds, those which grow closely together and form the rounded, rocky masses known as coral-heads, like the deep sea. They settle at a depth of ten or twelve fathoms, while the lighter branching kinds prefer shallower waters. Thus it happens that the foundation of a reef is always laid by those coral animals which, from their very nature and mode of growth, secure the soundest basis for the structure ; while the upper part is built by the lighter branching kinds.

14. We have seen the birth of an independent coral. But these animals have two ways of multiplying: one by which new communities are founded, another by which they spread and increase. A little germ, like the one described above, having undergone the changes I have mentioned, and assumed his permanent character, begins to put out little buds from either side, which grow into new beings exactly like himself, and multiply in their turn, till the community which he has founded is numbered by hundreds, thousands, nay, millions of distinct beings. All the members of this innumerable family are organically connected; that is, the cavities of their bodies open into each other, so that they lead a common life, the food absorbed by each one circulating through the whole mass, and nourishing all the rest.

15. There is a great difference in the mode of budding among the different kinds of coral. Some spread horizontally, budding from the base and pushing outward. In others, each animal gradually widens toward the summit as it grows, assuming a sort of trumpet-shape, and then divides, so that where there was but one mouth there are now two. All the curious and fantastic kinds of coral which we find in cabinets are the results of these different methods of budding. The study of the dead specimens, however, can convey a very inadequate idea of the beauty and wonder of the submarine wall, and of the living shrubbery which crowns its summit, as seen upon the reefs of Florida.

Mrs. Elizabeth C. Agassiz.

THE CORAL GROVE.

1. Deep in the wave is a coral grove,
   Where the purple mullet and gold-fish rove,
   Where the sea-flower spreads its leaves of blue,
   That never are wet with the falling dew,

But in bright and changeful beauty shine
Far down in the green and glassy brine.

2. The floor is of sand, like the mountain's drift,
    And the pearl-shells spangle the flinty snow;
From coral rocks the sea-plants lift
    Their boughs where the tides and billows flow;
The water is calm and still below,
    For the winds and waves are absent there,
And the sands are bright as the stars that glow
    In the motionless fields of upper air.

3. There, with its waving blade of green,
    The sea-flag streams through the silent water,
And the crimson leaf of the dulse is seen
    To blush like a banner bathed in slaughter.
There, with a light and easy motion,
    The fan-coral sweeps through the clear, deep sea;
And the yellow and scarlet tufts of ocean
    Are bending, like corn on the upland lea.

4. And life in rare and beautiful forms
    Is sporting amid those bowers of stone,
And is safe, when the wrathful spirit of storms
    Has made the top of the wave his own.
And when the ship from his fury flies,
    Where the myriad voices of ocean roar,
When the wind-god frowns in the murky skies,
    And demons are waiting the wreck on the shore—
Then, far below in the peaceful sea,
    The purple mullet and gold-fish rove,
There the waters murmur tranquilly
    Through the bending twigs of the coral grove.

Percival.

CRABS AND THEIR WAYS.

1. WITH one's eyes kept open, how very much there is to excite interest in a summer stroll beside the sea! Marine life—the creatures that represent the life-zone that belts or fringes the great murmuring world of waters—is so peculiar, some exquisitely beautiful, as the sea-anemones, others droll and grotesque, as the great class known as the *Crustacea*. The tide is out. See that bird with bill curving upward. A beautiful functional adaptation it is—for with it small stones are turned over so deftly, and thus its food, the sheltered worms, are exposed. It is the avocet.

2. So we turn avocet, using a stick in the operation. Ah! we have disturbed a poor polydactyled refugee in his retreat. See how threateningly he snaps at us his two pairs of pincers like formidable blacksmith-tongs. What a crusty-looking fellow he is! Now he is off, running sidewise; for they can go "forward, backward, and oblique." There is speed enough, but the gait is so comical. But crabs are given to flank movements. We determine to try one on him; so with the stick just touching him laterally, and a fillip, and he is on his back.

3. At this point, Frank, who is always facetious, and who had just been saying that he had come from the bowling green (he meant alley), says we have knocked the poor fellow off his pins, and that it was a ten-strike, adding for our enlightenment, "Don't you see that crab stands on ten pins?" Now, it so happens in this connection that it is just on this "ten-pin" arrangement that the naturalist founds his division *Decapoda* as one of the three orders of the great class *Crustacea*. The decapods, or ten-footed, include the crabs and lobsters, and rank the highest in their class.

4. All crustaceans exuviate, or cast their hard, shelly

covering at least once a year. It has been said quite graphically that "the new integument is so soft and yielding, and the muscles in such a flaccid condition, that the limbs are drawn through the small openings at the joints, much as a sack nearly filled with some fluid may be drawn through an opening much smaller than the sack itself." It should not be forgotten, however, that the neck in the great claws, or nippers, is crossed by thin, knife-like blades, or plates of shell; and it is certain that in drawing out the thumbs they are cut into long shreds, which doubtless, when drawn out, come together immediately and heal.

5. As giving a peep at the private life of the European crabs, let us skim off the cream of a paragraph from Gosse.

Edible Crab.

The naturalist has been exploring the rocks on the English coast, and says: "Peering into a hole, I saw a fine large crab. I pulled him out, and carried him home. There came out with him the claw of a crab of similar size, but quite soft, which I supposed might have been carried in there by my gentleman to eat. After I had got him out—it was a male—I looked in, and saw another at the bottom of the hole.

6. "Arrived at home, I found that I had left my pocket-knife at the mouth of the crab-hole. I returned; the crab had not moved. I drew it out. But lo! it was a soft crab, the shell being of the consistence of wet parchment. It was a female, too, and had lost one claw. What, then, are we to infer from this association? Do the com-

mon crabs live in pairs? And does one keep guard at the mouth of the cavern, while its consort is undergoing its change of skin? I have no doubt that the claw of its mate was unintentionally torn off in its efforts to effect some hold, when resisting my tugs in dragging him out."

7. But it is in America, after all, that the habits of crabs at their time of exuviation should be the best known. The soft-shell crab is condemned as food in Europe, it being considered as in a sickly state at that time, just as birds are when moulting. And may not this be so? However, in this country the procuring of the soft-shell crab is a great and profitable industry. Hence, any intelligent "crabber" knows a good deal of their habits. For many years we knew an old fisherman. He was quite illiterate, but of more than the average intelligence of his class. He was an old "crabber," too. As he long supplied my family with fish, I often got him into conversation.

8. "I hev ketched soft crabs for market many a year. The crab sheds every year, chiefly in early summer. At that time the he one is mighty kind to his mate. When she shows signs of shedding, the he one comes along, and gets on the she one's back, quite tenderly like, and entirely protects her from all enemies, whether of fishes or of their own kind. She is now getting ready to shed, and is called a *shedder*. Soon the back begins to burst nigh to the tail. She is then called a *buster*. The he one is then very anxious to find a good place for her, either by digging a hole in the sand or mud, or else looking up a good cover under some sea-weed. Here he brings her, all the time hovering nigh, and doing battle for her, if anything comes along. She now—and it only takes a few minutes—withdraws from the old shell. And she comes out perfect in every part, even to the inside of the hairs, the eyes, and long feelers, almost like the whiskers of a cat. At the first tide she is *fat*, and the shell is soft, just like a thin skin. She

is then called a *soft-shell*, and it's the first-tiders that bring the high price. At the second tide she is perfectly watery and transparent, and is then called a *buckler ;* but she is not worth much then. At the third tide she is again a *hard-shell*, as she always was, only bigger."

9. As mentioned, our edible crab literally backs out of the shell; that is, it comes out at an opening behind. The *Limulus*, or horseshoe-crab, acts directly contrariwise. The shell cracks open at the front, and the animal emerges forward, instead of from behind, or backward. In fact, the structure of the shell makes this the only possible mode. A few years ago the officers superintending the building of the fort at Sandy Hook became greatly interested at witnessing this exuviation of the shell of *Limulus Polyphemus*, and they declared that the fellow was spewing himself out of his mouth!

Rev. Samuel Lockwood.

FIDDLERS UPON THE SHORE.

1. THE fiddler-crab is truly a queer customer. Some call him the soldier-crab; and certainly, if agility and seeming courage make up the martial element, then a valorous little fellow he is. The males have one hand enormously large. This, when closed upon the front of the body, is suggestive of the attitude of a violinist—hence we boys used to call it the fiddler-crab. The naturalist names it *Gelasimus vocans*, a name highly expressive of its attributes. Some have rendered the words "calling-crab." This is too far short of their significance. The words are intended to indicate both the action of the crab and its effect upon the beholder. When alarmed, they go scuttling over the mud to their burrows, the males each holding his

great claw aloft, and waving it in a manner that looks ludicrously like beckoning, or challenging, and at the same time threatening, and this, too, while in full and masterly retreat.

2. Each seems, as it might be, a Liliputian Falstaff; and, if rendered in Homeric strain, *Gelasimus vocans* would signify the "laughter-provoking challenger." Indeed, Gelasimus never sees anybody, whether great or small, but forth he hurls his challenge in pantomime, for up goes that threatening huge member, so that its owner appears to be habitually bent on something high-handed. As this swaying of the great fiddle-like claw seems to start and direct or animate the retreat, it is ludicrously suggestive of a musical conductor beating time by swaying a bass-viol instead of his *báton*, the effect of his eccentricity being to cause a stampede of all the fiddlers.

Fiddler-Crab.

3. This crab excavates holes in the earth, a male and a female occupying one hole. Into this retreat it retires with astonishing celerity when alarmed, and, having gained its hole, it literally barricades the entrance, by turning round and closing it up with its big hand, leaving just room enough for the little keen eyes to keep a sharp lookout at whatever may be passing. In these burrows they spend the winter, probably in hibernation. More than once, when pursuing the fiddler, who, with fiddle aloft, ran swiftly, has the writer had the luxury of a slip and fall on the slimy clay of Fiddler Town, as we called a certain place in the salt-meadows,

where these fiddlers lived. Those mishaps were really enjoyable—that is, to those who looked on.

Rev. Samuel Lockwood.

SEA-HERMITS AND THEIR HOMES.

1. THERE is a group of crabs which has a curious habit, made necessary on account of the unprotected condition of the hinder part of their bodies. This is entirely naked; hence these crabs occupy the empty shells of sea-snails, winkles, and such univalves. It is called the hermit-crab, or *Pagurus*. The most common species on the Atlantic coast is the little hermit. A pair of nippers at the extremity of the tail, or naked abdomen, enables it to grip the columella, or upper part of the inside of the shell that it occupies, thus keeping itself snugly in place. As the crab increases in size by growth, it has to change its home for one more roomy; and this leads to some remarkable exhibitions of its instincts. The sight, which we have often beheld, is one of exciting interest. Watch, now, if you please.

2. Here is a fat little hermit-crab, whose domicile, like a strait-jacket, has become decidedly uncomfortable, and he is somewhat distracted about it. He is out a house-hunting—that is a literal fact. See, he has found an empty shell. It is not so handsome as the one he now occupies, but it is a little larger. Look, how he almost lifts it up among his ten feet, every one of which is an interested inspector, as each must bear its part in sustaining the establishment. Now he rolls it round and round, all over and over, delicately manipulating its sculpture occasionally; he is not only testing its specific gravity like a philosopher, but also seems to have an eye to appearances.

Now comes the most essential, the inspection of the interior. Will it fit? That is the chief consideration. He inserts his longest finger, and thoroughly probes the whole matter. One more trial—and now it seems that the antennæ, or feelers, enter into the consultation. And what an amount of feeling deliberation does this step involve! Well, the thing appears to be satisfactory. It is evidently decided that the new house will answer.

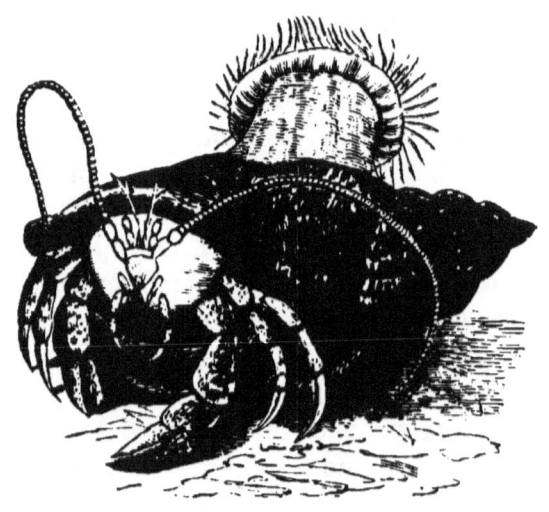

Hermit-Crab.

3. And now comes the most trying time of all—for "moving" is a trying time. But Pagurus is actuated by considerations that fall not to the lot of migratory mortals of the bipedal sort. His accountability is of the ten-talent order. With his eyes he surveys the entire situation. What! Yes, it is so! He has moved, and settled, and has got the house "all to rights." The whole thing was done in the twinkling of an eye. It vacates the old house, whisks its tail round, and enters the new one backward, as if shot into it from a gun. In fact, unless watching intently, the whole movement will elude the eye, like a trick

of legerdemain. And the cause is not far to seek. If that soft, nude, defenseless body were exposed but for an instant, it might become the prey of some darting fish.

4. These hermit-crabs are highly pugnacious. We once took a pair of them that we suspected of being anxious to change their houses. They were put in a vessel of sea-water, and, full in sight of them, was placed an empty winkle-shell, which we supposed was of the right size. How they did fight for it! It was a battle for life. One succumbed at last, and died. The survivor coolly surveyed his victim, and then surveyed the new premises. After this, he promptly entered into possession; and then, pitiful to relate, he fell to eating his defunct comrade. Oh, the cannibal! The cut given of a hermit-crab shows actinea, or zoöphite, upon the shell. These are sometimes called sea-anemones, and animal flowers, on account of their being real animals, with a flower-like form.

Rev. Samuel Lockwood.

PART IV.

HIGHER LIFE IN WATERS.

THE DEVIL-FISH AND HIS KIN.

1. The cuttle-fish has been an object of curiosity almost from time immemorial, both on account of its strange form and its habits. It seems to be a connecting link between the fishes and the lower forms of life in the waters. Like the sea-anemone, it consists of a sack-like body with tentacles, only with the cuttle-fish the body has attained a much greater consistency, and is provided with a bony substance known as cuttle-fish shell, and the tentacles are developed into ten long leathery arms, provided with suckers which can attach themselves to any hard substance. Just where the arms are attached to the body are two large, staring eyes, which give to the fish a very sinister appearance.

2. The cuttle-fish seeks its prey in the open sea, and is very voracious. Fishermen dread its presence in their nets, as it bites and mutilates other fish savagely. It is provided with a receptacle containing a dark-colored fluid, which it discharges when attacked, coloring the water, and so rendering itself invisible to its enemy. This fluid is sepia, from which sepia or India ink is made. The cuttle-fish sometimes attains the size of three feet in length.

3. A much more formidable member of this family of

fishes is the octopus, or devil-fish proper. This animal consists of a mouth and stomach combined, with usually eight, but sometimes ten long arms. The eyes are like those of the cuttle-fish. It can readily be seen how this creature seizes its prey. The arms are tough and leathery, and can not be easily cut with a knife. They are furnished their whole length with two rows of perfect sucking disks, or some two thousand air-pumps. The edges are sharp and saw-like, burying themselves in the flesh of their victims. With some of their arms attached to a rock, they throw out the others as lassos, and while in this position scarcely anything can resist their force.

4. The long appendages are used both as arms and legs. All the octopods swim freely at will, and associate in numbers, but the larger ones, as they become older, fly from community life and retire into the clefts and hollows of the rocks which have been worn by the waves, generally in places only a few feet below the level of low water. There, with one arm clasped close to the wall of its dwelling, the watchful savage extends the others, alert, like the boa-constrictor, for the approach of prey, and no less deadly in the crushing force of its folds. Its movements in seizing its victims are swift as an arrow.

The Octopus.

5. When the animal is swimming, its long tentacles would be in the way if extended or left pendent, so they

are drawn close alongside and allowed to float behind, where they act as the tail to a kite. Motion in the water is gained by drawing in and expelling water from the locomotory tube. The octopus thus swims backward instead of forward. Its food consists of crustaceans, fishes, and other mollusks; every kind of animal, in fact, which comes within its reach. But it disdains carrion flesh, and feeds only on living victims. The general life of the octopus, as of the other cuttle-fish, is about five or six years; and it lays eggs, which are large, and generally found in clusters. Fishermen call them sea-grapes.

6. The locomotion of the devil-fish is as easy on land as in the water. They have been known frequently to run up perpendicular cliffs, two hundred feet high, as easily as the fly runs up a wall, the machinery of attachment being very similar. They are said to move as fast on land as a man can run, and they frequently pursue their prey out of the sea, though on the land they are far more timid than in the water. The vulnerable portion of the octopus is the neck, and fishermen and others, who know their habits when attacked, always strive, if possible, to seize them by the throttle-valve, when they are easily killed. This is comparatively easy on land, but nearly impossible in the water.

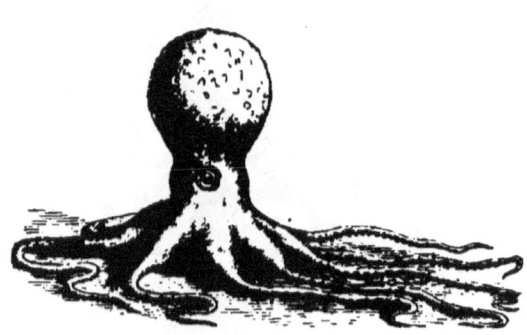

Octopus Running.

7. The octopus grows to an immense size, when it merits its name of devil-fish. Some years since one was cast ashore at Newfoundland with arms fifty feet in length. But the largest one of which we have an authentic account

was the one encountered near the Madeira Islands by the French steamer Alecton. This monster was estimated to be fifty feet long without reckoning its eight formidable arms, covered with suckers, and about twenty feet in circumference at its largest part, the head terminating in many arms of enormous size, the other extremity in two fleshy lobes or fins of great size, the weight of the whole being estimated at four thousand pounds; the flesh was soft, glutinous, and of reddish-brick color.

8. The commandant, wishing in the interests of science to secure the monster, actually engaged it in battle. Numerous shots were aimed at it, but the balls traversed its flaccid and glutinous mass without causing it any vital injury. But after one of these attacks the waves were observed to be covered with foam and blood, and, singular thing, a strong odor of musk was inhaled by the spectators. This musk odor is peculiar to many of the cephalopods.

9. The musket-shots not having produced the desired results, harpoons were employed, but they took no hold on the soft, impalpable flesh of the marine monster. When it escaped from the harpoon, it dived under the ship, and came up again at the other side. They succeeded at last in getting the harpoon to hold, and in passing a bowling hitch round the posterior part of the animal. But when they attempted to hoist it out of the water the rope penetrated deeply into the flesh, and separated it into two parts, the head with the arms and tentacles dropping into the sea and making off, while the fins and posterior parts were brought on board; they weighed about forty pounds.

10. Rev. Mr. Harvey, of Newfoundland, published an account a few years ago of the adventure of two fishermen in Conception Bay. Their boat passed near what appeared to be a floating bale of goods, which was presumed to be flotsam from some wreck. One of them struck the mass with the boat-hook, when it instantly opened, like a gigan-

tic umbrella without a handle, and a huge head, with fiery, threatening eyes that protruded ominously, and a long, curved beak, raised itself from the surface. While they stood paralyzed with fear, the monster flung at them a tentacle of livid, corpse-like hue, thirty feet long, which went far beyond the boat, or they would have been engulfed.

11. One of the fishermen seized a sharp hatchet, and, by a well-directed blow, severed this terrible lasso before another could be used, on which the savage apparition of the sea swiftly darted backward, and was lost to sight amid the ink-like discharge with which it blackened the waters. The tentacle was given to Mr. Harvey, and the fishermen avowed that there must have been at least ten feet more of it next the body of their assailant. The colored discharge would indicate that this monster was a kind of cuttle-fish rather than an octopus.

12. These terrible animals draw their prey to their formidable mouths and swallow it whole, where it is slowly digested as in the case of the boa. The soft elastic material of their body admits of an almost indefinite amount of extension, so that prey of almost any size is easily disposed of. Nature here, as elsewhere, however, has its compensations. All the cuttle-fish are the favorite food of the whale, the dolphin, and the porpoise. Michelet says: "These lords of the ocean are so delicate in their taste that they eat only the heads and arms, which are easy of digestion. The coasts are frequently covered with thousands of the mutilated cuttle-fish. The porpoises take most incredible bounds, at first, to frighten them, and afterward to run them down. After making a meal, they seem to express their satisfaction by a series of gymnastics."

SHOOTING AND ANGLING FISHES.

1. THE Eton boy hastening home for the holidays provides himself with a tin tube and a pocketful of peas. We beg the present Etonian's pardon; we should have said he used to do so formerly, when there were boys at Eton, and, backed by some skill as a marksman, therewith constituted himself an intolerable nuisance to every village and vehicle he passed on his road home. The Macoushee Indian makes a better use of his blow-tube; he puffs small arrows and hardened balls of clay through it with unerring aim, doing great execution among birds and other small game.

2. Now, the chætodon, which is an inhabitant of the Eastern seas from Ceylon to Japan, rather, perhaps, resembles the Macoushee Indian than the Eton boy, though his gun, shooting-tube, or blow-pipe, or whatever it may be termed, is a natural one. His nose is really a kind of "beak," through which he has the power of propelling a small drop of water with some force and considerable accuracy of aim. Near the edge of the water is perhaps a spray of weed, a twig, or a tuft of grass; on it sits a fly, making its toilet in the watery mirror below. Rostratus advances cautiously under the fly; then he stealthily projects his tube from the water, takes a deadly aim, and pop goes the watery bullet.

"Poor insect, what a little day of sunny bliss is thine!" Knocked over by the treacherous missile, drenched, stunned, half drowned, she drops from her perch into the waters below, to be sucked in by the chætodon.

3. But if we have fishes who can shoot their game, we have also fishes who can fish for it; ay, and fish for it with rod and line, and bait, as deftly as ever angler coaxed gudgeons from the ooze of the New River or salmon from

the flashing torrent of the Spey. Witness this clumsy-looking monster the fishing-frog, or angler-fish.

The Angler-Fish.

4. Frightful and hideous is he, according to our vulgar notions of loveliness, which the lophius possibly might disagree with. The beast is sometimes five or six feet in length, with an enormous head in proportion to the rest of its body, and with huge sacks like bag-nets attached to its gill-covers, in which it stows its victims; and what a cavernous mouth!

5. Surely a fish so repulsive, and with a capacity so vast and apparently omnivorous, would frighten from its

neighborhood all other fish, and would, if its powers of locomotion were in accordance with its size, be the terror of the seas to fish smaller than itself; but Providence knoweth how to temper its gifts, and the lophius is but an indifferent swimmer, and is too clumsy to support a predatory existence by the fleetness of its motions. How, then, is this huge capacity satisfied? Mark those two elongated tentacles which spring from the creature's nose, and how they taper away like veritable fishing-rods. To the end of them is attached, by a line or a slender filament, a small glittering morsel of membrane. This is the bait. The hooks are set in the mouth of the fisherman down below. But how is the animal to induce the fish to venture within reach of those formidable hooks?

6. Now mark this perfect feat of angling. How does the Thames fisherman attract the gudgeons? They are shy; he must not let them see him, yet he must draw them to him, and he does it by stirring up the mud upon the bottom. "In that cloud of mud is food," say the gudgeons. Then the angler plies his rod and bait. Just so the lophius proceeds, and he too stirs up the mud with his fins and tail. This serves not only to hide him, but to attract the fish. Then he plies *his* rod, and the glittering bait waves to and fro like a living insect glancing through the turbid water. The gudgeons, or rather gobies, rush toward it. "Beware! beware!" But when did gudgeon attend to warning yet? Suddenly, up rises the cavernous Nemesis from the cloud below, and "snap!" the gobies are entombed in the bag-net, thence to be transferred to the lophius's stomach, when there are enough of them collected to form a satisfactory mouthful.

7. The angler-fish is not left entirely undisturbed to carry on his work of destruction. A kind of eel ensconces himself in the branchial sack of the angler and makes it his permanent home, levying a toll upon all food which the

angler catches, and at the same time resists the efforts of the angler to convert him into food. Henceforth the angler is obliged to fish for two, and, in case of scarcity, it is not the eel that will first suffer from hunger.

Francis Francis.

HUNTING-FISHES.

1. MANY fish hunt their prey singly, as the pike and trout, and the way in which a large fish of these kinds will course and run down a smaller fish resembles nothing so much as a greyhound coursing a hare. Now the unhappy little fish turns from side to side in its efforts to escape, while its pursuer bends and turns to every motion, following close upon its track, and cutting him off exactly as the greyhound does the hare. Now he rushes among a shoal of his fellows, hoping to be lost sight of in the crowd and confusion; but the grim foe behind is not to be baffled or deceived, and, singling him out, and scattering the small fry, which fly in all directions, ruffling the surface of the water like a sudden squall of wind in their fright, follows up his victim with unerring instinct. In an agony of terror, the poor little quarry springs again and again frantically from the water, only to fall at last, exhausted, into the gaping jaws of his ravenous foe, who, griping his body crosswise, sails steadily away to his lair, there to devour his prey at leisure.

2. Some fish hunt their food, like dogs and wolves, in packs. The bonito hunting the flying-fish is an example. But the fiercest, most savage, and resolute of all the leagued banditti of the deep is the piräi of South America. So savage are these little pirates that, when their size and apparent capabilities are taken into consideration, their feats of destructiveness are little short of the marvelous.

3. Let us take the portrait of this fish. Doubtless the reader figures to himself a fish of "a lean and hungry look," a very Cassius of a fish, with the lantern-jaws of a pike. But, in fact, the piräi is somewhat aldermanic and like a bream in figure, with a fighting-looking kind of nose, and a wondrously expressive eye. The jaw is square, powerful, and locked into a very large head for the size of the fish; and that is a fat, plump head too, but radiated over with strong bone and gristle. The teeth—ah! they would condemn him anywhere, for here is a fish sixteen inches long with the teeth almost of a shark.

4. This voracious fish is found plentifully in all the rivers in Guiana, and is dreaded by every other inhabitant or visitor of the river. Their jaws are so strong that they are able to bite off a man's finger or toe. They attack fish of ten times their own weight, and devour all but the head. They begin with the tail, and the fish, being left without the chief organ of motion, is devoured with ease, several going to participate of the meal. Indeed, there is scarcely any animal which it will not attack, man not excepted. Large alligators which have been wounded on the tail afford a fair chance of satisfying their hunger, and even the toes of this formidable animal are not free from their attacks. The feet of ducks and geese, where they are kept, are almost invariably cut off, and young ones devoured altogether. In these places it is not safe to bathe, or even to wash clothes, many cases having occurred of fingers and toes being cut off by them.

5. Of course, the lines which are used to capture them have to be armed with metal, to prevent their being cut through. Their voracity is marvelous, and any bait will attract them the instant it is thrown into the water. Precaution is necessary, however, when the fish is lifted out of the water, or it will inflict serious wounds in its struggles. The fisherman, therefore, has a small bludgeon

ready, with which he breaks their skulls as soon as they are caught.

6. Some fish-hunters use other fish to hunt their game, as we use pointers and setters, such as the little pilot-fish, which leads the huge shark to his prey; though this has been disputed, because the pilot-fish has been known to follow and play about a vessel just as it does usually about the body of a shark. The probability is, that the pilot-fish is a species of parasite or diner-out, who will make particular friends with any big person who will feed him, and no doubt would find food in the refuse cast from the vessel, even as he would from the fragments torn off by the shark when feeding on any large body. Doubtless, too, there is a certain amount of protection obtained from consorting with monsters against other predaceous fish. The fact of the pilot-fish conducting the shark to his prey has been disputed, but veritable instances related by eye-witnesses leave no doubt that at times it does fulfill this office for the shark. Nor is there anything singular in the fact. The pilot-fish is on the lookout for his own dinner, probably, but will not venture on it until his protector has helped himself. We have numerous similar instances both in human and in beast life.

7. The reader, possibly, has never witnessed a skäll in Scandinavia. It is a species of hunt in which a number of sportsmen take in a wide space of ground where game exists, drawing a cordon around it, narrowing their circle little by little, and driving the game together into a flock, when they shoot them down. Now there are fish who hunt their game in the same way. Mr. Lonce, while fishing off the Channel Islands, witnessed a skäll of this kind. His attention was called to several porpoises, which seemed to be engaged in a water-frolic, swimming after one another in a circle, and he pointed it out to Peter, the fisherman who accompanied him.

8. "That is no frolic, but very sober earnest for the sand-eels," said Peter. "Now," he continued, "I will show you a sight which I have only chanced to see two or three times in my life, and you are therefore very lucky to have the opportunity of seeing it at all. There is a great shoal of sand-eels yonder, and the porpoises are driving them into a mass; for you see the sand-eel is only a very small morsel for a porpoise, and to pick them up one by one would not suit Mr. Porpoise, who would get hungry again by the time he had done feeding on them singly; so they drive the eels into a thick crowd, in order that when they make a dash at them they may get a dozen or two at a mouthful. But as we want some for bait, we will join in the hunt."

9. They edged down to the spot until they were within the circle. The porpoises, following one another pretty closely, were swimming around, now rising to the surface, now diving below, and gradually contracting the circle. The terrified sand-eels were driven closer and closer, and in their fear came to the surface all about the boat, and, just as two or three porpoises made a dash into the crowd, snapping right and left, the fishermen plunged their nets into the water, and brought them up quite full of these little fish. The shoal was soon dispersed, but the skill with which the skäll had been conducted looked very much like reasoning.

Francis Francis.

FISHES ARMED WITH LIGHTNING.

1. AMONG other powers, offensive and defensive, commanded by fish and men alike, is the very remarkable one of electricity. Several species of fish are literally armed with lightning, which they can discharge at enemies or prey with fatal effect. These animated electric batteries

are so powerful that even the shark, the terror of all the finny tribe, after one encounter never seeks another, but gives them a wide berth. As all varieties of the electric fishes live quietly, and usually in the mud in shallow waters, they would be peculiarly exposed to the attacks of the larger fish, but their power of self-defense renders them invulnerable. For purposes other than defense it is not certainly known how this peculiar apparatus serves the fish, but the most reasonable hypothesis appears to be that the shock both stuns the prey so that it is easily caught, and effects a change by which digestion is facilitated. In support of this latter point, we have the fact that the alimentary canal in the electric fishes, where digestion takes place, is much shorter than in any other of the vertebrated animals.

2. The electric discharge from the fish is precisely the same as that from a battery, as is shown by rendering the needle magnetic, by its effect upon chemical compounds, and by the heat evolved and the electric spark obtained. Upon an examination of the fishes, the electric apparatus is found to consist of cells arranged and connected as in a galvanic battery, the electric conditions probably being maintained through the nervous structure of the animal.

3. The most widely scattered of the electric fishes is the torpedo, which belongs to the rays or skates. The body is smooth and rounded, the tail short and thick, cylindrical at the end and keeled on the sides. The torpedo, take it all in all, is an innocent-looking fish, and the quizzical expression of its face adds to the harmlessness of its aspect. But woe be unto man or animal which ventures to trench on its dignity!

4. The electrical apparatus is arranged in two masses, one on each side of the skull. It is composed of a multitude of perpendicular columns, in the shape of eight-sided prisms, separated by walls of membrane containing a fluid freely supplied with blood, and laced with an immense

number of nervous filaments. This apparatus is something like the galvanic pile. John Hunter counted twelve hundred columns in a very large fish, and about one hundred and fifty plates to the inch. In one specimen, Professor Wyman estimated the number of plates in an American torpedo, a species which sometimes reaches a length of four and one half feet, and a width of three feet, at the enormous number of three hundred thousand, the prisms being about two inches in height and containing one hundred plates to the inch. The intervals between the plates

The Torpedo.

were filled with an albuminous fluid, mostly water, but containing salt in solution.

5. In the torpedo the shock is most powerful when connection is made between the back and the abdomen. Actual contact with the fish, however, is not necessary, as it is well known by the Neapolitan fishermen that the shock is felt when the water is dashed on it, the electric current passing up along the stream, the circuit being completed through the earth to the stomach of the fish. The torpedo never uses its power for aggressive uses, as it is rather a timid fish; but it makes itself dreaded by other fish, which soon learn to let this living electric battery alone.

It lives on small fish, and keeps near the bottom, preferring a muddy bed to any other. There are about twenty species of the torpedo found in the different seas of the world.

6. The most powerful of all the electric fishes, however, is the gymnotus, or electric eel, of the South American rivers. It has been well described as an electric battery with an eel attachment. The electric apparatus of this strange creature occupy a large portion of the length of the body, and are four in number, two on each side. They consist of an assemblage of membranous, horizontal plates, intersected by delicate vertical plates, and the cells thus formed are filled with a glutinous matter. Each inch in length of the gymnotus contains, according to Hunter, two hundred and forty cells. There is thus an enormous surface of the electric machinery. The discharge is so great that it is computed by Professor Faraday as equal to that of fifteen Leyden-jars of three thousand five hundred square-inch surfaces.

7. This creature is rather sluggish in its movements, and is only dangerous when disturbed by interference. It differs from other eels in the completeness of its jaws and in the possession of ribs. The skin is smooth and scaleless, and the head is flat and oval, like that of a venomous serpent. It has more than a hundred sharp-pointed teeth, but it never bites, except when eating its food.

8. In the rivers of tropical South America it is frequently found in such numbers as to render both bathing and fishing extremely dangerous. It is found, however, that after five or six discharges it becomes exhausted, and can produce no more shocks until after a period of rest. The Indians have learned to take advantage of this, and they drive wild horses into the streams, who trample about in the mud, receiving the electric discharges until the eels are exhausted. In this condition they are speared without inconvenience.

PART V.

PYGMY WORKERS AND BUILDERS.

ANTS: THEIR HOMES AND HABITS.

1. "Go to the ant, thou sluggard, observe her ways, and be wise," is an injunction as old as Solomon, but it may be followed as profitably to-day as when first made three thousand years ago. When we go to the ants, we observe a well-ordered community, each individual performing its allotted task for the good of the whole, and examples of constructive ability, industry, thrift, and the wise adaptation of means to ends perfectly marvelous in so tiny a creature. What we are accustomed to call instinct here seems to approach human reason, and it may be questioned whether the ants do not possess an intelligence that places them in a very high rank among organized beings.

2. Observe the little ants of our fields and paths, and see how they work. Watch how they dig their tunnels and cover them in, like so many railway engineers. See how they stop, every now and then, to study out their plans; how they consider all obstacles, and avoid them; how they use every leaf and stick and straw to make a wall or a roof for their galleries. Who is the foreman, or "boss," as men sometimes say? Sometimes a single ant has hit upon a new plan; he goes to work on it; the others soon adopt the improvement, and help the skillful inventor; they are

all as busy as possible, and yet they all have their common plan. The queen lays her eggs; the workers take care of them, and keep running with them from place to place, always with some object. Almost all ants have several stories or sets of cells for their houses in this way.

3. Then they watch the state of the weather very carefully. If the sun is warm, and it will do the eggs good to be in the upper galleries, every little ant begins tugging them along to put them in a warm place. Then if it grows very hot indeed, so as to make the upper galleries too sultry, the eggs are carried down into the next row, where it is cooler. Then if a sudden rain comes, making these middle galleries too damp, up run the little busy workers, and carry all the eggs to safe chambers far underground. We sometimes think that a single baby makes a great deal of work in a house. But suppose that in every house there were a thousand babies, and that every baby had a nurse, and that all these nurses were running to and fro all day with the babies in their arms, carrying them from room to room, to sun them or air them or dry them, what a scene there would be, and how the nurses and babies would tumble over each other, up stairs and down! And yet that is what goes on all the time in the ants' nurseries.

4. With almost human intelligence ants also show human passion and pugnacity. Henry Thoreau once saw a battle between two tribes of ants which exhibited all the rage and destructive tendencies usually seen upon battle-fields. He says: "One day when I went out to my wood-pile I observed two large ants, the one red, the other much larger, nearly half an inch long, and black, fiercely contending with one another. Having once got hold, they never let go, but struggled and wrestled and rolled on the chips incessantly. Looking farther, I was surprised to find that the chips were covered with such combatants, that it was a war between two races of ants, the red always pitted

against the black, and frequently two red ones to one black. On every side they were engaged in deadly combat, yet without any noise that I could hear, and human soldiers never fought so resolutely. I watched a couple that were fast locked in each other's embraces, in a little sunny valley amid the chips, now at noonday prepared to fight till the sun went down, or life went out.

5. "The smaller red champion had fastened himself like a vise to his adversary's front, and through all the tumblings on that field never for an instant ceased to gnaw at one of his feelers near the root, having already caused the other to go by the board; while the stronger black one dashed him from side to side, and, as I saw on looking nearer, had already divested him of several of his members. They fought with more pertinacity than bull-dogs. Neither manifested the least disposition to retreat. It was evident that their battle-cry was 'Conquer or die.' In the mean time there came along a single red ant on the hillside of this valley, evidently full of excitement, who either had dispatched his foe or had not yet taken part in the battle. He saw this unequal combat from afar—for the blacks were nearly twice the size of the reds—he drew near with rapid pace till he stood on his guard within half an inch of the combatants; then, watching his opportunity, he sprang upon the black warrior, and commenced his operations near the root of his right fore-leg, leaving the foe to select among his own members; and so there were three united for life, as if a new kind of attraction had been invented which put all other locks and cement to shame.

6. "I should not have wondered by this time to find that they had their respective musical bands stationed on some eminent chip, and playing their national airs the while to excite the slow and cheer the dying combatants. I was myself excited somewhat as if they had been men. The more you think of it, the less the difference. I never

learned which party was victorious, nor what the cause of the war; but I felt for the rest of that day as if I had had my feelings excited and harrowed by witnessing the struggle, the ferocity and carnage of a human battle before my door."

7. In another respect ants show their kinship to the human. Some ant tribes make a business of capturing and holding slaves. At the head of the slave-makers are the little red ants, known as the Amazon ants. They set about their raids in a systematic manner, always starting at nightfall. Their victims are usually the industrious little miner ants. When they have issued from their abode, the Amazons array themselves in serried columns, and their army takes its way to the ants' nest which they are about to despoil. In vain do the warriors of the beleaguered city seek to bar the entrance; in spite of all such efforts the others penetrate into the very heart of the place, and pry into all the compartments in order to choose their victims, the larvæ and nymphs, this latter being the name given to the larvæ after they have spun their cocoons, whence they are to emerge perfect insects. The workers which oppose those raids are simply thrown down; they are not made prisoners, because they would adapt themselves with difficulty to the yoke; the assailants want only young individuals which they can mold to their will.

8. When the place is completely sacked, each conqueror takes a nymph or larva delicately between its teeth and prepares to return. Those who can not find nymphs or larvæ, carry off the mutilated dead bodies of their enemies in order to feed on them. Then the whole army, laden with booty, and sometimes stretching out in a line of a hundred and fifty feet in length, triumphantly regains its city in the same order as at its departure.

9. As soon as the young ants torn from their homes reach the abode of their spoilers, the slaves already there

lavish the most attentive care upon them; they give them food, cleanse them, and warm their chilled bodies.

10. In the slave-making republics conquerors and slaves finish by changing places. The warrior-robbers only display courage in fighting. The instant they have stowed away their booty in the nest, the Amazons refresh themselves after battle by the pleasures of laziness. But they soon become enervated, and the spoilers pass under the yoke of those they have conquered. This dependence is so great that, if they were deprived of their slaves, privations and inaction would speedily destroy the tribe.

11. The warrior ants, ardent in battle and the chase, revolt against all domestic work, for they only understand fighting. Incapable of building their own abodes, or nourishing their young, they leave these duties to their slaves. When the tribe is forced to abandon a nest on account of its being too old or too small, the slaves decide the question of emigration. They do not, however, run off and leave their helpless tyrants, but each one takes one of its degenerate masters in its mandibles and bears it to the new dwelling, just as a cat carries its kitten in its mouth.

THE APHIDES AND THEIR KEEPERS.

1. THE aphides are the small green insects, generally known as plant-lice, which infest our gardens. Insignificant as may be a single aphis, these insects are most formidable from their numbers, as all gardeners know to their cost. Roses are often so thickly covered with these pestilential insects that the leaves and buds are completely hidden, the latter never being permitted to develop themselves into flowers.

2. These insects are prolific almost beyond belief. As

a general rule, insects lay eggs which are hatched, pass through the state of larva and pupa, and then become perfect insects. But the plant-lice go on a very different plan. A female aphis takes her place on a branch—say of the rose—plunges her beak into the tender bark, and begins to suck the sap. After a short time she begins to produce young aphides at an average rate of fourteen per diem. These young creatures are just like their mother, only less, and immediately follow her example by first sucking the sap of the plant and then producing fresh young.

3. It is in consequence of this remarkable mode of production that the twigs and buds become so rapidly covered with aphides, the quickly succeeding generations crawling over the backs of their predecessors, so as to arrive at an unoccupied spot of bark in which they can drive their beaks. Thus, at the beginning of a week, say on Monday, a rose-tree may be apparently free from aphides, or have at the most six or seven of the "blight" upon it, but by Thursday the whole plant will be so thickly covered with aphides that scarcely a particle of the bark can be seen, the whole being crowded with the green bodies of the insect, each with its beak dug deeply into the plant, and draining it of its juices.

4. The natural foe of the aphides is the bright little spotted beetle known as the lady-bug, or lady-bird. Beautiful as are the lady-birds, it is not for their beauty alone that they are valued, inasmuch as they are among the greatest benefactors of civilized man, and preserve many a harvest which, but for their aid, would be hopelessly lost. For in their larval state they feed upon the aphides, and, being exceedingly voracious, devour vast numbers of these destructive insects. Few persons would suppose, on looking at the coccinella larva, what was its real condition of life. It looks as harmless, dull, sluggish a creature as can be imagined, and much more likely to be eaten itself

than to eat other insects. Yet, with all this innocence of aspect, it is so ruthless a destroyer of animal life that, if a few of them be placed on a bush or plant which is infested with aphides, in a day or two not an aphis will be left.

5. From the back of the aphides, and toward the tail, there are two slender projections. These are tubes, from which exudes a sweet liquid, which, with the aid of the microscope, can be seen starting, in minute drops, from the end of each tube. When the aphides are in great profusion upon a tree, this liquid falls from them, and covers the leaves with the sweet, sticky substance which is so familiar to us under the name of "honey-dew." Trees thus distinguished are always overrun by swarms of ants, which lick the sweet droppings from the leaves and hold high revels on this substance, whose origin was once so mysterious.

6. The ants even go farther than this. Not content with taking the honey-dew that has fallen from the aphides, they anticipate its fall, and eagerly lap up the sweet secretion as it exudes from the insects. In fact, they make much the same use of the aphides as we do of cows, and even carry off the ant-cows, as they may be called, to their own nests, and there keep them. That the ants do this has long been known, but the notion of keeping milch-cows seemed so far beyond the capacities of an insect that many persons refused to give credence to so romantic a story.

7. I have often watched an ant go from one aphis to another, stand behind each, and gently squeeze the body with its fore-legs; perhaps one aphis in ten, not more, will give out a small drop of honey as clear as crystal, which the ants instantly swallow. The ants take much more care of the aphides than the aphides do of themselves; they are sad, dull, stupid creatures. It is very pretty to see the licking and washing and cleaning and caressing which the ants constantly bestow on them. When the aphides cast

their skin, the ants instantly carry it away, nor will they let any dirt or rubbish remain among them or on them.

8. But the most amusing care of the ant is guarding the aphides from the attacks of that little parasitic fly whose operations Mr. Haliday has so well described. You must have seen a sheep-dog run over the backs of a whole flock of sheep, when closely crowded together, in order to bring back some sinner that has gone astray; so will the ants, in the hot sunshine, run about over an establishment of aphides, driving away the rascally parasite that is forever hovering over to destroy them.

9. The mode in which the ichneumon-flies operate on the aphis is very remarkable. As may be inferred from the size of the aphides, on which they are parasitic, they are of very small dimensions, and one of these tiny creatures, when standing on the back of an aphis which it is about to wound, looks much like a rook perched on a sheep's back.

10. When the fatal egg has been introduced under the skin of the aphis, the wounded insect, like the stricken hart, separates itself from its fellows and passes to the under-side of a leaf, and there fixes itself. Its body soon begins to swell, and at last becomes quite globular and horny, the change being caused by the death of the aphis and the rapid growth of the parasite within it. The ichneumon passes rapidly through its changes, and in a short time assumes the perfect form, always with its head next the tail of its victim, pushes off the last two or three segments of the dead aphis, and makes its escape into the world. The dead and empty skins of such hapless aphides may be found plentifully toward the end of summer sticking firmly to the leaf, and showing the round aperture through which the destroying parasite has crept.

11. Sometimes there is a sort of contest between the aphis and the ichneumon-fly; the former, however, hav-

ing no more chance against its tiny foe than has a rabbit against a weasel. If the aphis have its beak deeply plunged into the bark, the ichneumon-fly has an easy task, for the aphis can do nothing but kick and struggle, while anchored to the spot by its proboscis, and all that the ichneumon-fly has to do is to make its deadly lunge. But, if the aphis be wandering about the plant, the ichneumon-fly has to walk about with it, and try first one side and then the other, until she can find an opportunity of depositing her egg.
Rev. J. G. Wood.

SPINNERS OF THE MULBERRY-TREES.

1. OF all the insect tribes, the ways and transformations of the mulberry silk-worm are probably the best known. The accurate and minute knowledge which we have of this insect is owing to the fact that success in the production of silk is rendered possible only by carefully studying every phase of the life of the silk-worm, and by providing the conditions necessary to its healthful development. There are many varieties of silk-producing worms, each feeding upon the leaves of some special plant, but only a few whose products can be successfully and economically manufactured. Within a short time past successful experiments have been made with the varieties which feed upon the oak and the ailanthus, but still the spinners of the mulberry-trees continue to furnish the greater part of the world's supply of silk.

2. The silk-worms are hatched from eggs about the size of a mustard-seed, an ounce of eggs producing from thirty thousand to forty thousand worms. Scarce is the worm born than he begins to eat. Indeed, it has no time to lose, for, before reaching maturity, it must gain seventy-two thousand times its own weight; so, to acquit itself con-

scientiously of its task, it does nothing but eat, digest, and sleep. In about five days this devouring appetite ceases; the little worm becomes almost motionless, hangs itself by its hind feet, raising and holding a little inclined the anterior part of its body. This repose lasts twenty-four, thirty-six, or forty-eight hours, according to temperature; then the dried-up skin splits open behind the head, and soon along the length of the body. The caterpillar comes out with a new skin, which has been formed during this sleep.

3. The process of insects shedding their old skin and emerging in a new one is usually termed *moulting*, but in silk-culture it is termed *sickness;* for this is a critical period in the life of a silk-worm, and many of the weaker ones do not survive it. Before reaching maturity, the skin is changed four times, in periods varying from three to eight days, the worm eating voraciously after each moulting, and becoming nearly dormant for a brief period before the next change. After the skin is shed for the last time, the growth becomes very rapid, and maturity is reached in about ten days, giving the insect a life of about thirty-two days in the larva state.

4. At this point it ceases to eat, and the alimentary canal is entirely emptied of food; it appears restless, wanders about, and seeks to climb. When furnished with a proper kind of branch, it mounts upon it, and, choosing a convenient place, it hangs itself by its hind feet, and soon through its spinner a thread of silk makes its appearance. This is at first cast out in any direction, and forms a collection of cords, which shall attach the cocoon to be spun to the surrounding twigs. Next the form of the cocoon is outlined, and then for some hours we can see the worker performing his task through the transparent gauze with which he surrounds himself. Little by little this gauze thickens and grows opaque, until finally it becomes

a perfect cocoon. At the end of about seventy-two hours the work is done.

5. Having once commenced, the worm continues to spin, and the thread is unbroken from one end to the other. The cocoon is thus seen to be really a ball wound

The Silk-worm.

from the inside. The thread which forms it is eleven miles long, and weighs about six grains. Let us for a moment consider the prodigious activity of the silk-worm while spinning its thread. To dispose of the silk, it moves its head in all directions, each movement being about one sixth of an inch. To finish his task in the seventy-two hours requires about three hundred thousand motions in a day, or sixty-nine every minute. No weaver can equal this in activity for a single hour, and much less would any one be able to keep up to the highest rate of speed for three days in succession.

6. The silk-worm has now changed from the larva to the pupa state. After finishing his cocoon he becomes torpid once more. His body is inclosed in a kind of shell, the color of which is a golden yellow. A very slight movement of the posterior part, which requires the closest attention to observe, is the only sign of life. Yet, within, a most remarkable change is taking place, and in about fifteen days is complete. The shell of the pupa now splits open, as did the skin of the larva, and there emerges a complete butterfly—a creature as unlike the forms through which it has already passed as can well be imagined.

7. This butterfly is almost an inch long and two inches across when its wings are spread. It is of a whitish or pale yellow color. Sex in the silk-worm is developed only in the butterfly form. The male flies about chiefly in the evening, but the females have but little activity. In three days the female deposits about five hundred eggs, and as her work is ended she immediately dies; the life of the male has about the same duration.

8. When the cocoons are spun they are separated into two parts—those which are to be wound, and those which are reserved for hatching the butterflies from which the new supply of eggs is to be obtained. The former are placed in hot water, which kills the pupa within, and the silk is wound off from the outside.

9. Such is a brief history of the life of an insect which forms the basis of one of the greatest industries of the world. Silk-making probably originated in China, and is now extensively carried on in that country and in Japan.

In Europe the principal silk-producing countries are France and Italy. The manufacture has spread into other countries, and it is becoming a quite important industry in the United States.

10. In raising cocoons, two things are necessary — a climate and soil that will produce mulberry-trees (and this is found in the United States almost anywhere south of latitude 43°), and intelligent care during the brief period of the silk-worm's existence. This part of the silk-culture is essentially a home industry. The silk-worms require such delicate and individual care that the best results are attained from small orchards of mulberries and a limited amount of worms in one establishment. By devoting an acre or two to the cultivation of the trees, the children and unproductive members of the family can do the very light work necessary during the six weeks' care of the worms. In this way the family can receive a substantial benefit, the profits often being greater from this small number of trees than from all the remainder of the farm. The demand for cocoons is so great that there is no danger of overstocking the market.

HONEY-GATHERERS.

1. In all ages the bee communities have been regarded with great interest by observers of nature. The facts resulting from even a cursory observation are such as to excite admiration and astonishment. Here, among diminutive insects, is found a society perfectly organized and well ordered; the members continually industrious and showing a wise thrift in regard to the future, and displaying a high degree of seeming intelligence in adapt-

ing means to ends. It is observed, also, that they are architects of no mean order, constructing communal homes perfectly adapted to the needs of the individual, and serving in the highest degree the wants of the whole. In constructing hexagonal cells, they choose the only form that would economically fill the entire space, leaving no waste room, and in this they show that they possess geometric art, though they may not be acquainted with geometric science.

2. A little closer observation reveals other facts of great interest. A single queen is found in each community, who is at once the mother and the ruler of the society, and to her loyal homage is paid by all the members. The society itself is divided into drones and workers, the former males and few in number, and the latter neuters, constituting the mass of the community. It is seen, also, that the cells are used for different purposes, and for each use they are of somewhat different structure. The mass of the cells are for the purpose of storing honey, and this forms the honey-comb which is brought to the table. In other cells the eggs are deposited and the young bees kept while in their pupa state. These cells are of three kinds, as adapted, respectively, to the queen, the workers, and the drones, the royal cell being several times larger than the others. In other cells is stored the food known as bee-bread, upon which the larva is fed, the royal jelly, fed to prospective queens exclusively, being kept by itself.

3. The workers gather honey principally from flowers, storing it in the honey-cells for food during the winter; and at a certain time before the honey season ends they expel the drones from the hive, and leave them to perish for want of food. The phenomenon of swarming is also well known. At a period, usually in early summer, the whole hive seems to be in a state of commotion, and great numbers of bees collect in masses upon the outside of their hive.

After hanging there for a time they set off together to find a new home, leaving a portion still in possession of the old one. Those who take care of bees prepare for this, and have a home ready for the new swarm.

4. So far, these facts, patent to every observer, have long been well known, but the more minute details of bee life were revealed for the first time about the close of the last century by Francis Huber, the Swiss naturalist, who devoted most of his life to the study of their ways. What is most remarkable about these discoveries is that Huber was blind, and was obliged to see exclusively through the eyes of others. He had a mind, however, wonderfully keen, alert, and well trained, and his affliction obliged him to verify his work at every step, so as to preclude the possibility of mistake. His discoveries, published in 1792, were first received with incredulity, but all subsequent observation has served to confirm them. Indeed, since his time nothing has been added to our knowledge of the bees save the settlement of a few points which he raised, and about which he expressed some doubt. Some of the most interesting of his discoveries are as follows:

5. The neuter or worker bees are all imperfectly developed females, and, with proper treatment, the larva of any one of them may become a queen. The queen, when perfectly developed, lays its eggs, from which the different kinds of bees are hatched, without mistake, in the cells prepared for each; but when the queen is imperfect she makes mistakes, and deposits drones' eggs in worker cells, and *vice versa*. The workers, however, rectify these mistakes, and change the cells to meet the new conditions. In one respect, however, they are at fault: if a drone's egg is deposited in a royal cell, they dose the poor fellow to death trying to make a queen of him.

6. Just before the swarming season begins the workers construct royal cells, sometimes to the number of twenty-

seven. In these the queen deposits eggs on successive days, so that when she leads off the new swarm another queen will be ready to take her place; and also that, if the swarm be vigorous enough to throw off several colonies, each may be provided with a leader. About the time the new queens are coming out the old queen seems to be possessed with a complete frenzy, fiercely attacking the royal cells and stinging the occupants to death. The first new queen that comes out also shows the same rage, and endeavors to kill all the larvæ in the other queen cells. At this time the instinct of the workers seems reversed; they no longer implicitly obey, but, gathering about the royal cells, they interpose their bodies in such a manner as to frustrate the intentions of the queen until the paroxysm of her anger has passed. Their resistance is entirely passive, and as soon as she becomes quiet they again become faithful and obedient subjects.

7. If a swarm of bees finds itself suddenly queenless, the workers immediately select the larva of a worker bee, not over three days old, and enlarge the cell by cutting down the partition-walls between it and two adjoining cells, destroying the inmates, and then they supply the larva thus selected with royal jelly. The nursery of the royal heir is thus elongated, and is capped over with a peculiar covering. In sixteen days from the time it is hatched it becomes a queen. Under such circumstances, the new queen, upon her birth, is allowed to kill all her possible rivals in the royal cells. Should two queens emerge at the same time, the workers form a ring, so as to insure fair play, and let them fight until one is killed, when they give their adhesion to the other.

8. If a strange queen be introduced into a swarm possessing one of their own, the workers surround her and quietly detain her as prisoner until she perishes with hunger, but they offer her no direct violence. Should the strange

queen pass all the sentinels and guards, until she comes in presence of the old queen, a battle is inevitable, as the workers will detain either if they seem disposed to fly.

9. After the loss of a queen by a swarm, if a strange queen be introduced, her reception will depend entirely upon the time which has elapsed since their bereavement. At first they refuse to be comforted, and reject any attempt to replace their loss. After eighteen hours they begin to consider the matter, and in twenty-four receive, with royal honors, any queen which may be offered them.

10. A common bee, when it reaches its maturity, emerges from its cell without help, but for some time it is too weak to fly. A queen, however, is guarded by the workers; she is closely watched, and constantly fed through a small aperture in the covering of her cell, until she has attained sufficient strength to fly. The presence of a developed and imprisoned queen is generally made known by a peculiar note which she utters, called "piping." Above the busy hum of the hive this sound may be distinguished; it seems to be the expression of her impatience at her imprisonment, and is the usual precursor of swarming.

11. When the swarming season arrives, and the drones and some of the new queens have nearly arrived at maturity, the old queen becomes violently agitated, and rapidly passes over the combs, communicating her agitation to all she meets. In a short time the whole swarm appears to be in a violent state of excitement. Within the hive the thermometer rises from between 90° and 95° to 104°, a heat intolerable to the bees, and, with the queen at their head, they rush impetuously out of the hives. The initial cause of the queen's agitation is not known, but the swarming is as much occasioned by the excessive heat as by the overstocked hive.

12. Honey is not directly obtained from flowers, but is a saccharine substance which is worked over by the inter-

nal organs of the bees. The pollen of flowers is collected in a like manner, swallowed, and regurgitated in the form of bee-bread or food for the larva. When wax is needed, the bees gorge themselves with honey and hang suspended in festoons or curtains for about twenty-four hours, when the wax is found secreted in the form of a little scale between the overlapping rings of the abdomen, which spaces are called wax-pockets. So that when we see bees hang in clusters in other than the swarming season we may know that they are engaged in the manufacture of wax.

13. Of the treatment of these wax-scales Huber says: "The worker disengages it by means of pincers on his legs, and by seizing it in his mouth. We remarked that with its claws it turned the wax in every necessary direction; that the edge of the scale was immediately broken down, and the fragments, having been accumulated in the hollow of the mandibles, issued forth like a very narrow ribbon, impregnated with a frothy liquid by the tongue. The tongue assumed the most varied shapes, and performed the most complicated operations, being sometimes flattened like a trowel, and at other times pointed like a pencil; and, after imbuing the whole substance of the ribbon, pushing it forward into the mandibles, where it was drawn out a second time, but in an opposite direction."

14. The lenses of the bees' eyes are not adjustable, and, though they can see accurately at great distances, they seem blind to objects close by. Bees dart down to the door of their hives with a precision that is generally unerring, but if, from any cause, they miss the opening, they are obliged to rise in the air in order to take another observation. If bees hear at all, it is only such sounds as affect their own welfare. Their sense of smell appears to be very keen: the presence of honey they detect in the most carefully concealed places. The sense which appears to be the most perfect with them is touch, which resides wholly in the

antennæ. In the language of Huber, "the bee constructs its comb in darkness; it pours its honey into the magazines, feeds its young, judges of their age and necessities, recognizes its queen—all by aid of its antennæ, which are much less adapted for becoming acquainted with objects than our hands. Therefore, shall we not grant to this sense modifications and perfections unknown to the touch of man?"

THE HUMBLEBEE.

1. Burly, dozing humblebee,
   Where thou art is clime for me.
   Let them sail for Porto Rique,
   Far-off heats through seas to seek;
   I will follow thee alone,
   Thou animated torrid zone!
   Zigzag steerer, desert cheerer,
   Let me chase thy waving lines;
   Keep me nearer, me thy hearer,
   Singing over shrubs and vines.

2. Insect lover of the sun,
   Joy of thy dominion!
   Sailer of the atmosphere;
   Swimmer through the waves of air;
   Voyager of light and noon;
   Epicurean of June;
   Wait, I prithee, till I come
   Within earshot of thy hum—
   All without is martyrdom.

3. When the south wind in May days,
   With a net of shining haze,

Silvers the horizon wall,
And, with softness touching all,
Tints the human countenance
With the color of romance;
And, infusing subtle heats,
Turns the sod to violets—
Thou, in sunny solitudes,
Rover of the underwoods,
The green silence doth displace
With thy mellow, breezy bass.

4. Hot midsummer's petted crone,
Sweet to me thy drowsy tone
Tells of countless sunny hours,
Long days, and solid banks of flowers;
Of gulfs of sweetness without bound
In Indian wildernesses found!
Of Syrian peace, immortal leisure,
Firmest cheer, and bird-like pleasure.

5. Aught unsavory or unclean
Hath my insect never seen;
But violets and bilberry-bells,
Maple-sap and daffodels,
Grass with green flag half-mast high,
Succory to match the sky,
Columbine with horn of honey,
Scented fern and agrimony,
Clover, catchfly, adder's-tongue,
And briar-roses, dwelt among;
All beside was unknown waste,
All was picture as he passed.

6. Wiser far than human seer,
Yellow-breeched philosopher!

Seeing only what is fair,
Sipping only what is sweet,
Thou dost mock at fate and care,
Leave the chaff and take the wheat.
When the fierce northwestern blast
Cools sea and land so far and fast,
Thou already slumberest deep ;
Woe and want thou canst outsleep ;
Want and woe, which torture us,
Thy sleep makes ridiculous.

Emerson.

PART VI.

QUEER LITTLE FOLKS.

THE PIT-DIGGER AND ITS VICTIM.

1. WHEN I lived in a tent in South Carolina, I had all around me the curious little holes of a creature that feeds on ants, though it is no bigger than they are—the ant-lion. I had read about this little insect, as most children have, but I had never before seen it, except in its complete state, when it is a pretty lace-winged fly. But the remarkable part of its life is passed in the grub or larva state. Then it is a soft, heavy little thing, with feeble legs, and nothing strong about it but its appetite and jaws. But how is it to get its living? It feeds on other insects, but as it can not chase them, it must find a way to bring them to it; just as if we should sit at table, and the turkeys and chickens should come flying into our mouths. This is the way.

2. The ant-lion chooses a sandy place, and then crawls round in a circle two or three inches in diameter. Then it makes another round inside of the first a little deeper and jerks the sand outward with its head. Then it makes an inner circle deeper still, and so on, always scooping up the sand and throwing it out, until at last it has made a regular little pitfall, shaped like a cone, and then it lies at the bottom with its jaws and forceps just sticking out of the sand, waiting for dinner to come.

3. Dinner comes by and by in the shape of some little ant, roaming round for its own dinner, and attracted by this queer little pit. Almost all animals have some curiosity, and so the ant looks over the edge. His feet slip in the soft sand, the more he struggles the faster he slips down, and the ant-lion, wriggling up half-way to meet him, soon has him in his strong jaws, that never let go. In the struggle the sand is thrown about, and the pitfall is often so destroyed that it is easier to make a new one than to repair the old.

4. I have seen a hundred of these tiny burrows beside each other in the woods, and have often put into them little pieces of stick or straw, that I might see how easily these obstructions slid down, and how eagerly the little ant-lion seized upon them. It seemed a selfish and lonely way of getting one's food, besides the treacherousness of it. For I never saw two ant-lions in the same dining-room, and you can not have as much sympathy for them as for those who are collecting food to keep their families from starving. At any rate, it shows that if ants have sharp wits, they are needed to resist such very intelligent enemies.

T. W. Higginson.

HOW MOSQUITOES MANAGE.

1. THE following account of the mosquito is condensed from Réaumur, the distinguished French naturalist, and is mostly in his own language :

2. The mosquito is our declared enemy, and a very troublesome enemy it is. However, it is well to make its acquaintance ; for, if we pay a little attention, we shall be forced to admire it, and even to admire the instrument with which it wounds us. Besides which, throughout the whole course of its life, it offers most interesting matter of

investigation to those who are curious to know the wonders of nature. During a period in its life the observer, forgetting it will at some time annoy him, feels the greatest interest in its life-history.

3. The body of the mosquito is long and cylindrical. When in a state of repose, one wing is crossed over the other. The eyes are so large as to cover nearly the whole of the head. The instrument which it uses for puncturing the skin, and which is called the trunk, is well worthy of attention. Under the microscope the trunk appears to be straight and cylindrical, terminating in a small knob at the end. This is only the case, which opens and allows the stings, which are six in number, to come in play. These stings are exceedingly minute, pointed, and are used very much like a surgeon's lancet. This little instrument in itself would scarcely be felt, but the sting is accompanied by the emission of a fluid, which causes the irritation which we know so well.

4. The mosquito is not always in the form of a winged insect greedy for our blood. After its brief but very active life of from two to three weeks the female lays its eggs and dies. These eggs are in clusters, which when magnified appear like a fragment of honey-comb, with from fifty to one hundred and fifty cells. They are deposited in the water, or as close to it as possible. In wet seasons the water rises and floats the eggs, producing an abundant harvest; but in dry seasons many fail to reach the water, and so perish.

5. When first hatched in the water, they are very small, and remarkably active. They get all the food necessary for their sustenance from the water, and they seem to be incessantly in the search of it. While in the larva state, in the course of two or three weeks, they change their skin three times, each change being preceded by a period of repose, and succeeded by one of activity and voracity.

6. When it throws off its skin for the fourth time, it changes its shape and condition, and passes into the pupa state. Its body is shortened and rounded, presenting a much plumper appearance. It has lost the little fan-like

Mosquitoes.

membrane which the larva possessed, but is still able to swim by bending its body and straightening it again. While in this state it does not eat, and has no digestive apparatus. Its outside covering is a kind of sack, within which the perfect insect develops itself in the course of two or three days. While in the water the larva and pupa are both familiarly known as wigglers.

7. When about to undergo its last change, the pupa lies extended on the surface of the water with its thorax a little raised. In a moment the skin splits, beginning at the head and extending along the back. As soon as it is enlarged—and to do so sufficiently is but the work of a moment—the forepart of the perfect insect is not long in showing itself; and soon afterward the head appears, rising above the opening. But this moment, and those that follow, until the mosquito has entirely left its covering, are most critical, and when it is exposed to great danger. This insect, which lately lived in the water, is suddenly in a position in which it has nothing to fear so much as the water. If it were upset on the water, and the water were to touch its thorax or body, it would be fatal.

8. This is the way in which it acts in this critical position: As soon as it has got out its head and thorax, it lifts them as high as it is able above the opening through which they had emerged, and then draws the posterior part of the body toward the same opening; or, rather, that part pushes itself forward by contracting a little, and then lengthening again, the roughness of the covering from which it desires to extricate itself serving as an assistance.

9. A large portion of the mosquito is thus uncovered, and at the same time the head is advanced farther toward the anterior end of the covering; but as it advances in this direction it rises more and more, both ends of the sheath thus becoming quite empty. The sheath is now a kind of boat, into which the water does not enter; and it would be fatal if it did. Large boats, which pass under bridges, have masts which can be lowered; as soon as the boat has passed the bridge, the mast is hoisted up by degrees until it is vertical. The mosquito rises until it be-

comes the mast of its own little boat, and a vertical mast also.

10. The forepart of the boat is much more loaded than the other, but it is also much broader. It is difficult to imagine how the insect is able to put itself in such a singular, though for it necessary, position, and how it can keep it. Any one who observes how deep the forepart of the boat is, and how near the edges of its sides are to the water, forgets, for the time being, that the mosquito is an insect that he would willingly destroy at other times. One feels uneasy for its fate; and the more so if the wind happens to arise so as to disturb the surface of the water. But one sees with pleasure that there is air enough to carry the mosquito along quickly; it is carried from side to side; it makes voyages in the boat in which it is borne. The boat, as yet, has only a mast, because its wings and legs are fixed close to its body, but in proportion it is a larger sail than one would dare to put on a real vessel; one can not help fearing that the little boat will capsize. Should the boat capsize, there is no chance for the mosquito. I have seen the water covered with mosquitoes which had perished as soon as they were born. Happily, all dangers may be passed over in a minute.

11. The mosquito, after raising itself perpendicularly, draws its two front legs from the sheath and brings them forward, and then draws out the two next. It now no longer tries to maintain its erect position, but leans toward the water, gets near it, and places its feet upon it; the water is sufficiently firm and solid to support the insect's body. As soon as it is thus in the water it is safe; its wings are unfolded and dried, which is done sooner than it takes to tell it, and it then is in a condition to fly away and commence experiments on the observer.

Réaumur.

PLANT-EATING AND OMNIVOROUS ANTS.

1. ANT communities everywhere have the same general characteristics in regard to orderly government, to the construction of communal habitations, to the care of the young, to industry, and to the division of labor; but it is in tropical regions only that they exhibit some of their most remarkable peculiarities. The plant-eating ant is the pest of the agriculturist, but the omnivorous ants are such fearful scourges that they frequently render large sections of country entirely uninhabitable by man. In Africa the owners of large and flourishing plantations have been driven away by these ants, and upon the banks of the Parana, in Brazil, a large territory has been almost transformed into a desert.

2. In South America, the sauba, or leaf-cutting ants, are among the pests which make regular farming almost impossible. These ants build nests about two feet high and often forty feet in diameter. The interiors are divided into galleries, some of which extend deep into the ground. It is said that these ants always build where they can have direct access to water, and in one instance it was found that they had constructed a well twelve inches in diameter and thirty feet deep. These ants ascend trees and plants in immense swarms, taking possession of the entire plant. Then each ant cuts a circular piece from a leaf, and, descending, bears it away to the nest. In this way the tree is soon denuded of its leaves, and the vast army of ants, following the same route, form regular beaten paths. While engaged in this work their columns are said to look like a multitude of animated leaves on a march.

3. The leaves are stored up in chambers constructed for that purpose, and for a long time the object of this accumulation was a matter of conjecture. Late investigations, however, have shown that in the moist and warm atmosphere

of the nests the leaves ferment and produce minute fungi, upon which the larva of the ants feed. In effecting this object they seem to have long anticipated man in the construction of under-ground beds for the production of mushrooms and truffles. To a large extent these insects decide upon the kind of vegetation which shall grow in the regions which they inhabit. Only the kinds which the ants do not use can survive. The farm crop to which they take a fancy is destroyed at once.

4. One of the most noted of the destructive insect communities are the termites, which, though scientifically placed in another genus, are usually ranked among the ants, and are popularly known as white ants. In organization the termites resemble the bees, each community owing allegiance to a single queen, and otherwise divided into males or drones and workers. Unlike the bees, they have a distinct class of soldiers to preserve order and to defend the home. The queen grows to such monstrous size that she can not move, but devotes herself to the business of laying eggs, which she does at the rate of eighty thousand per day.

5. Some varieties of these termites build dwellings often twenty feet high, pyramidal in shape, and frequently adorned with turrets. These structures are so solid that the wild cattle often climb upon them without crushing their walls. The interiors are divided into chambers, with galleries, that often extend many feet under ground. A village consisting of the dwellings of the termites presents a very remarkable appearance, and it is almost impossible to believe that it is the work of so diminutive an insect. Were man to build as high proportionally, his structures would be five times as high as the pyramids of Egypt.

6. Another variety of termites do not build for themselves, but take possession of human habitations. From their galleries under ground they make their way into

dwellings in myriads. They do not appear to the sight, but eat their way into the wood through tiny holes which would be scarcely observable even by minute investigation. Once inside, they literally eat up the whole woody fiber, leaving nothing but a thin outside shell. The posts, the

Warrior Termites.

beams, the rafters of the houses, and every wooden thing connected with them, share the same fate. To the eye everything seems right, but suddenly the whole collapses like the Deacon's one-horse shay, nothing remaining but dust, and the uneaten wafer-like surface of the wood.

7. In Sierra Leone, after a short absence from home,

the owner will return and find only the ghosts of furniture remaining, which disappear at the first rude touch. A whole staircase is destroyed in two weeks, and tables, chairs, and book-cases in much less time. In Southern France, where the termites have lately made their appearance, papers and clothing have to be protected in metal safes as against burglars. On one occasion the wooden supports of a dining-room were eaten through, and the flooring gave way while a party were dining, much to the derangement of the dinner and to the consternation of the host and guests.

8. The fire-ants of the Amazon, another omnivorous tribe, are even a worse scourge than the termites. Mr. Bates, the naturalist, says: "The village of Aveyros may be called the head-quarters of the fire-ant, which may be fittingly termed the scourge of this fine river. It is found only in sandy soil and in open places, and seems to thrive most in the neighborhood of houses and weedy villages; it does not make its home in the shades of the forest. Aveyros was deserted a few years before my visit on account of this little tormentor, and the inhabitants had only recently returned to their houses, thinking its numbers had decreased. It is a small species, not greatly differing from the red ant of our own country, except that the pain and irritation caused by its sting are much greater.

9. "The soil of the whole village is undermined by them; the ground is perforated with the entrances to their subterranean galleries, and a little sandy dome shows itself here and there, where the insects bring their young to receive warmth near the surface. The houses are overrun with them; they dispute every fragment of food with the inhabitants, and destroy clothing for the sake of the starch. All eatables are obliged to be suspended in baskets from the rafters, and the cords well soaked in copaiba-balsam, which is the only means known to prevent them from climbing.

10. "They seem to attack persons out of sheer malice. If we stood a few moments in the street, even at a distance from their nests, we were sure to be overrun with them, and severely punished, for the moment an ant touched the skin he secured himself with his jaws, doubled in his tail, and stung with all his might. When we were seated on chairs in the evenings, in front of the house, to enjoy a chat with our neighbors, we had stools to support our feet, the legs of which, as well as those of the chairs, were well anointed with the balsam. The cords of hammocks were obliged to be smeared in the same way, to prevent the ants from paying sleepers a visit."

CARNIVOROUS AND AGRICULTURAL ANTS.

1. Du Chaillu has given an admirable description of the driver or army ant of tropical Africa. These ants collect in vast armies and march off together in search of food. They belong to the true carnivora, and do no injury to vegetation. The marching column is usually about two inches wide, and it often is several miles in length. They shun the glare of the day, and take up their line of travel by night, or in the dense shade of the woods. When possible, they form covered passage-ways, as through hollow logs and under the fallen leaves, and through these the entire army moves. They attack every form of animal life. When they strike a decayed log, or a heap of vegetable refuse, they at once spread out and enter every crevice, so that the object appears to be a living mass of ants inside and out. They find and instantly devour every insect, grub, and larva which may exist, and then they fall into line and resume their march.

2. Lions, tigers, and elephants flee at their approach,

and woe to any crippled animal that is unable to get out of their way; he is doomed, and the ants never leave him until the very marrow is picked out of his bones. The carcass of an elephant or a rhinoceros would stay the march but a few hours. The huge python, lying dormant after he has gorged himself, often falls a prey to these marching hordes and is literally eaten up alive. They destroy vast quantities of the eggs of serpents and crocodiles, and so help man by keeping down the numbers of these obnoxious reptiles.

3. Their visit to a human domicile is both welcomed and dreaded. Their presence is first made known by squeakings and an unusual commotion among the various pests which infest such habitations. The young and the old now lay hands on their household gods and flee for their lives, happy if they escape from personal molestation from the advanced guards of the grand army. The ants enter into possession, and the work of purgation is soon finished. Rats, mice, and roaches are tracked to their most secret lairs and ruthlessly devoured; nor do fleas and other such small deer escape. The ants are literally everywhere; and, when they leave, the house is swept of every living thing, a condition which, on the whole, amply pays for the brief inconvenience to which the family has been subjected. In some cases sick and aged people have been abandoned in the hasty flight of the family, and have shared the fate of all animal life which comes in the way of these ants.

4. The ecitons, or foraging ants of tropical America, in habits are nearly allied to the drivers. Of these Mr. Belt, the naturalist of Nicaragua, says: "The moving columns of ecitons are composed almost entirely of workers of different sizes, but, at intervals of two or three yards, there are larger and lighter-colored individuals that often stop and sometimes run a little backward,

stopping and touching some of the ants with their antennæ. They look like officers giving orders and directing the march of the column.

5. "My attention was generally first called to them by the twittering of some small birds belonging to different species. On approaching, a dense body of the ants, three or four yards wide, and so numerous as to blacken the ground, would be seen moving rapidly in one direction, examining every cranny and underneath every fallen leaf. On the flanks, and in advance of the main body, smaller columns would be pushed out. These smaller columns would generally first flush the cockroaches, grasshoppers, and spiders. The pursued insects would rapidly make off, but many, in their confusion and terror, would bound right into the midst of the main body of ants. At first, the grasshopper, when it found itself in the midst of its enemies, would give vigorous leaps, with perhaps two or three of the ants clinging to its legs. Then it would stop a moment to rest, and that moment would be fatal, for the tiny foes would swarm over the prey, and, after a few more ineffectual struggles, it would succumb to its fate, and soon be bitten to pieces and carried off to the rear.

6. "The greatest catch of the ants was, however, when they got among some fallen brushwood. The cockroaches, spiders, and other insects, instead of running right away, would ascend the fallen branches and remain there, while the host of ants were occupying all the ground beneath. By and by, up would come some of the ants, following every branch, and driving before them their prey to the ends of the small twigs, where nothing remained for them but to leap, and they would alight in the very throng of their foes, with the result of being certainly caught and pulled to pieces.

7. "The ants send off exploring parties up the trees, which hunt for nests of wasps, bees, and probably birds.

If they find any, they soon communicate the intelligence to the army below, and a column is sent up immediately to take possession of the prize. I have seen them pulling out the larvæ and pupæ from the cells of a large wasps' nest, while the wasps hovered about, powerless, before the multitude of the invaders, to render any protection to their young.

8. "One day, when watching a small column of these ants, I placed a little stone on one of them to secure it. The next that approached, as soon as it discovered its situation, ran backward in an agitated manner, and soon communicated the intelligence to the others. They rushed to the rescue: some bit at the stone and tried to move it; others seized the prisoner by the legs, and tugged with such force that I thought the legs would be pulled off; but they persevered until they got the captive free. I next covered one up with a piece of clay, leaving only the ends of the antennæ projecting. It was soon discovered by its fellows, who set to work immediately, and, by biting off pieces of the clay, soon liberated it.

9. "Another time I found a very few of them passing along at intervals. I confined one of these under a little piece of clay, with his head projecting. Several ants passed it, but at last one discovered it, and tried to pull it up, but it could not. It immediately set off at a great rate, and I thought it had deserted its comrade; but it had only gone for assistance, for in a short time about a dozen ants came hurrying up, evidently fully informed of the circumstances of the case, for they made directly for their imprisoned comrade, and soon set him free. The excitement and ardor with which they carried on their exertions for the rescue could not have been greater if they had been human beings."

10. Of all these tribes, however, the claim for greatest intelligence must be accorded to the agricultural ants of

western Texas. This species, which has been carefully studied by Dr. Lincecum for the space of twelve years, is, save man, the only creature which does not depend for its sustenance on the products of the chase or the spontaneous fruits of the earth. As soon as a colony of these ants have become sufficiently numerous they clear a tract of ground, some four or five feet in width, around their city. In this plot all existing plants are eradicated, all stones and rubbish removed, and a peculiar species of grass is sown, the seeds of which resemble very minute grains of rice. The field—for so we must call it—is carefully tended by the ants, kept free from weeds, and guarded against marauding insects. When mature, the crop is reaped, and the seeds are carried into the nest. If they are found to be too damp, they are carefully carried out, laid in the sunshine till sufficiently dry, and then housed again.

11. This formation of a plot of cleared land is a critical point in the career of a young community. Any older and larger city which may lie within some fifty or sixty paces looks upon the step as a cause of war, and at once marches its armies to the attack. After a combat ensues, which may be prolonged for days, Providence declares in favor of the largest battalions, and the less numerous community is exterminated, fighting literally to the last ant. When a colony is unmolested, it increases rapidly in population, and undertakes to lay out roads : one of these, from two to three inches in width, has been traced to one hundred yards from the city. These ants are not very carnivorous, nor do they damage the crops of the neighboring farmers.

12. Persons who intrude upon their premises are bitten with great zeal, but otherwise the species may be regarded as harmless. One creature alone they seem to tolerate near them, and that is the small, black "erratic ant," which Dr. Lincecum conjectures may be of some use to them, and which is therefore allowed to build its small cities in their

immediate neighborhood. If it becomes too numerous, however, it is got rid of not by open war, but by a course of systematic, and yet apparently unintentional, annoyance. The agriculturists suddenly find it necessary to extend their field and enlarge the base of their city. In carrying out these alterations they literally bury the nests of their neighbors under heaps of the small pellets of soil thrown up by the prairie earth-worms, and continue this process until the erratic ants, in sheer despair, remove to a quieter spot.

THE PRAYING MANTIS.

1. SPECIES of insects known as mantids belong to the order *Orthoptera*, which includes crickets, grasshoppers, cockroaches, locusts, etc. The following figure illustrates the appearance of one of these. They are of bright, variegated colors, and are sometimes quite large, even three or four inches in length. The mantis lays its eggs at the end of summer, in rounded, fragile shells, which it attaches to the branches of trees, and which do not hatch till the following summer. It differs in locomotion from its orthopterous relatives, which travel by jumps, while the mantis crawls so slowly that its progress can only be appreciated by careful and prolonged watching. This trait is connected with another character by which the mantis differs from the foregoing groups, for, while they are vegetarians, this insect is carnivorous, and its insidious movements are part of the policy by which it captures the various creatures upon which it feeds.

2. But the mantis is not only a carnivore which lives by killing and devouring other insects, it is also a creature of the most quarrelsome disposition; in fact, it is a ferocious cannibal. If two of these insects be shut up together,

they engage in a desperate combat; they deal each other blows with their front legs, and do not leave off fighting until the stronger has succeeded in eating off the other's head. From their very birth the larvæ attack each other. In their contests, the male, being smaller than the female,

The Praying Mantis.

is often the victim. This pugnacity of the mantis is the source of amusement to children in China. Two mantids are shut up together in a bamboo cage, and the young heathen view with delight the inevitable battle, and the resulting cannibal feast.

3. And yet, while its inoffensive orthopterous brethren have got but little credit for their virtues, and are generally reviled as nuisances, this atrocious little savage has had the fortune to acquire a peculiar reputation for wisdom and saintliness. For thousands of years, and in all parts of the world, it has borne this character. The cause has been that it habitually assumes an attitude that appears devotional, and it was supposed to spend a large portion of its life in prayer. Settled on the ground, it raises its head and thorax, clasps together the joints of its front legs (see cut), and raises them as if in supplication, and remains in this posture for hours together.

4. A naturalist, who has carefully studied his habits, observes: "He is a very remarkable fellow, powerful alike upon wing or leg, but much given to fits of lethargy and brown-study. His traditional religious exercise, indeed, is simply lying in wait for what the gods may send him in the way of food. He fixes himself, as if in rapt contemplation, upon some convenient stalk or leaf, and then bends up his chest and shoulders into an almost erect position, pressing together his arms in front, and looking well out before him, with the palpi of his lips slightly vibrating. In this expectant mood he allows himself to be coaxed with the finger, merely staggering back a pace or two, and fixing his goggle-eyes upon the biped who vouchsafes this personal attention. If he lights upon a perpendicular window or wall when in this vein of "religious" ecstasy, he seems to remain for hours together without motion, but all the while he mounts imperceptibly up and up until he reaches the ceiling or roof which limits the chamber in the upward direction.

5. "The closest watching does not show how this most gradual of all climbings is accomplished. Not a limb can be seen to move, yet up, minute after minute, he glides. It is while he is in these fits of expectant ecstasy that he

seizes his prey. He is essentially a carnivorous feeder, and pounces stealthily upon any unwary insect that settles within convenient reach, seizing the victim between his upraised legs, and fixing it there between the row of spikelets with which these prehensile limbs are fringed. After a deliberate inspection of the morsel held in this position, he goes to work with his jaws."

Science Monthly.

THE KATYDID.

1. I LOVE to hear thine earnest voice,
      Wherever thou art hid,
   Thou testy little dogmatist,
      Thou pretty katydid!
   Thou mindest me of gentlefolks—
      Old gentlefolks are they—
   Thou say'st an undisputed thing
      In such a solemn way.

2. Thou art a female katydid,
      I know it by the trill
   That quivers through thy piercing notes,
      So petulant and shrill.
   I think there is a knot of you
      Beneath the hollow tree—
   A knot of spinster katydids—
      Do katydids drink tea?

3. Dear me! I'll tell you all about
      My fuss with little Jane,
   And Ann, with whom I used to walk
      So often down the lane;

And all that tore their hairs of black,
  Or wet their eyes of blue.
Pray tell me, sweetest katydid,
  What did poor Katy do?

4. Ah, no! the living oak shall crash,
  That stood for ages still,
The rock shall rend its mossy base,
  And thunder down the hill,
Before the little katydid
  Shall add one word, to tell
The mystic story of the maid
  Whose name she knows so well.

5. Peace to the ever-murmuring race!
  And when the latest one
Shall fold in death her feeble wings
  Beneath the autumn sun,
Then shall she raise her fainting voice
  And lift her drooping lid,
And then the child of future years
  Shall hear what Katy did.

Holmes.

PART VII.

CURIOUS DWELLERS OF SWAMP AND FOREST.

THE MONARCH OF THE SWAMP.

1. In the old, old time geologists tell us that the earth was inhabited by monstrous beasts, birds, and reptiles, compared with which their present representatives are mere pygmies. Prominent among these were many species of saurians, reptiles with enormous bodies, short legs, huge jaws, and immense tails, who found the earth a congenial abiding-place before the lands and the waters were separated, and who evidently lorded it over their amphibious companions. They could swim in the water, or paddle through the mud, and even learned to rest upon the dry land for a brief space when it appeared. The alligators are the survivals of these old saurians, wonderfully shrunk from the dimensions of their progenitors, but still sufficiently powerful to remain monarch of the swamp, to which position their structure is eminently fitted.

2. Like the knights of old, all the exposed parts of their bodies are covered with an impenetrable armor, so that they fear neither the claws of the panther, the fangs of the copperhead, nor the close embrace of the constrictor. The scales which constitute this armor are even rifle-proof, and sportsmen along the Florida rivers see their bullets glance off, producing upon the animal probably only a

slightly uncomfortable shock. Achilles could be wounded only in the heel, but the one vulnerable spot of the alligator is the eye, which, cold, cruel, and relentless, is always on the lookout for prey. The soft parts of the body, on the under-side, can scarcely be approached by an enemy, and the only danger to which they are exposed is in the waters of Guiana, where the ferocious little piräri fish nips off their toes.

3. The tail, which is but a tapering elongation of the body, constituting nearly half the length of the animal, is used as a weapon offensive and defensive. One fair blow of the tail of an adult alligator is enough to dampen the ardor of the fiercest of tigers, and to induce a meditative pause on the part of the most thick-hided rhinoceros. Deer and other animals, which come down to the water to drink, are stunned by a blow of this enormous flail, and are easily borne off into the water to appease an appetite which appears to be insatiable.

4. But if the alligator were interrogated, he would probably claim that he prided himself upon his jaws more than anything else; and this with good reason. Its jaw capacity is more largely developed than in any other animal. The head is enormous, extending straight forward in a line with the body and ending in a snout. It is protected by the hardest of bones, and furnished with the toughest and strongest of muscles. It literally splits in two from one extremity to the other, the upper half being hung upon a hinge, which enables it to open as freely as a pair of shears. The cavity thus exposed is armed with a formidable set of teeth, the whole constituting an apparatus admirably calculated to crush out all opposition when occasion requires. The old lady, listening to the description of an alligator from her sailor son, exclaimed, "Oh, la! wasn't he a horrid-looking critter?" "Well," was the reply, "he did not have the most amiable expression in the

world, but there was much openness about his countenance when he smiled."

5. His color is a muddy brown, and, as he slowly swims along the streams or floats down the current, he can scarcely be distinguished from driftwood; or, as he lies stretched out on the shore, he may easily be mistaken for a half-de-

Alligators in Florida Swamp.

cayed log. But let any animal approach him, and the log at once shoots into astonishing activity, one end being changed into a threshing-machine, and the other into a veritable mill ready to crush and grind any grist which may be offered. The larger animals are glad to make off, congratulating themselves if no bones are broken, while the smaller ones remain, to form a permanent connection with an individual of whose business activity they have had such convincing proofs.

6. In fierceness of disposition these saurians seem to vary in just the ratio of their length of jaw, and of their ability to make a wide opening for the accommodation of their friends. The crocodiles of Egypt and India have the longest and most pointed snouts, and are the least amiable of all. They attack man and beast with almost uniform success. They grow to the length of twenty feet, the head comprising about one seventh of the body. Unlike their American cousins, they prefer the flow of the streams to the stagnant waters of the swamp.

7. Next to these are the alligators of our Southern States. They grow to a length of about fifteen feet, with a nose a little less pointed than that of the crocodile. They are formidable enemies, and are dreaded by all who have occasion to visit the swamps. When captured young, they may be partially tamed, and, while small, they are often treated as household pets. But as they grow up they become too voracious for profit, and there is a constant danger of the old instinct asserting itself as against their artificial training. So, on the whole, they are not considered desirable members of a civilized community.

8. The cayman of South America is smaller than the alligator, has a blunter nose, and is less ferocious. He is savage enough, however, and the natives of those regions hold him in great fear. Sometimes a cayman-hunt will be organized on a grand scale, and then, if one is hooked and killed, there are great rejoicings. It often happens, however, that the hunted cayman either escapes or in his turn becomes hunter, in which case the rejoicings give place to mourning.

9. The eggs of these saurians are deposited in the sand near the streams. The cayman pays little attention to

them when once deposited, but the crocodiles and alligators watch their nests with jealous care. During March, which is the breeding season, the crocodiles deposit their eggs in the sand on the banks, or, in preference, in small sand-banks or islands on the stream. The eggs, which are white and hard, in size resemble those of a domestic goose. One found on the White Nile measured exactly three inches and a half in length, and five inches and thirteen

The Nile Crocodile.

sixteenths in circumference. The care and anxiety bestowed by these ferocious creatures upon their eggs is astonishing. When about to lay, the female crocodile will dig with her claws a hole in the sand, six inches deep, drop her egg therein, and cover it up. She will then make several holes around the first, to mislead those in search of her treasure. Every day she will add a fresh egg to her store, at the same time carefully enlarging the excavation, turning them and re-covering them with sand. After they are hatched by the sun's rays, the mother will place her young in the shallow water of a retired creek, where she will nourish them until they are capable of feeding themselves.

10. An Egyptian sportsman, who supported himself and his family by the produce of his gun, with three of his neighbors, went to an island—a favorite resort of crocodiles—to hunt for their eggs. As they were going round the island, three crocodiles escaped into the river. On examining the spot, a quantity of eggs was discovered in the sand. These they secured, and were proceeding back to their tent, when a crocodile who had watched the transaction rushed to the place of her deposit, and as rapidly returned to the river, and, swimming, followed them opposite to their abode, where until nightfall her eyes were seen above the water. The sportsmen feasted sumptuously upon their spoil; but as soon as the last embers of their fire had died away, the crocodile charged them furiously, repeating her attacks several times during the night; and it was only by the frequent discharge of their fire-arms that they kept her off at all.

11. This crocodile, which had hitherto remained harmless, now became furious, and attacked all the cattle it could catch upon the river-side. Among the victims was a fine mare in a neighboring village, who, as usual, was allowed to graze in the coarse, abundant pasturage. One day, while drinking, she was seized in the back of the neck by the jaws of the crocodile. The mare, being a powerful animal, in an agony of pain threw up her head. The crocodile dropped upon her back, and with her strange burden the mare galloped off to her stable. The astonished villagers immediately set upon the crocodile with their stout sticks, until she was induced to let go her hold and dismount; but the mare died from the joint effect of her wounds and the fright.

CAPTURE OF A CAYMAN.

1. The cayman is the terror and scourge of all the large rivers in South America near the line. Perhaps no animal in existence bears more decided marks of cruelty and malice than the cayman. His mouth is armed with thirty-two formidable teeth in each jaw, but he has no grinders; he is made to snatch and swallow. The back of the cayman may be said to be almost impenetrable to a musket-ball, but his sides are not nearly so hard; indeed, were the sides as hard and unyielding as the other parts of his body, there would not be elasticity enough to admit of expansion after taking in a supply of food.

2. I was exceedingly anxious to capture a cayman for the purpose of dissection. To this end we went up the Essequibo River to a creek which abounded in the game we were seeking. Here I baited hooks for several nights, and, although caymans were seen in plenty, they were too wary to be caught. Several times they came up and took the bait off the hooks. The Indians told me the cayman would never be captured by a hook like the one we used, and I finally became convinced that this was true. As a last resort, one of the Indians prepared a hook and bait of his own and placed it carefully in the water. He then took the empty shell of a tortoise and gave it some heavy blows with an axe. I asked him why he did that. He said that it was to let the cayman hear that something was going on. In fact, the Indian meant it for the cayman's dinner-bell.

3. Having done this, we went back to the hammocks, not intending to visit it again till morning. During the night the jaguars roared and grumbled in the forest, as though the world was going wrong with them, and at intervals we could hear the distant cayman. The roaring

of the jaguars was awful, but it was music to the dismal noise of these hideous and malicious reptiles. About half past five in the morning the Indian stole off silently to take a look at the bait. On arriving at the place, he set up a tremendous shout. We all jumped out of our hammocks and ran to him. The Indians got there before me, for they had no clothes to put on, and I lost two minutes in looking for my trousers and in slipping into them.

4. We found a cayman, ten and a half feet long, fast at the end of the rope. Nothing now remained to do but to get him out of the water without injuring his scales. We mustered eight strong. I informed the Indians it was my intention to draw him quietly out of the water, and then secure him. They looked and stared at each other, and said I might do it myself, but they would have no hand in it; the cayman would worry some of us. On saying this, they squatted on their hams with the most perfect indifference.

5. Daddy Quashi, my negro factotum, was for applying to our guns as usual, considering them our best and safest friends. I immediately offered to knock him down for his cowardice, and he shrunk back, begging that I would be cautious and not get worried. My Indian was now in conversation with the others, and they asked if I would allow them to shoot a dozen arrows into him, and thus disable him. This would have ruined all. I had come above three hundred miles on purpose to get a cayman uninjured, and not to carry back a mutilated specimen. I rejected this proposition with firmness, and darted a disdainful eye upon the Indians.

6. Daddy Quashi was again beginning to remonstrate, and I chased him on the sand-bank for a quarter of a mile. He told me afterward he thought he should have dropped down dead with fright, for he was firmly persuaded, if I had caught him, I should have bundled him into the cay-

man's jaws. Here, then, we stood in silence. They wanted to kill him, and I wanted to take him alive.

7. I now walked up and down the sand, revolving a dozen projects in my head. The canoe was at a considerable distance, and I ordered the people to bring it round to the place where we were. The mast was eight feet long, and not much thicker than my wrist. I took it out of the canoe and wrapped the sail around the end of it. Now it appeared clear to me that, if I went down upon one knee, and held the mast in the same position as a soldier holds his bayonet when rushing to a charge, I could force it down the cayman's throat, should he come open-mouthed at me. When this was told to the Indians they brightened up, and said they would help me pull him out of the river.

8. "Brave squad!" said I to myself, "now that you have got me between yourselves and danger." I then mustered all hands for battle. We were, four South American Indians, two negroes from Africa, a creole from Trinidad, and myself, a white man from Yorkshire. Daddy Quashi hung in the rear. I showed him a large Spanish knife which I carried; it spoke volumes to him, and he shrugged his shoulders in absolute despair.

9. The sun was just peeping over the high forests on the eastern hills, as if coming to look on and bid us act with becoming fortitude. I placed all the people at the end of the rope, and ordered them to pull till the cayman appeared on the surface of the water; and then, should he plunge, to slacken the rope and let him go again into the deep. I now took the mast in my hand, and sunk down upon one knee about four yards from the water's edge. The people pulled the cayman to the surface; he plunged furiously as soon as he arrived in these upper regions, and went below again on their slackening the rope. I saw enough not to fall in love with him at first sight.

10. I now told them we would run all risks, and have him on land immediately. They pulled again, and out he came. This was an interesting moment. I kept my position firmly, with my eyes fixed steadfast on him. By this time he was within two yards of me. I saw he was in a state of fear and perturbation. I instantly dropped the mast, sprang up, and jumped upon his back, turning half round as I vaulted, so that I gained my seat in the right position. I immediately seized his fore-legs, and, by main force, twisted them on his back; thus they served me for a bridle.

11. He now seemed to have recovered from his surprise, and, probably fancying himself in hostile company, he began to plunge furiously, and lashed the sand with his powerful tail. I was out of reach of the strokes of it by being near the head. He continued to plunge and strike, and made my seat very uncomfortable. It must have been a fine sight for an unconcerned spectator. The people roared out in triumph, and were so vociferous that it was some time before they heard me tell them to pull me and my steed farther inland. I was apprehensive the rope might break, and then there would be every chance of my going down to the regions under water with the cayman. The people now dragged us about forty feet on the sand; it was the first and last time I was ever on a cayman's back.

12. After repeated attempts to regain his liberty, the cayman gave in, and became tranquil through exhaustion. I now managed to tie up his jaws, and firmly secured his fore-feet in the position I had held them. We had now another severe struggle for superiority, but he was soon overcome, and again remained quiet. While some of the people were pressing upon his head and shoulders, I threw myself on his tail, and, by keeping it down in the sand, prevented him from kicking up another dust. He was

finally conveyed to the canoe, and then to the place where we had suspended our hammocks. Here he was put to death as gently as possible, and, after breakfast was over, I commenced the work of dissection.

Charles Waterton.

TUSSLE WITH A CONSTRICTOR.

1. I WISHED to find a good-sized snake, and capture him if possible, and I offered a reward to any of the negroes who would find one in the forest and come and let me know. One Sunday morning I met one of them in the forest with a little dog with him, and he told me he was going to hunt armadillos. On coming back, about noon, the little dog began to bark at the root of a large tree, and, on going up to see what was the matter, he discovered a snake, and hastened back to inform me.

2. The sun had just passed the meridian in a cloudless sky; there was scarcely a bird to be seen, for the winged inhabitants of the forest, as though overcome by heat, had retired to the thickest shade; all would have been like midnight silence were it not for the shrill voice of the pe-pe-yo every now and then resounding from a distant tree. I was sitting on the steps of an old, dismantled building when the negro and his little dog came down the hill in haste, and I was soon informed that a snake had been discovered; but it was a young one, called the bushmaster, a rare and poisonous reptile.

3. I instantly rose up, and, laying hold of the eight-foot lance, which was close by—"Well, then," said I, "we'll go and have a look at the snake." I was barefoot, with a hat and check shirt and trousers on, and a pair of braces to keep them up. The negro had his cutlass, and, as we ascended the hill, another negro, armed with a cutlass,

joined us, judging from our pace that there was something to do. The little dog came along with us, and when we had got about a mile into the forest the negro stopped, and pointed to the fallen tree. I told the negroes not to stir from the place where they were, and to keep the little dog in, and that I would go on and reconnoiter.

4. I advanced up to the place slowly and cautiously. The snake was well concealed, but at last I made him out; it was a coulacanara, not poisonous, but large enough to have crushed any of us to death. He was something more than fourteen feet long. This species of snake is very rare, and is much thicker, in proportion to his length, than any other snake in the forest. A coulacanara fourteen feet in length is as thick as a common boa of twenty-four. On ascertaining the size of the snake, I retired slowly the way I came. Aware that the day was on the decline, and that the approach of night would be detrimental to the dissection, a thought struck me that I could take him alive.

5. When I told this to the negroes, they begged and entreated me to let them go for a gun and more force, as they were sure the snake would kill some of us. But I had been in search of a large serpent for years, and now, having come up with one, it did not become me to turn soft. So, taking the cutlass from one of the negroes, and ranging them both behind me, I told them to follow me, and that I would cut them down if they offered to fly. I smiled as I said this, but they shook their heads in silence, and seemed to have but a bad heart of it.

6. When we got to the place, the serpent had not stirred, but I could see nothing of his head. A species of woodbine had formed a complete mantle over the fallen tree, almost impervious to the rain or the rays of the sun. Probably he had resorted to this sequestered place for a length of time, as it bore the marks of ancient settlement. I now took my

knife to cut away the woodbine and twigs till I could get a good view of his head. One negro stood guard close behind me with the lance, and near him the other with a cutlass. The cutlass which I had taken from the first negro was on the ground close by in case of need.

7. After working in dead silence for a quarter of an hour, with one knee all the time on the ground, I had cleared away enough to see his head. It appeared coming out between the first and second coil of his body, and was flat on the ground. This was the very position I wished him to be in. I rose in silence, and retreated very slowly, making a sign to the negroes to do the same. The dog was sitting at a distance in mute observance. I could now read in the faces of the negroes that they considered this a very unpleasant affair, and they made another attempt to persuade me to let them go for a gun. I smiled in a good-natured manner, and made a feint to cut them down with the weapon I had in my hand. This was all the answer I made to their request, and they looked very uneasy.

8. We were now about twenty yards from the snake's den. I ranged the negroes behind me, and told him who stood next me to lay hold of the lance the moment I struck the snake, and that the other must attend to my movements. It now only remained for me to take their cutlasses from them, for I was sure, if I did not disarm them, they would be tempted to strike the snake in time of danger, and thus for ever spoil his skin. They seemed to regard this as an act of intolerable tyranny in me, and probably nothing kept them from bolting but the consolation that I was to be between them and the snake. Indeed, my own heart, in spite of all I could do, beat quicker than usual.

9. We went slowly on in silence, without moving our arms or heads, in order to prevent all alarm as much as possible, lest the snake should glide off, or attack us in

self-defense. I carried the lance perpendicularly before me, with the point about a foot from the ground. The snake had not moved; and, on getting up to him, I struck him with the lance on the near side, just behind the neck, and pinned him to the ground. That moment the negro next me seized the lance and held it firmly in its place, while I dashed head foremost into the den to grapple with the snake and get hold of his tail before he could do any mischief.

10. On pinning him to the ground with the lance, he gave a tremendous loud hiss, and the little dog ran away, howling as he went. We had a sharp fray in the den, the rotten sticks flying upon all sides, and each party struggling for superiority. I called out to the second negro to throw himself upon me, as I found I was not heavy enough. He did so, and the additional weight was of great service. I had now got firm hold of his tail, and, after a violent struggle or two, he gave in, finding himself overpowered. This was the moment to secure him. So, while the first negro continued to hold the lance firm to the ground, and the other was helping me, I contrived to unloose my braces, and with them tied up the snake's mouth.

11. The snake, now finding himself in an unpleasant situation, tried to better himself, and set resolutely to work, but we overpowered him. We contrived to make him twist himself round the shaft of the lance, and then prepared to convey him out of the forest. I stood by the head, and held it firmly under my arm; one negro supported the middle, and the other the tail. In this order we began to move slowly toward home, and reached it after resting ten times, for the snake was too heavy for us to support him without stopping to recruit our strength. As we proceeded onward with him he fought hard for freedom, but all in vain. The day was now too far spent to think of dissecting him. If I killed him, a partial putre-

faction would take place before morning, so I concluded to put him into a very strong bag which I had brought with me, and keep him alive till daylight. After securing his mouth afresh, we forced him into the bag, and left him to his fate.

12. I can not say that he allowed me to have a very quiet night. My hammock was in the loft just above him, and the floor between us had half gone to decay. He was very restless and fretful; and, had Medusa been my wife, there could not have been more disagreeable hissing in my bed-chamber that night. At daybreak I borrowed ten negroes to assist in taking him out of the bag. We held him down by main force until I killed him. By six in the evening he was completely dissected. On examining his teeth, I observed that they were all bent like tenter-hooks, pointing down his throat, and not large or strong; but they are exactly suited to what they are intended by nature to perform. The snake does not masticate his food, and thus the only service his teeth have to perform is to seize the prey and hold it till he swallows it alive.

13. During this fray my old negro, Daddy Quashi, was absent, and returned just in time to help me take off the skin. He had a particular horror for snakes, and the next week I had an opportunity to put this weakness to the test. Having left my umbrella in the forest, I took Daddy Quashi to help me look for it. While he was searching about, I came to the scene of my late conflict, and in an old timber path I observed a young coulacanara, ten feet long, slowly moving onward; I saw he was not thick enough to break my arm in case he got twisted around it. There was not a moment to be lost. I laid hold of his tail with my left hand; with my right I took off my hat, and held it as you would hold a shield for defense.

14. The snake instantly turned and came on to me, with his head about a yard from the ground, as if to ask

me what business I had to take liberties with his tail. I let him come, hissing and open-mouthed, within two feet of my face, and then, with all the force I was master of, I drove my fist, shielded by my hat, full in his jaws. He was stunned and confounded by the blow, and, ere he could recover himself, I had seized his throat with both hands in such a position that he could not bite me; I then allowed him to coil himself about my body, and marched off with him as my lawful prize. He pressed me hard, but not alarmingly so. Daddy Quashi now came up with the umbrella. As soon as he saw me, and in what company I was, he ran off home, I after him, shouting to increase his fear. On scolding him for his cowardice, the old rogue begged that I would forgive him, for that the sight of the snake had positively made him sick at the stomach.

Charles Waterton.

CHAMELEONS; THEIR HABITS AND COLOR-CHANGES.

1. IN consequence of the incredible stories anciently told of the chameleon, one is hardly disposed to regard that animal as a reality; it appears to find its proper place in mythology rather than in natural history—among fabled dragons, centaurs, and griffins, rather than among the actualities of the animal kingdom. The chameleon, however, has a real existence; and, after fiction and fable are brushed aside, a very curious creature indeed remains. It belongs to the Saurian order (lizards). The genus *Chamæleo* embraces about twenty species, none of them American. With one exception, the *common chameleon*, which is naturalized in Southern Spain and in Sicily, these animals are found only in the warmer parts of Africa and Asia.

2. The chameleon is from ten to fifteen inches in length, whereof one half is represented by the prehensile tail. The body is roughly pyramidal in shape; the skin is covered with papillous elevations instead of scales, and these, in some of the species, assume the shape of spiny processes along the ridge of the back and the median line of the chest and belly. The toes, five in number, are divided into two opposable sets of two and three, the toes of each set being webbed down to the claws, which are long and sharp. The head is angular, rising into a pyramidal occiput. The

The Chameleon.

eyeball is very large, protruding, covered with a single lid, which has a minute aperture in the center for the very small pupil. There is no external ear.

3. The tongue is extensible to the length of half of the total length of the animal—that is, from five to seven inches. The lungs are large, and connect with air-cells underlying the skin. The neck is so short as to prevent the head being turned from side to side. Though the chameleon is arboreal in its habits, it is very slow in its movements. It is unprovided with any weapons of defense against its ene-

mies. The female lays about thirty eggs, which are deposited in a hollow in the ground, and covered with loose earth.

4. The immobility of the chameleon distinguishes it markedly from the rest of the lizard tribe, which are generally active and quick in their movements. Alfred Brehm states that the chameleon never moves at all except from necessity; it will remain in one position on a branch or twig for hours at a time, firmly grasping with tail and paws the object on which it is perched. The eyes, on the contrary, are nearly always in motion. In their battles they use their teeth, but without doing serious injury; and they have a curious way of solemnly lashing one another with their tails. But such activity as this is exceptional in the chameleon: it is to be seen especially in the pairing season.

5. When preying on winged insects, the chameleon is seen occasionally to protrude the knobbed end of his tongue, and in an instant that member is shot forth and again retracted, bearing the prey into the captor's mouth. The extremity of the tongue exudes a sticky substance on which the prey is caught. When flies and other winged insects are not to be had, the chameleon's swivel-eyes scan the trunk of the tree, and the branches above, below, and on all sides around, to see if any creeping thing may be caught. If any such creature is approaching the spot where the chameleon is lying, he waits till it comes within striking distance, and then "discharges" his tongue at it.

6. But, if the creature is traveling away from him, he pursues, though with grave deliberation. If the prey comes very near to his muzzle, the chameleon retreats a little, to increase the distance, and then darts out his tongue. In performing this act, the chameleon displays very great activity; otherwise, all his movements are the reverse of precipitate. Thus, if he would change from his normal

position of absolute quietude—his belly resting on a horizontal branch, which he grasps as firmly as he can with all five hands (for his tail is a fifth hand)—he first advances one of the fore-paws one step; then the tail is relaxed, advanced an equal distance, and again coiled tight; next the other feet are advanced a step, one after another; and so on. It is not easy to recognize the propriety of the name *little lion* (*Chamæleon*) given to this reptilian tardigrade by the ancient Greeks. And the animal is as harmless as it is slow of movement, though the ancients supposed that in the dog-days it assumes some of the lion's ferocity.

7. The large, projecting eyeballs of the chameleon are capable of a great variety of movements; and, what is very curious, each of them may, and usually does, act independently of the other. This circumstance compensates for the fixedness of the head, enabling the animal to direct its glances on all sides, without the necessity of calling into play any muscles save those of the eyeball. Still, when about to strike, the chameleon brings both of its eyes to bear upon the object.

8. "Notwithstanding," says Weissenbaum, "the strictly symmetrical construction of the chameleon as to its two halves, the eyes move independently of each other, and convey different impressions to the different centers of perception: the consequence is that, when the animal is agitated, its movements appear like those of two animals glued together. Each half wishes to move its own way, and there is no concert of action. The chameleon, therefore, is not able to swim like other animals; it is so frightened when put into water that the faculty of concentration is lost, and it tumbles about as if in a state of intoxication. Nay, more, the chameleon may be asleep on one side and awake on the other."

9. The chameleon is often seen to inhale air, gulp after gulp, with great avidity, thus inflating its body enormously,

even to the feet and tail. As has been already stated, the animal's lungs are very large—so large, indeed, that it was supposed by Pliny, who simply transcribes the accounts given by Greek authors, that the lungs almost filled the entire cavity of the body; these lungs connect with the air-cells beneath the skin. By taking air into the lungs, whence it passes into the air-cells, the chameleon is able to inflate itself to as much as twice its ordinary size; and often it remains so inflated for a long time, now slightly collapsing, again swelling out, till the skin becomes as tense as the head of a drum. No doubt it was this power of self-inflation which led the ancients to suppose that, "alone among animals, the chameleon neither eats nor drinks, its only sustenance being air."

10. But the color-changes of the chameleon form perhaps the most interesting phenomenon connected with this animal. We need not repeat the fabulous stories told about these color-changes: the facts which can be strictly verified by direct observation are wonderful enough without the adornments of imagination. These changes of color range from whity-yellow, through yellow, bright and dark green, to dull black; and these diversities of coloration may affect the entire surface of the animal, or one or other of its sides, or may appear only in spots. When the chameleon is asleep, and not exposed to the direct rays of the sun, its color is a whity-yellow; when basking in the sun, it is a dingy black or dusky brown. On being aroused from sleep, the side which is first awakened assumes a darker shade. There is reason for believing that sunlight, apart from the warmth which accompanies it, is very grateful to the chameleon, and, in response to this stimulus, he at once begins his play of color.

Science Monthly.

THE CHAMELEON.

1. OFT has it been my lot to mark
   A proud, conceited, talking spark,
   Returning from his finished tour,
   Grown ten times perter than before:
   Whatever word you chance to drop,
   The traveled fool your mouth would stop.
   "Sir, if my judgment you'll allow,
   I've seen, and sure I ought to know."
   So begs you pay a due submission,
   And acquiesce in his decision.

2. Two travelers of such a cast,
   As o'er Arabia's wilds they passed,
   And on their way, in friendly chat,
   Now talked of this, and then of that;
   Discoursed a while, 'mongst other matter,
   Of the chameleon's form and nature.

3. "A stranger animal," cried one,
   "Sure never lived beneath the sun:
   A lizard's body, lean and long,
   A fish's head, a serpent's tongue,
   Its tooth with triple claws disjoined,
   And what a length of tail behind!
   How slow its pace! and then its hue,
   Whoever saw so fine a blue!"

4. "Hold there!" the other quick replies;
   "'Tis green: I saw it with these eyes,
   As late with open mouth it lay,
   And warmed itself in the sunny ray;
   Stretched at its ease the beast I viewed,
   And saw it eat the air for food."

5. "I've seen it, sir, as well as you,
    And must again affirm it blue;
    At leisure I the beast surveyed,
    Extended in the cooling shade."

6. "'Tis green! 'tis green, sir, I assure ye."
    "Green!" cries the other, in a fury;
    "Why, sir, d'ye think I've lost my eyes?"
    "'Twere no great loss," the friend replies;
    "For if they always serve you thus,
    You'll find them but of little use."

7. So high at last the contest rose,
    From words they almost came to blows,
    When luckily came by a third;
    To him the question they referred,
    And begged he'd tell them if he knew
    Whether the thing was green or blue.

8. "Sirs," cried the umpire, "cease your pother;
    The creature's neither one nor t'other;
    I caught the animal last night,
    And viewed him o'er by candle-light;
    I marked it well, 'twas black as jet—
    You stare, but, sirs, I've got it yet,
    And can produce it." "Pray, sir, do;
    I'll lay my life the thing is blue."

9. "And I'll be sworn that when ye've seen
    The reptile, you'll pronounce it green."
    "Well, then, at once to end this doubt,"
    Replies the man, "I'll turn him out;
    And when before your eyes I've set him,
    If you don't find him black, I'll eat him,"
    He said; then full before their sight
    Produced the beast, and lo! 'twas white.

Merrick.

PART VIII.

OUR FOREST CHORISTERS.

SONGSTERS OF THE GARDEN.

1. For many years I have been in the habit of noting down some of the leading events of my embowered solitude, such as the coming of certain birds and the like, after the fashion of White of Selborne, rather than properly digested natural history. I thought it not impossible that a few simple stories of my winged acquaintances might be found entertaining by persons of kindred taste.

2. The return of the robin is commonly announced by the newspapers, like that of eminent and notorious people to a watering-place, as the first authentic notification of spring. And such his appearance in the orchard and garden undoubtedly is. But, in spite of his name of migratory thrush, he stays with us all winter, and I have seen him when the thermometer marked fifteen degrees below zero, armed impregnably within like Emerson's titmouse, and as cheerful as he.

3. The robin has a bad reputation among people, who do not value themselves less, for being fond of cherries. There is, I admit, a spice of vulgarity in him, and his song, rather of the Bloomfield sort, too largely ballasted with prose. His ethics are of the Poor Richard school, and the main chance which calls forth all his energies is altogether

of the belly. He never has those fine intervals of lunacy into which his cousins, the cat-bird and the mavis, are apt to fall. But, for a' that and twice as muckle 's a' that, I would not exchange him for all the cherries that ever came out of Asia Minor. With whatever faults, he has not wholly forfeited that superiority which belongs to the children of nature.

4. The robins are not good solo-singers, but their chorus, as, like primitive fire-worshipers, they hail the return of light and warmth, is unrivaled. There are a hundred singing like one. They are noisy enough then, and sing, as poets should, with no afterthought. But when they come after cherries to the tree near my window, they muffle their voices, and their faint "pip, pip, pop!" sounds far away at the bottom of the garden, where they know I shall not suspect them of robbing the great walnut-tree of its bitter-rinded store. They are feathered Pecksniffs, to be sure, but then how brightly their breasts, that look rather shabby in the sunlight, shine on a rainy day against the dark green of the fringe-tree! After they have pinched and shaken all the life out of an earthworm, as Italian cooks pound all the spirit out of a steak, and then gulp him, they stand up in honest self-confidence, expand their red waistcoats with the virtuous air of a lobby member, and outface you with an eye that calmly challenges inquiry. "Do I look like a bird that knows the flavor of raw vermin? I throw myself upon a jury of my peers."

5. Ask any robin if he ever ate anything less ascetic than the frugal berry of the juniper, and he will answer that "his vows forbid him." Can such a bosom cover such depravity? Alas, yes! I have no doubt his breast was redder at that very moment with the blood of my raspberries. On the whole, he is a doubtful friend of the garden. He makes his dessert on all kinds of berries, and is not averse to early pears. But when we remember how om-

nivorous he is, eating his own weight in an incredibly short time, and that Nature seems exhaustless in her invention of new insects hostile to vegetation, perhaps we may reckon that he does more good than harm. For my part, I would rather have his cheerfulness and kind neighborhood than many berries.

6. For his cousin, the cat-bird, I have a still warmer regard. Always a good singer, he sometimes nearly equals the brown thrush, and has the merit of keeping up his music later in the evening than any bird of my familiar acquaintance. Ever since I can remember, a pair of them have built in a gigantic syringa near our front door, and I have known the male to sing almost uninterruptedly, during the evenings of early summer, till twilight darkened into dark. They differ greatly in vocal talent, but all have a delightful way of crooning over, and, as it were, rehearsing their song in an undertone, which makes their nearness always unobtrusive. Though there is the most trustworthy witness to the imitative propensity of this bird, I have only once, during an intimacy of more than forty years, heard him indulge it. In that case the imitation was by no means so close as to deceive, but a free reproduction of the notes of some other birds, especially of the oriole, as a kind of variation of his own song.

7. The cat-bird is as shy as the robin is familiar. Only when his nest or his fledglings are approached does he become noisy and aggressive. I have known him to station his young in a thick cornel-bush, on the edge of the raspberry-bed, after the fruit began to ripen, and feed them there for a week or more. In such cases he shows none of that conscious guilt which the robin shows. On the contrary, he will maintain his post in the thicket, and sharply scold the intruder who ventures to steal *his* berries. After all, his claim is only for tithes, while the robin will bag your entire crop if he gets a chance.

8. Dr. Watts's statement that "birds in their little nests agree," like too many others intended to form the infant mind, is far from being true. On the contrary, the most peaceful relations of the different species to each other is that of armed neutrality. They are very jealous of their neighbors. A few years ago I was much interested in the house-building of a pair of summer yellow-birds. They had chosen a very pretty site near the top of a tall white lilac, within easy eye-shot of a chamber-window. A very pleasant thing it was to see their little home growing with mutual help, to watch their industrious skill interrupted only by little flirts and snatches of endearment, frugally cut short by the common sense of the tiny housewife. They had brought their work nearly to an end, and had already begun to line it with fern-down, the gatherings of which demanded more distant journeys and longer absences.

9. But, alas! the syringa, immemorial manor of the catbirds, was not more than twenty feet away, and these "giddy neighbors" had, as it appeared, been all along jealously watchful, though silent, witnesses of what they deemed an intrusion of squatters. No sooner were the pretty mates fairly gone for a new load of lining than

"To their unguarded nests these weasel Scots came stealing."

Silently they flew back and forth, each giving a vengeful dab at the nest in passing. They did not fall to and deliberately destroy the nest, for they might have been caught at their mischief. As it was, whenever the yellow-birds came back, their enemies were hidden in their own sight-proof bush. Several times their unconscious victims repaired damages, but at length, after counsel taken together, they gave it up. Perhaps, like other unlettered folk, they came to the conclusion that the devil was in it, and yielded to the invisible persecutions of witchcraft.

10. The robins, by constant attacks and annoyances, have succeeded in driving off the blue-jays who used to build in our pines, their gay colors and quaint, noisy ways making them welcome and amusing neighbors. I once had a chance to do a kindness to a household of them, which they received with very friendly condescension. I had had my eye for some time past upon a nest, and was puzzled by a constant fluttering of what seemed full-grown wings in it whenever I drew nigh. At last I climbed the tree, in spite of the angry protests from the old birds against my intrusion. The mystery had a very simple solution. In building the nest, a long piece of pack-thread had been somewhat loosely woven in, three of the young had contrived to entangle themselves in it, and had become full-grown without being able to launch themselves into the air. One was unharmed; another had so tightly twisted the cord about its shank that one foot was curled up and seemed paralyzed; the third, in his struggles to escape, had sawn through the flesh of the thigh and so much harmed itself that I thought it humane to put an end to its misery.

11. When I took out my knife to cut their hempen bonds, the heads of the family seemed to divine my friendly intent. Suddenly ceasing their cries and threats, they perched quietly within reach of my hand, and watched me in my work of manumission. This, owing to the fluttering terror of the prisoners, was an affair of some delicacy; but ere long I was rewarded by seeing one of them fly away to a neighboring tree, while the cripple, making a parachute of his wings, came lightly to the ground, and hopped off as well as he could with one leg, obsequiously waited upon by his elders. A week later I had the satisfaction of meeting him in the pine walk, in good spirits, and already so far recovered as to be able to balance himself with the lame foot. I have no doubt that in his old age he accounted for his lameness by some handsome story of

a wound received at the famous Battle of the Pines, when one tribe, overcome by numbers, was driven away from its ancient camping-ground.

12. Orioles are in great plenty with me. I have seen seven males flashing about the garden at once. A merry crew of them swing their hammocks from the pendulous boughs. Last year a pair of orioles built on the lowest trailer of a weeping elm, which hung within ten feet of our drawing-room window, and so low that I could reach it from the ground. The nest was wholly woven and felted with ravelings of woolen carpet, in which scarlet predominated. They were very bold in the quest of cordage, and I have often watched them stripping the fibrous bark from the honeysuckle growing over the very door.

13. But, indeed, all my birds look upon me as if I were a mere tenant at will, and they were landlords. With shame I confess it, I have been bullied even by a humming-bird. This spring, as I was cleansing a pear-tree of its lichens, one of these little zigzagging blurs came hurrying toward me, couching his long bill like a lance, his throat sparkling with angry fire, to warn me off from a Missouri currant whose honey he was sipping. And many a time he has driven me out of a flower-bed.

14. The bobolinks are generally chance visitors, tinkling through the garden in blossoming-time; but this year, owing to the long rains early in the season, their favorite meadow was overflowed, and they were driven to the upland. So I had a pair of them domiciled in my grass-field. The male used to perch in an apple-tree, then in full bloom, and, while I stood perfectly still close by, he would circle away, quivering round the entire field of five acres, with no break in his song, and settle down again among the blossoms, to be hurried away again almost immediately by a new rapture of music. He had the volubility of an Italian charlatan at a fair, and, like him, appeared to be

proclaiming the merits of some quack remedy. *Opodeldoc-opodeldoc-try-Doctor-Lincoln's-opodeldoc!* he seemed to repeat over and over again, with a rapidity that would have distanced the deftest-tongued Figaro that ever rattled.

15. The bobolinks build in considerable numbers in a meadow within a quarter of a mile of us. When they are breeding, if I chance to pass, one of the male birds always accompanies me like a constable, flitting from post to post of the rail-fence, with a short note of reproof continually repeated till I am fairly out of the neighborhood. Then he will swing away into the air and run down the wind, gurgling music without stint over the unheeding tussocks of meadow-grass and dark clumps of bulrushes that mark his domain. We have no bird whose song will match the nightingale's in compass, none whose note is so rich as that of the European blackbird, but for mere rapture I have never heard the bobolink's rival.

16. A pair of pewees have built immemorially on a jutting brick in the arched entrance of the ice-house. Always on the same brick, and never more than a single pair, though two broods of five each are raised there every summer. How do they settle their claim to the homestead? By what right of primogeniture? Once the children of the man employed about the place *oölogized* the nest, and the pewees left us for a year or two. I felt toward these boys as the messmates of the Ancient Mariner did toward him after he shot the albatross. But the pewees came back at last, and one of them is now on his wonted perch, so near my window that I can hear the click of his bill as he snaps at a fly with unerring precision.

17. The pewee is the first bird to pipe in the morning; and during the early summer he preludes his matutinal ejaculation of *pewee* with a slender whistle, unheard at any other time. He saddens with the season, and as summer declines he changes his note to *cheu, pewee!* as if in lam-

entation. Had he been an Italian bird, Ovid would have had a plaintive tale to tell about him. He is so familiar as often to pursue a fly through the open windows of my library.

18. There is something inexpressibly dear to me in these old friendships of a lifetime. There is scarce a tree of mine but has had, at some time or other, a happy homestead among its boughs, to which can I not say,

"Many light hearts and wings,
Which now be dead, lodged in thy living bowers."

My walk under the pines would lose half its summer charm were I to miss that shy anchorite, the Wilson's thrush, nor hear in haying-time the metallic ring of his song, that justifies his rustic name of *scythe-whet*.

19. I protect my game as jealously as an English squire. If anybody had oölogized a certain cuckoo's-nest I know of, it would have left a sore place in my mind for weeks. I love to bring these aborigines back to the mansuetude they showed to the early voyagers, and before they had grown accustomed to man and his savage ways. And they repay your kindness with a sweet familiarity too delicate ever to breed contempt. I have made a Penn-treaty with them, preferring that to the Puritan way with the natives, which converted them to a little Hebraism and a great deal of Medford rum. If they will not come near enough to me —as most of them will—I bring them close with an opera-glass, a much better weapon than a gun. I would not, if I could, convert them from their pretty pagan ways.

20. The only one I sometimes have savage doubts about is the red squirrel. *I think* he oölogizes. I know he eats cherries, and he gnaws off the small ends of the pears to get the seeds. He steals the corn from under the noses of my poultry. But what would you have? He will come down upon the limbs of a tree I am lying under till he is within a yard of me. He and his mate will scurry up and

down the great black-walnut for my diversion, chattering like monkeys. Can I sign his death-warrant who has tolerated me about his grounds so long? Not I. Let them steal and welcome. I am sure I should, had I the same bringing up and the same temptation. As for the birds, I do not believe there is one of them but does more good than harm; and of how many featherless bipeds can this be said?

James Russell Lowell.

THE SONG OF BIRDS.

1. IN proportion as we have been trained to be agreeably affected by the outward forms of nature and the sounds that proceed from the animate and inanimate world, are we capable of being made happy without resorting to expensive and vulgar recreations. It ought, therefore, to be one of the chief points in the education of youth, while teaching them the still more important offices of humanity, to cultivate and enliven their susceptibility to the charms of natural objects. Then would the aspects of nature, continually changing with the progress of the seasons and the sounds that enliven their march, satisfy, in a great measure, that craving for agreeable sensations which leads mankind away from humble and healthful pursuits to those of a more artificial and exciting life. The value of such pleasures consists not so much in their cheapness as in their favorable moral influences, which improve the heart, while they lead the mind to observations that pleasantly exercise and develop, without tasking its powers. The quiet emotions, half musical and half poetical, which are awakened by listening to the song of birds, belong to this class of refined enjoyments.

2. But the music of birds, though agreeable to all, conveys positive and durable pleasure only to those who have

learned to associate with their notes, in connection with the scenes of nature, a thousand interesting and romantic images. To many persons of this character it affords more delight than the most brilliant music of the opera or the concert. In vain, therefore, will it be said, as an objection, that the notes of birds have no charm save that which is derived from association, and that, considered as music, they do not equal that of the most simple reed or flageolet.

3. It is sufficient to remark that the most delightful influences of nature proceed from those sights and sounds that appeal to the imagination and affections through the medium of slight and almost insensible impressions made upon the eye and ear. At the moment when these physical impressions exceed a certain mean, the spell is broken, and the enjoyment becomes sensual, not intellectual. How soon, indeed, would the songs of birds lose their effect if they were loud and brilliant, like a band of instruments! It is their simplicity which gives them their charm.

4. As a further illustration of this point, it may be remarked that simple melodies have among all people exercised a greater power over the imagination than louder and more complicated music. Nature employs a very small amount of physical sensation to create an intellectual passion, and when an excess is used a diminished effect is produced. I am persuaded that the effect of a great part of our sacred music is lost by an excess of harmony and a too great volume of sound. On the same principle, a loud crash of thunder deafens and terrifies; but its low and distant rumbling produces an agreeable emotion of sublimity.

5. The songs of birds are as intimately allied with poetry as with music. The lark has been aptly denominated a "feathered lyric" by one of the English poets; and the analogy becomes apparent when we consider how much the song of a bird resembles a lyrical ballad in its influence on the mind. Though it utters no words, how

plainly it suggests a long train of agreeable images of love, beauty, friendship, and home!

6. The voice of every singing-bird has its associations in the minds of all susceptible persons who were born and nurtured within the precincts of its untutored minstrelsy. The music of birds is modulated in pleasant unison with all the chords of affection and imagination, filling the soul with a lively consciousness of happiness and beauty, and soothing it with romantic visions of memory—of love, when it was an ethereal sentiment of adoration and not a passion, and of friendship, when it was a passion and not an expedience; of dear and simple adventures, and of comrades who had part in them; of dappled mornings and serene and glowing sunsets, of sequestered nooks and mossy seats in the old wood, of paths by the riverside and flowers that smiled a bright welcome to our rambling, of lingering departures from home, and of old by-ways overshadowed by trees and hedged with roses and viburnums, that spread their shade and their perfume around our path to gladden our return. By this pleasant instrumentality has Nature provided for the happiness of those who have learned to be delighted with the survey of her works, and with the sound of those voices which she has appointed to communicate to the human soul the joys of her inferior creation.

7. The singing-birds, with reference to their songs, may be divided into four classes. First, the rapid singers, whose song is uninterrupted, of considerable length, and uttered with fervor, and in apparent ecstasy. Second, the moderate singers, whose notes are slowly modulated, but without pauses or rests between their different strains. Third, the interrupted singers, who seldom modulate their notes with rapidity, and make decided pauses between their several strains, of which there are in general from five to eight or nine. Fourth, the warblers, whose notes consist of only one or two strains, not combined into a song.

8. The canary, among foreign birds, and the linnet and bobolink, among American birds, are familiar examples of the first class; the common robin and the veery of the second; the wood-thrush, the cat-bird, and the mocking-bird, of the third; and the blue-bird, the pewee, and the purple martin, of the fourth class. It may be added that some birds are nearly periodical in their habits of singing, preferring the morning and evening, and occasional periods in other parts of the day, while others sing almost indifferently at all hours. The greater number of species, however, are more tuneful in the early morning than at any other hour.

9. June, in this part of the world, is the most vocal month of the year. Many of our principal songsters do not arrive until the middle of May; and all, whether they come early or late, continue in song throughout the month of June. The bobolink, which is one of the first to become silent, continues vocal until the second week in July. So nearly simultaneous is the discontinuance of the songs of this species, that it might seem as if their silence were preconcerted, and that by a vote they had on a certain day adjourned over to another year.

10. If an unusually genial day occurs about the seventh of July, we may hear multitudes of them singing merrily on that occasion. Should this time be followed by two or three successive days of chilly and rainy weather, their tunefulness is so generally brought to a close during this period that we may not have another musical note from a single individual after the seventh. The songs of birds are discontinued as soon as their care of their offspring has ceased. Hence, those birds that raise but one brood of young during the season, like the bobolink, are the first to become silent.

11. No one of the New England birds is an autumnal warbler, though the song-sparrow often greets the fine

mornings in October with his lays, and the shore-lark, after spending the summer in Labrador and about the shores of Hudson's Bay, is sometimes heard in autumn, soaring and singing at the dawn of day, while on their passage to the South. The bobolink, the veery, or Wilson's thrush, the red thrush, and the golden robin are silent after the middle of July; the wood-thrush, the cat-bird, and the common robin, not until a month later; but the song-sparrow alone continues to sing throughout the summer. The tuneful season of the year in New England embraces a period of about four months—from the middle of April to the middle of August.

12. There are certain times of the day, as well as certain seasons of the year, when the birds are most musical. The grand concert of the feathered tribe takes place during the hour between dawn and sunrise. During the remainder of the day they sing less in concert, though many species are very musical at noonday, and seem, like the nocturnal birds, to prefer the hour when others are silent. At sunset there is an apparent attempt to unite once more in chorus, but this is far from being so loud or so general as in the morning. The little birds which I have classed in the fourth division are a very important accompaniment to the anthem of dawn, their notes, though short, serving agreeably to fill up the pauses made by the other musicians. Thus, the hair-bird has a sharp and trilling note, without any modulation, and not at all melodious when heard alone; but in the morning it is the chief harmonizer of the whole chorus, and seems, more than any other voice, to give unity and symphony to the multitude of miscellaneous parts.

13. There are not many birds whose notes could be accurately described upon the gamut. The nearest approach we can make to accuracy is to give some general idea of their time and modulation. Their musical intervals can be

distinguished but with difficulty, on account of the rapidity of their utterance. I have often attempted to transcribe some of their notes upon the musical scale, but I am persuaded that such sketches can be only approximations to literal correctness. As different individuals of the same species sing very differently, the notes as transcribed from the song of one individual will never exactly represent the song of another. If we listen attentively, however, to a number of songs, we will detect in all of them a *theme*, as it is termed by musicians, of which the different individuals of the species warble their respective variations. Every song is, technically speaking, a *fantasia* constructed upon this theme, from which none of the species ever departs.

J. Elliot Cabot.

LIFE AND SONG IN THE WOODS.

1. WALKING the other day in an old hemlock wood, I counted over forty varieties of birds, though this is an unusual number for a single forest. I descended a hill and approached the hemlocks through a large sugar-bush. When twenty rods distant, I hear all along the line of the forest the incessant warble of the red-eyed fly-catcher, cheerful and happy as the merry whistle of a school-boy. He is one of our most common and widely distributed birds. Approach any forest, at any hour of the day, in any kind of weather, from May to August, in any of the middle or eastern districts, and the chances are that the first note you hear will be his. Rain or shine, before noon or after, in the deep forest or in the village grove—when it is too hot for the thrushes or too cold and windy for the warblers—it is never out of time or place for this little minstrel to indulge his cheerful strain.

2. There is nothing plaintive or especially musical in his performance, but the sentiment expressed is eminently that of cheerfulness. Indeed, the songs of most birds have some human significance, which, I think, is the source of the delight we take in them. The song of the bobolink, to me, expresses hilarity; the song-sparrow's, faith; the bluebird's, love; the cat-bird's, pride; the white-eyed fly-catcher's, self-consciousness; that of the hermit-thrush, spiritual serenity; while there is something military in the call of the robin, and unalloyed contentment in the warble of the red-eyed vireo.

3. Passing down through the maple arches, barely pausing to observe the antics of a trio of squirrels—two gray ones and a black one—I cross an ancient brush-fence and am fairly within the old hemlocks, and in one of the most primitive, undisturbed nooks. In the deep moss I tread as with muffled feet, and the pupils of my eyes dilate in the dim, almost religious light. The irreverent red squirrels, however, run and snicker at my approach, or mock the solitude with their ridiculous chattering and frisking.

4. This nook is the chosen haunt of the winter wren. This is the only place, and these are the only woods, in which I find him in this vicinity. His voice fills these dim aisles, as if aided by some marvelous sounding-board. Indeed, his song is very strong for so small a bird, and unites in a remarkable degree brilliancy and plaintiveness. I think of a tremulous, vibrating tongue of silver. You may know that it is the song of a wren from its gushing, lyrical character; but you must needs look sharp to see the little minstrel, especially while in the act of singing. He is nearly the color of the ground and the leaves; he never ascends the tall trees, but keeps low, flitting from stump to stump, and from root to root, dodging in and out of his hiding-places, and watching all intruders with a suspicious eye.

He has a very perk, almost comical look. His tail stands more than perpendicular; it points straight toward his head. He is the least ostentatious singer I know of. He does not strike an attitude and lift up his head in prepara-

A Forest Warbler.

tion, and, as it were, clear his throat; but he sits there on the log and pours out his music, looking straight before him, or even down at the ground.

5. I am attracted by another warble in the same locality, and experience a like difficulty in getting a good view of

the author of it. It is quite a noticeable strain, sharp and sibilant, and sounds well amid the old trees. In the upland woods of beech and maple it is a more familiar sound than in these solitudes. On taking the bird in your hand, even if you are not a young lady, you will probably exclaim, "How beautiful!" So tiny and elegant, the smallest of the warblers; a delicate blue back, with a slight, bronze-colored, triangular spot between the shoulders; upper mandible black; lower mandible yellow as gold; throat yellow, becoming a dark bronze on the breast. Blue yellow-back he is called, though the yellow is much nearer a bronze. He is remarkably delicate and beautiful — the handsomest, as he is the smallest, of the warblers known to me. It is never without surprise that I find amid these rugged, savage aspects of nature, creatures so fairy and delicate. But such is the law. Go to the sea or climb the mountain, and with the ruggedest and the savagest you will find likewise the fairest and the most delicate. The greatness and the minuteness of nature pass all understanding.

6. In a little opening quite free from brush and trees I step down to bathe my hands in the brook, when a small, light, slate-colored bird flutters out of the bank, not three feet from my head, as I stoop down, and, as if severely lamed or injured, flutters through the grass and into the nearest bush. As I do not follow, but remain near the nest, she *chips* sharply, which brings the male, and I see it is the speckled Canada warbler. I find no authority in the books for this bird to build upon the ground, yet here is the nest, made chiefly of dry grass, set in a slight excavation in the bank, not two feet from the water, and looking a little perilous to anything but ducklings or sandpipers.

7. There are two young birds and one little speckled egg, just pipped. But how is this? what mystery is here? One nestling is much larger than the other, monopolizes

most of the nest, and lifts its open mouth far above that of its companion, though obviously both are of the same age, not more than a day old. Ah! I see—the old trick of the cow-bunting, with a stinging human significance. Taking the interloper by the nape of the neck, I deliberately drop it into the water, but not without a pang, as I see its naked form, convulsed with chills, float down the stream. Cruel! So is nature cruel. I take one life to save two. In less than two days this pot-bellied intruder would have caused the death of the two rightful occupants of the nest; so I step in and divert things into their proper channel again.

8. It is a singular freak of nature, this instinct which prompts one bird to lay its eggs in the nests of others, and thus shirk the responsibility of rearing its own young. The cow-buntings always resort to this cunning trick, and, when one reflects upon their numbers, it is evident that these little tragedies are quite frequent. In Europe the parallel case is that of the cuckoo, and occasionally our own cuckoo imposes upon a robin or a thrush in the same manner. The cow-bunting seems to have no conscience about the matter, and, so far as I have observed, invariably selects the nest of a bird smaller than itself. Its egg is usually the first to hatch; its young overreaches all the rest when food is brought; it grows with great rapidity, spreads and fills the nest, and the starved and crowded occupants soon perish, when the parent bird removes their dead bodies, giving its whole energy and care to the foster-child.

9. The warblers and smaller fly-catchers are generally the sufferers, though I sometimes see the slate-colored snow-bird unconsciously duped in like manner; and the other day, in a tall tree in the woods, I discovered the black-throated, green-backed warbler devoting itself to this dusky, overgrown foundling. An old farmer to whom I

pointed out the fact was much surprised that such things should happen in his woods without his knowledge.

10. Ever since I entered the woods, even while listening to the lesser songsters, or contemplating the silent forms about me, a strain has reached my ear from out the depths of the forest that to me is the finest sound in nature—the song of the hermit-thrush. I often hear him thus a long way off—sometimes over a quarter of a mile away, when only the stronger and more perfect parts of his music reach me; and through the general chorus of wrens and warblers I detect this sound rising pure and serene, as if a spirit from some remote height were slowly chanting a divine accompaniment. This song appeals to the sentiment of the beautiful in me, and suggests a serene, religious beatitude as no other sound in nature does. It is, perhaps, more of an evening than a morning hymn, though I hear it at all hours of the day. It is very simple, and I cãn hardly tell the secret of its charm. "O spheral, spheral!" he seems to say; "O holy, holy! O clear away, clear away! O clear up, clear up!" interspersed with the finest trills and the most delicate preludes.

11. It is not a proud, gorgeous strain, like the tanager's or the grosbeak's; suggests no passion or emotion—nothing personal—but seems to be the voice of that calm, sweet solemnity one attains to in his best moments. It realizes a peace and a deep, solemn joy that only the finest souls may know. A few nights ago I ascended a mountain to see the world by moonlight; and when near the summit the hermit commenced his evening hymn a few rods from me. Listening to this strain on the lone mountain, with the full moon just rounded from the horizon, the pomp of your cities and the pride of your civilization seemed trivial and cheap.

12. But the declining sun and the deepening shadows admonish me that this ramble must be brought to a close.

In a secluded, swampy corner of the old barkpeeling, where I find the great purple orchis in bloom, and where the foot of man or beast seems never to have trod, I linger long, contemplating the wonderful display of lichens and mosses that overrun both the smaller and the larger growths. Every bush and branch and sprig is dressed up in the most rich and fantastic of liveries; and, crowning all, the long, bearded moss festoons the branches or sways gracefully from the limbs. Every twig looks a century old, though green leaves tip the end of it. A young yellow birch has a venerable, patriarchal look, and seems ill at ease under such premature honors. A decayed hemlock is draped as if by hands for some solemn festival.

13. Mounting toward the upland again, I pause reverently as the hush and stillness of twilight come upon the woods. It is the sweetest, ripest hour of the day. And, as the hermit's evening hymn goes up from the deep solitude below me, I experience that serene exaltation of sentiment of which music, literature, and religion are but the faint types and symbols.

John Burroughs.

BIRD LIFE AND MOTION.

1. WHEN one thinks of a bird, one fancies a soft, swift, aimless, joyous thing, full of nervous energy and arrowy motions, a song with wings. So remote from ours their mode of existence, they seem accidental exiles from an unknown globe, banished where none can understand their language; and men only stare at their darting, inexplicable ways, as at the gyrations of the circus. Watch their little traits for hours, and it only tantalizes curiosity. Every man's secret is penetrable, if his neighbor be sharp-sighted. But this bird that hovers and alights beside me,

peers up at me, takes its food, then looks again, attitudinizing, jerking, flirting its tail, with a thousand inquisitive and fantastic motions, although I have power to grasp it in my hand and crush its life out, yet I can not gain its secret thus, and the center of its consciousness is really farther from mine than the remotest planetary orbit. "We do not steadily bear in mind," says Darwin, with a noble scientific humility, "how profoundly ignorant we are of the condition of existence of every animal."

2. What "sympathetic penetration" can fathom the life, for instance, of yonder mysterious, almost voiceless humming-bird, smallest of feathery things, and loneliest, whirring among birds, insect-like, and among insects, bird-like, his path untraceable, his home unseen? An image of airy motion, yet it sometimes seems as if there were nothing joyous in him. He seems like some exiled pygmy prince, banished, but still regal, and doomed to wings. Did gems turn to flowers, flowers to feathers, in that long-past dynasty of the humming-birds? It is strange to come upon his tiny nest, in some gray and tangled swamp, with this brilliant atom perched disconsolately near it, upon some mossy twig; it is like visiting Cinderella among her ashes. And from humming-bird to eagle, the daily existence of every bird is a remote and bewitching mystery.

3. Pythagoras has been charged, both before and since the days of Malvolio, with holding that "the soul of our grandam might haply inhabit a fowl," that delinquent men must revisit earth as women, and delinquent women as birds. Malvolio thought nobly of the soul, and in no way approved his opinion; but I remember that Harriet Rohan, in her school-days, accepted this, her destiny, with glee. "When I saw the oriole," she wrote to me, "from his nest among the plum-trees in the garden, sail over the air and high above the Gothic arches of the elm, a stream of flashing light, or watched him swinging silently on pendent

twigs, I did not dream how near akin we were. Or when a humming-bird, a winged drop of gorgeous sheen and gloss, a living gem, poising on his wings, thrust his dark, slender, honey-seeking bill into the white blossoms of a little bush beside my window, I should have thought it no such bad thing to be a bird, even if one next became a bat, like the colony in our eaves, that dart and drop and skim and skurry, all the length of moonless nights, in such ecstasies of dusky joy." Was this weird creature, the bat, in very truth a bird, in some far primeval time? and does he fancy, in unquiet dreams at nightfall, that he is one still? I wonder whether he can enjoy the winged brotherhood into which he has thrust himself—victim, perhaps, of some rash quadruped-ambition—an Icarus doomed for ever *not* to fall.

4. I think that, if required, on pain of death, to name instantly the most perfect thing in the universe, I should risk my fate on a bird's egg. There is, first, its exquisite fragility of material, strong only by the mathematical precision of that form so daintily molded. There is its absolute purity from external stain, since that thin barrier remains impassable until the whole is in ruins—a purity recognized in the household proverb of "An apple, an egg, and a nut."

·5. Then, its range of tints, so varied, so subdued, and so beautiful, whether of pure white, like the martin's, or pure green, like the robin's, or dotted and mottled into the loveliest of browns, like the red thrush's, or aqua marine, with stains of moss-agate, like the chipping sparrow's, or blotched with long, weird ink-marks on a pale ground, like the oriole's, as if it bore inscribed some magic clew to the bird's darting flight and pensile nest. Above all, the associations and predictions of this little wonder, that one may bear home between his fingers all that winged splendor, all that celestial melody, coiled in mystery within these tiny walls! Even the chrysalis is less amazing, for its form always preserves some trace, however fantastic, of the perfect insect, and it is but molting a skin; but this egg appears to the eye like a separate unit from some other kingdom of nature, claiming more kindred with the very stones than with feathery existence; and it is as if a pearl opened and an angel sang.

6. The nest which is to contain these fair things is a wondrous study also, from the coarse masonry of the robin to the soft structure of the humming-bird, a baby-house among nests. Among all created things, the birds come nearest to man in their domesticity. Their unions are usually in pairs, and for life; and with them, unlike the practice of most quadrupeds, the male labors for the young. He chooses the locality of the nest, aids in its construction, and fights for it, if needful. He sometimes assists in hatching the eggs. He feeds the brood with exhausting labor, like yonder robin, whose winged picturesque day is spent in putting worms into insatiable beaks, at the rate of one morsel in every three minutes. He has to teach them to fly, as among the swallows, or even to hunt, as among the hawks. His life is anchored to his home.

7. Yonder oriole fills with light and melody the thousand branches of a neighborhood; and yet the center for all this divergent splendor is always that one drooping dome upon one chosen tree. This he helped to build in May, confiscating cotton as if he were a Union provost-marshal, and singing many songs, with his mouth full of plunder; and there he watches over his household, all through the leafy June, perched often upon the airy cradle-edge, and swaying with it in the summer wind. And from this deep nest, after the pretty eggs are hatched, will he and his mate extract every fragment of the shell, leaving it, like all other nests, save those of birds of prey, clean and pure, when the young are flown. This they do chiefly

from an instinct of delicacy, since wood-birds are not wont to use the same nest a second time, even if they rear several broods in a season.

8. In comparing modes of flight, the most surprising, of course, is that of the swallow tribe, remarkable not merely for its velocity, but for the amazing boldness and instantaneousness of the angles it makes; so that eminent European mechanicians have speculated in vain upon the methods used in its locomotion, and prizes have been offered, by mechanical exhibitions, to him who could best explain it. With impetuous dash, they sweep through our perilous streets, these wild hunters of the air, "so near, and yet so far"; they bathe flying, and flying they feed their young. In my immediate vicinity, the chimney-swallow is not now common, nor the sand-swallow; but the cliff-swallow, that strange emigrant from the far West, the barn-swallow, and the white-breasted species, are abundant, together with the purple martin.

9. I know no prettier sight than a bevy of these bright little creatures, met from a dozen different farm-houses to picnic at a wayside pool, splashing and fluttering, with their long wings expanded like butterflies, keeping poised by a constant hovering motion, just tilting upon their feet, which scarcely touch the moist ground. You will seldom see them actually perch on anything less airy than some telegraph-wire; but, when they do alight, each will make chatter enough for a dozen, as if all the rushing hurry of the wings had passed into the tongue.

10. Between the swiftness of the swallow and the stateliness of the birds of prey, the whole range of bird motion seems included. The long wave of a hawk's wings seems almost to send a slow vibration through the atmosphere, tolling upon the eye as yon distant bell upon the ear. I never was more impressed with the superior dignity of these soarings than in observing a bloodless contest in the

air last April. Standing beside a little grove, on a rocky hillside, I heard crows cawing near by, and then a sound like great flies buzzing, which I really attributed, for a moment, to some early insect. Turning, I saw two crows flapping their heavy wings among the trees, and observed that they were teasing a hawk about as large as themselves, which was also on the wing.

11. Presently all three had risen above the branches, and were circling higher and higher in a slow spiral. The crows kept constantly swooping at their enemy, with the same angry buzz, one of the two taking decidedly the lead. They seldom struck at him with their beaks, but kept lumbering against him, and flapping him with their wings, as if in a fruitless effort to capsize him, while the hawk kept carelessly eluding the assaults, now inclining on one side, now on the other, with a stately grace, never retaliating, but seeming rather to enjoy the novel amusement, as if it were a skirmish in balloons. During all this, indeed, he scarcely seemed once to wave his wings; yet he soared steadily aloft, till the crows refused to follow, though already higher than I ever saw crows before, dim against the fleecy sky; then the hawk flew northward, but soon after he sailed over us once again, with loud, scornful *chirr*, and they only cawed, and left him undisturbed.

Atlantic Monthly.

BIRDS IN AUTUMN.

1. AFTER July, most of our birds grow silent, and, but for the insects, August would be almost the stillest month in the year—stiller than the winter, when the woods are often vocal with the crow, the jay, and the chickadee. But with patient attention one may hear, even far into the autumn, the accustomed notes. As I sat in my boat,

one sunny afternoon of last September, beneath the shady western shore of our quiet lake, with the low sunlight striking almost level across the wooded banks, it seemed as if the last hoarded drops of summer's sweetness were being poured over all the world. The air was full of quiet sounds. Turtles rustled beside the brink and slid into the water; cows plashed in the shallows; fishes leaped from the placid depths; a squirrel sobbed and fretted on a neighboring stump; a katydid across the lake maintained its hard, dry croak; the crickets chirped pertinaciously, but with little fatigued pauses, as if glad that their work was almost done; the grasshoppers kept up their continual chant, which seemed thoroughly melted and amalgamated into the summer, as if it would go on indefinitely, though the body of the little creature were dried into dust.

2. All this time the birds were silent and invisible, as if they would take no more part in the symphony of the year. Then, as if by preconcerted signal, they joined in: crows cawed anxiously afar; jays screamed in the woods; a partridge clucked to its brood, like the gurgle of water from a bottle; a kingfisher wound his rattle, more briefly than in spring, as if we now knew all about it and the merest hint ought to suffice; a fish-hawk flapped into the water, with a great, rude splash, and then flew heavily away; a flock of wild ducks went southward overhead, and a smaller party returned beneath them, flying low and anxiously, as if to pick up some lost baggage; and, at last, a loon laughed loud from behind a distant island, and it was pleasant to people these woods and waters with that wild shouting, linking them with Katahdin Lake and Amperzand.

3. But the later the birds linger in the autumn, the more their aspect differs from that of spring. In spring, they come, jubilant, noisy, triumphant, from the South, the winter conquered and the long journey done. In au-

tumn, they come timidly from the North, and, pausing on their anxious retreat, lurk within the fading copses and twitter snatches of song as fading. Others fly as openly as ever, but gather in flocks, as the robins, most piteous of all birds at this season—thin, faded, ragged, their bold note sunk to a feeble quaver, and their manner a mere caricature of that inexpressible military smartness with which they held up their heads in May.

4. Yet I can not really find anything sad even in November. When I think of the thrilling beauty of the season past, the birds that came and went, the insects that took up the choral song as the birds grew silent, the procession of the flowers, the glory of autumn, and when I think that, this also ended, a new gallery of wonder is opening, almost more beautiful, in the magnificence of frost and snow, there comes an impression of affluence and liberality in the universe, which seasons of changeless and uneventful verdure would never give. The catkins already formed on the alder, quite prepared to droop into April's beauty; the white edges of the May-flower's petals, already visible through the bud—show in advance that winter is but a slight and temporary retardation of the life of nature, and that the barrier which separates November from March is not really more solid than that which parts the sunset from the sunrise. *Atlantic Monthly.*

ROBERT OF LINCOLN.

1. MERRILY swinging on brier and weed,
   Near to the nest of his little dame,
   Over the mountain-side or mead,
   Robert of Lincoln is telling his name:

OUR FOREST CHORISTERS.

      Bob-o'-link, bob-o'-link,
        Spink, spank, spink;
Snug and safe is that nest of ours,
Hidden among the summer flowers.
        Chee, chee, chee.

2. Robert of Lincoln is gayly drest,
    Wearing a bright black wedding-coat;
White are his shoulders and white his crest.
    Hear him call in his merry note:
      Bob-o'-link, bob-o'-link,
        Spink, spank, spink;
Look, what a nice new coat is mine,
Sure there was never a bird so fine.
        Chee, chee, chee.

3. Robert of Lincoln's Quaker wife,
    Pretty and quiet, with plain brown wings,
Passing at home a patient life,
    Broods in the grass while her husband sings:
      Bob-o'-link, bob-o'-link,
        Spink, spank, spink;
Brood, kind creature; you need not fear
Thieves and robbers while I am here.
        Chee, chee, chee.

4. Modest and shy as a nun is she;
    One weak chirp is her only note.
Braggart and prince of braggarts is he,
    Pouring boasts from his little throat:
      Bob-o'-link, bob-o'-link,
        Spink, spank, spink;
Never was I afraid of man;
Catch me, cowardly knaves, if you can!
        Chee, chee, chee.

5. Six white eggs on a bed of hay,
   Flecked with purple, a pretty sight!

Bobolink.

There as the mother sits all day,
Robert is singing with all his might:

Bob-o'-link, bob-o'-link,
Spink, spank, spink ;
Nice good wife, that never goes out,
Keeping house while I frolic about.
Chee, chee, chee.

6. Soon as the little ones chip the shell,
   Six wide mouths are open for food ;
Robert of Lincoln bestirs him well,
   Gathering seeds for the hungry brood.
      Bob-o'-link, bob-o'-link,
      Spink, spank, spink ;
This new life is likely to be
Hard for a gay young fellow like me.
      Chee, chee, chee.

7. Robert of Lincoln at length is made
   Sober with work, and silent with care ;
Off is his holiday garment laid,
   Half forgotten that merry air :
      Bob-o'-link, bob-o'-link,
      Spink, spank, spink ;
Nobody knows but my mate and I
Where our nest and our nestlings lie.
      Chee, chee, chee.

8. Summer wanes ; the children are grown ;
   Fun and frolic no more he knows ;
Robert of Lincoln's a humdrum crone ;
   Off he flies, and we sing as he goes :
      Bob-o'-link, bob-o'-link,
      Spink, spank, spink ;
When you can pipe that merry old strain,—
Robert of Lincoln, come back again.
      Chee, chee, chee. *Bryant.*

THE MOCKING-BIRD.

1. Among the many novelties which the discovery of this part of the western continent first brought into notice we may reckon that of the mocking-bird, which is not only peculiar to the new world, but inhabits a very considerable extent of both North and South America, having been traced from the States of New England to Brazil, and also among many of the adjacent islands. These birds are, however, much more numerous in those States south than in those north of the river Delaware, being generally migratory in the latter, and resident in the former. A warm climate, and low country, not far from the sea, seem most congenial to their nature; accordingly, we find the species less numerous to the west than east of the great range of the Alleghany, in the same parallels of latitude. The berries of the red cedar, myrtle, holly, cassine shrub, many species of smilax, together with gum-berries, gall-berries, and a profusion of others with which the luxuriant swampy thickets of those regions abound, furnish them with a perpetual feast. Winged insects, also, of which they are very fond, and remarkably expert at catching, abound there even in winter, and are an additional inducement to residency. Though rather a shy bird in the Northern States, in the South he appeared almost half domesticated, feeding on the cedars and among the thickets of smilax that lined the roads, while I passed within a few feet; playing around the planter's door, and hopping along the shingles.

2. The precise time at which the mocking-bird begins to build his nest varies according to the latitude in which he resides. There are particular situations to which he gives the preference. A solitary thorn-bush, an almost impenetrable thicket, an orange-tree, cedar- or holly-bush, are favorite spots, and frequently selected. It is no great

objection with him that these happen, sometimes, to be near the farm- or mansion-house : always ready to defend, but never over-anxious to conceal, his nest, he very often builds within a small distance of the house, and not unfrequently in a pear or apple tree; rarely at a greater height than six or seven feet from the ground. The nest varies a little with different individuals, according to the conveniency of collecting suitable materials. A very complete one is now lying before me, and is composed of the following substances : First, a quantity of dry twigs and sticks; then withered tops of weeds of the preceding year, intermixed with fine straws, hay, pieces of wool and tow; and, lastly, a thick layer of fine fibrous roots, of a light-brown color, lines the whole. The eggs are four, sometimes five, of a cinereous blue, marked with large blotches of brown. The female sits fourteen days, and generally produces two broods in the season, unless robbed of her eggs, in which case she will even build and lay the third time. She is, however, extremely jealous of her nest, and very apt to forsake it if much disturbed. It is even asserted by some of our bird dealers that the old ones will actually destroy the eggs, and *poison* the young, if either the one or the other have been handled. But I can not give credit to this unnatural report. I know, from my own experience, at least, that it is not always their practice; neither have I ever witnessed a case of the kind above mentioned.

3. During the period of incubation, neither cat, dog, animal, or man can approach the nest without being attacked. The cats, in particular, are persecuted whenever they make their appearance, till obliged to retreat. But his whole vengeance is most particularly directed against that mortal enemy of his eggs and young, the black-snake. Whenever the insidious approaches of this reptile are discovered, the male darts upon it with the rapidity of an arrow, dexterously eluding its bite, and striking it violently

and incessantly about the head, where it is very vulnerable. The snake soon becomes sensible of its danger, and seeks to escape; but the intrepid defender of his young redoubles his exertions, and, unless his antagonist be of great magnitude, often succeeds in destroying him. All its pretended powers of fascination avail it nothing against the vengeance of this noble bird. As the snake's strength begins to flag, the mocking-bird seizes and lifts it up partly from the ground, beating it with his wings, and, when the business is completed, he returns to the repository of his young, mounts the summit of the bush, and pours out a torrent of song in token of victory.

4. The plumage of the mocking-bird, though none of the homeliest, has nothing gaudy or brilliant in it, and, had he nothing else to recommend him, would scarcely entitle him to notice; but his figure is well proportioned, and even handsome. The ease, elegance, and rapidity of his movements, the animation of his eye, and the intelligence he displays in listening and laying up lessons from almost every species of the feathered creation within his hearing, are really surprising, and mark the peculiarity of his genius. To these qualities we may add that of a voice full, strong, and musical, and capable of almost every modulation, from the clear, mellow tones of the wood-thrush to the savage scream of the bald eagle. In measure and accent he faithfully follows his originals. In force and sweetness of expression he greatly improves upon them.

5. In his native groves, mounted on the top of a tall bush or half-grown tree, in the dawn of a dewy morning, while the woods are already vocal with a multitude of warblers, his admirable song rises pre-eminent over every competitor. The ear can listen to *his* music alone, to which that of all the others seems a mere accompaniment. Neither is this strain altogether imitative. His own native notes, which are easily distinguishable by such as are well

acquainted with those of our various song-birds, are bold and full, and varied, seemingly, beyond all limits. They consist of short expressions of two, three, or, at the most, five or six syllables; generally interspersed with imitations, and all of them uttered with great emphasis and rapidity; and continued, with undiminished ardor, for half an hour, or an hour, at a time—his expanded wings and tail glistening with white, and the buoyant gayety of his action arresting the eye, as his song most irresistibly does the ear. He sweeps round with enthusiastic ecstasy—he mounts and descends as his song swells or dies away; and, as my friend Mr. Bartram has beautifully expressed it, "He bounds aloft with the celerity of an arrow, as if to recover or recall his very soul, expired in the last elevated strain."

6. While thus exerting himself, a bystander destitute of sight would suppose that the whole feathered tribe had assembled together, on a trial of skill, each striving to produce his utmost effect, so perfect are his imitations. He many times deceives the sportsman, and sends him in search of birds that perhaps are not within miles of him, but whose notes he exactly imitates; even birds themselves are frequently imposed on by this admirable mimic, and are decoyed by the fancied calls of their mates; or dive, with precipitation, into the depths of thickets, at the scream of what they suppose to be the sparrow-hawk.

7. The mocking-bird loses little of the power and energy of his song by confinement. In his domesticated state, when he commences his career of song, it is impossible to stand by uninterested. He whistles for the dog; Cæsar starts up, wags his tail, and runs to meet his master. He squeaks out like a hurt chicken, and the hen hurries about, with hanging wings and bristled feathers, clucking to protect its injured brood. The barking of the dog, the mewing of the cat, the creaking of a passing wheel-

barrow, follow, with great truth and rapidity. He repeats the tune taught him by his master, though of considerable length, fully and faithfully. He runs over the quiverings of the canary, and the clear whistlings of the Virginia nightingale, or redbird, with such superior execution and effect that the mortified songsters feel their own inferiority, and become altogether silent, while he seems to triumph in their defeat by redoubling his exertions.

8. This excessive fondness for variety, however, in the opinion of some, injures his song. His elevated imitations of the brown thrush are frequently interrupted by the crowing of cocks; and the warblings of the bluebird, which he exquisitely manages, are mingled with the screaming of swallows or the cackling of hens; amid the simple melody of the robin we are suddenly surprised by the shrill reiterations of the whip-poor-will; while the notes of the kildeer, blue jay, martin, baltimore, and twenty others, succeed, with such imposing reality, that we look round for the originals, and discover, with astonishment, that the sole performer in this singular *concert* is the admirable bird now before us. During this exhibition of his powers he spreads his wings, expands his tail, and throws himself around the cage in all the ecstasy of enthusiasm, seeming not only to sing, but to dance, keeping time to the measure of his own music. Both in his native and domesticated state, during the solemn stillness of night, as soon as the moon rises in silent majesty, he begins his delightful solo, and serenades us the livelong night with a full display of his vocal powers, making the neighborhood ring with his inimitable medley.

Alexander Wilson.

THE PERSEVERING SONGSTER.

1. A CURIOUS circumstance, quite aside from the ordinary dictates of instinct, occurred in the case of a young bobolink, in the family of the Rev. J. W. Turner, of Great Barrington, Massachusetts. He was caged at first apart from a pair of canaries, which were in another cage in the same room. The bobolink never sung at all from June to December, until he was permitted to share in the same cage the civilities and sympathies of his neighbors, the canaries, who had been so long entertaining him with their sweet and unwearied strains. When admitted to the same cage with them, he tried most assiduously to learn their song, at first, however, for a long time, with miserable success enough. He would stand and watch them with an agony of attention, and then try to imitate their notes. He would swell out his throat, and stretch up his neck as they did, and then, with a violent effort, try to sound one note, which, in spite of all his zeal and labor, proved to be a mere rough scream.

2. At this humiliating failure he would be so provoked and enraged that he would fly at his inoffensive and well-meaning mates and teachers, and peck them most unmercifully, and drive them from their perch. So he did for three or four weeks, before any apparent progress was made in his studies. But his perseverance was equal to the difficulties he had to overcome. At length he could sound one note well, and one only. And so he continued for some six weeks longer, learning one note at a time, till he had finally completed the whole canary song, and could sing it to perfection. Then he would sing with them in perfect harmony and perfect time, always closing at the exact note with them.

3. It is also a little singular that, although through all

this training he was never known to begin to make a sound till the canaries had first struck the key-note, yet, after he had acquired the skill to sing their song, *he* must always himself now give the signal by a significant *cluck*, when, instantly, the canaries, generously forgetting or forgiving his former incivilities, would strike in with, and perform the piece with the greatest perfection, and with the highest delight to themselves and the listening family, who enjoyed this singular concert through the early part of every day for the whole summer.

4. It is also worthy of remark that this successful essayist in foreign music was never known to utter a note, or to attempt to utter a note, in his native tongue, till he had mastered the canary. Then, after a few weeks, when he found himself something of an independent singer, and capable, as he thought, of leading the choir, he at last ventured to go without the chorus and attempt his own native melody. In his first attempts at the solo, it was most diverting to hear him in confused notes—part in his native bobolink, and part in canary, till at length he was able to expel all foreign element from his style and sing only the pure bobolink.

5. Having now succeeded in this, he proposed to the canaries to try the chorus again, and gave the "*cluck*," when the canaries, instant to the sign, started off singing their own native song. But not so the bobolink; he threw himself on his "reserved rights" and sang bobolink; and so they have continued to the present time, he singing bobolink, and they canary. And as he is the chorister, they begin when he does, and end when he ends, precisely at the same instant.

6. When this bobolink was first caught, his colors were a bright, beautiful black and white. After molting, he, for some reason not stated, never resumed his original spring dress, but has continued the plain brown, like the

female, now for two years; and sings in the winter as well as in the summer, especially when the sun shines brightly, and the winds whistle in the trees around the dwelling; and now, since his character is matured, he is a sprightly, happy, gentlemanly sort of a bird.

Boston Traveler, 1851.

BIRD-NOTES.

1. THE winged tribes have various sounds and voices, adapted to express their various passions, wants, and feelings—such as anger, fear, love, hatred, hunger, and the like. All species are not equally eloquent; some are copious and fluent, as it were, in their utterance, while others are confined to a few important sounds; no bird, like the fish-kind, is quite mute, though some are rather silent. The language of birds is very ancient, and, like other ancient modes of speech, very elliptical: little is said, but much is meant and understood.

2. The notes of the eagle-kind are shrill and piercing, and, about nest-making season, much diversified. The notes of our hawks resemble those of the king of birds. Owls have very expressive notes; they hoot in a fine vocal sound, much resembling the *vox humana,* and reducible by a pitch-pipe to a musical key. This note seems to express complacency and rivalry among the males; they use, also, a quick call and a horrible scream, and can snore and hiss when they mean to menace. Ravens, besides their loud croak, can exert a deep and solemn tone that makes the woods to echo; the low note of the crow sounds strange and ridiculous; rooks, in the breeding season, attempt sometimes, in the gayety of their hearts, to sing, but with no great success; the parrot-kind have many modulations of voice, as appears by their aptitude to learn hu-

man sounds; doves coo in a mournful manner, and are emblems of despairing lovers; the woodpecker sets up a sort of loud, hearty laugh; the fern-owl or goat-sucker, from the dusk till daybreak, serenades his mate with the clattering of castanets.

3. All the tuneful *Passeres* express their complacency by sweet modulations and a variety of melody. The swallow, by a shrill alarm, bespeaks the attention of his fellows, and bids them to beware, the hawk is at hand. Aquatic and gregarious birds, especially the nocturnal, that shift their quarters in the dark, are very noisy and loquacious, as cranes, wild geese, wild ducks, and the like: their perpetual clamor prevents them from dispersing and losing their companions.

4. In so extensive a subject, sketches and outlines are as much as can be expected, for it would be endless to instance in all the infinite variety of the feathered tribes. We will, therefore, confine the remainder of this letter to the few domestic fowls of our yards which are most known, and, therefore, best understood. And first the peacock, with his gorgeous train, demands our attention; but, like most of the gaudy birds, his notes are grating and shocking to the ear; the yelling of cats and the braying of an ass are not more discordant. The voice of the goose is trumpet-like and clanking, and once saved the Capitol at Rome, as grave historians assert; the hiss, also, of the gander is formidable and full of menace, and "protective of his young."

5. Among ducks the sexual distinction of voice is remarkable, for, while the quack of the female is loud and sonorous, the voice of the drake is inward and harsh and feeble, and scarce discernible. The cock-turkey struts and gobbles in a most uncouth manner; he hath also a pert and petulant note when he attacks his adversary. When a hen-turkey leads forth her young brood she keeps a

watchful eye, and if a bird of prey appear, though ever so high in the air, the careful mother announces the enemy with a little inward moan, and watches him with a steady and attentive look; but, if he approach, her note becomes earnest and alarming, and her outcries are redoubled.

6. No inhabitants of a yard seem possessed of such a variety of expression and so copious a language as common poultry. Take a chicken of four or five days old and hold it up to a window where there are flies, and it will immediately seize the prey with little twitterings of complacency; but if you tender it a wasp or a bee, at once its note becomes harsh, and expressive of disapprobation and a sense of danger. When a pullet is ready to lay, she intimates the event by a joyous and easy, soft note. Of all the occurrences of her life, that of laying seems to be the most important; for no sooner has a hen disburdened herself than she rushes forth with a clamorous kind of joy, which the cock and other hens immediately adopt. The tumult is not confined to the family concerned, but catches from yard to yard, and spreads to every homestead within hearing, till at last the whole village is in an uproar.

7. As soon as a hen becomes a mother, her new relation demands a new language; she then runs clucking and screaming about, and seems agitated as if possessed. The father of the flock has also a considerable vocabulary. If he finds food, he calls the hens to partake; and if a bird of prey passes over, with a warning voice he bids his family beware. The gallant chanticleer has at command his love-phrases and his terms of defiance. But the sound by which he is best known is his crowing; by this he has been distinguished in all ages as the countryman's clock or larum, as the watchman that proclaims the divisions of the night. Thus the poet elegantly describes him:

". . . . the crested cock, whose clarion sounds
The silent hours."

8. A neighboring gentleman one summer had lost most of his chickens by a sparrow-hawk, that came gliding down between a fagot-pile and the end of his house to the place where the coops stood. The owner, inwardly vexed to see his flock thus diminished, hung a setting-net adroitly between the pile and the house, into which the caitiff dashed and was entangled. Resentment suggested the law of retaliation; he therefore clipped the hawk's wings, cut off his talons, and, fixing a cork on his bill, threw him down among the brood-hens. Imagination can not paint the scene that ensued; the expressions that fear, rage, and revenge inspired were new, or at least such as had been unnoticed before: the exasperated matrons upbraided, they execrated, they insulted, they triumphed. In a word, they never desisted from buffeting their adversary till they had torn him into a hundred pieces.

White's Selborne.

ODE TO THE SKY-LARK.

1. HAIL to thee, blithe spirit!
   Bird thou never wert,
   That from heaven, or near it,
   Pourest thy full heart
In profuse strains of unpremeditated art.

2. Higher still and higher,
   From the earth thou springest
   Like a cloud of fire;
   The blue deep thou wingest,
And singing still dost soar, and soaring ever singest.

3. In the golden lightning
    Of the sunken sun,
   O'er which clouds are bright'ning,
    Thou dost float and run,
Like an unbodied joy whose race is just begun.

4. The pale purple even
    Melts around thy flight;
   Like a star of heaven
    In the broad daylight,
Thou art unseen, but, yet, I hear thy shrill delight.

5. What thou art, we know not;
    What is most like thee?
   From rainbow clouds there flow not.
    Drops so bright to see,
As from thy presence showers a rain of melody.

6. Like a poet hidden
    In the light of thought,
   Singing hymns unbidden,
    Till the world is wrought
To sympathy with hopes and fears it heeded not.

7. Teach us, sprite or bird,
    What sweet thoughts are thine;
   I have never heard
    Praise of love or wine
That panted forth a flood of rapture so divine.

8. Chorus hymeneal,
    Or triumphal chaunt,
   Matched with thine would be all
    But an empty vaunt—
A thing wherein we feel there is some hidden want.

9. What objects are the fountains
    Of thy happy strain ?
  What fields, or waves, or mountains ?
    What shapes of sky or plain ?
What love of thine own kind ? what ignorance of pain ?

10. Waking or asleep,
    Thou of death must deem
  Things more true and deep
    Than we mortals dream,
Or how could thy notes flow in such a crystal stream ?

11. We look before and after,
    And pine for what is not :
  Our sincerest laughter
    With some pain is fraught :
Our sweetest songs are those that tell of saddest thought.

12. Teach me half the gladness
    That thy brain must know :
  Such harmonious madness
    From my lips would flow,
The world should listen then as I am listening now.

Shelley.

PART IX.

OTHER NEIGHBORS IN THE TREES.

HOMES IN THE WOODS.

1. OF course, in the deep, primitive woods there are nests; but how rarely we find them! The simple art of the bird consists in choosing common, neutral-tinted material, as moss, dry leaves, twigs, and various odds and ends, and placing the structure on a convenient branch, where it blends in color with its surround-

ings; but how consummate is this art, and how skillfully is the nest concealed! We occasionally light upon it, but who, unaided by the movements of the bird, could find it out? During the present season I went to the woods nearly every day for a fortnight, without making any discoveries of this kind; till one day, paying them a farewell visit, I chanced to come upon several nests.

2. A black and white creeping warbler suddenly became much alarmed as I approached a crumbling old stump in a dense part of the forest. He alighted upon it, chirped sharply, ran up and down its sides, and finally left it with much reluctance. The nest, which contained three young birds nearly fledged, was placed upon the ground at the foot of the stump, and in such a position that the color of the young harmonized perfectly with the bits of bark, sticks, etc., lying about. My eye rested upon them for the second time before I made them out. They hugged the nest very closely, but, as I put down my hand, they all scampered off with loud cries for help, which caused the parent-birds to place themselves almost within my reach. The nest was merely a little dry grass arranged in a thick bed of dry leaves.

3. This was amid a thick undergrowth. Moving on into a passage of large, stately hemlocks, with only here and there a small beech or maple rising up into the perennial twilight, I paused to make out a note which was entirely new to me. It is still in my ear. Though unmistakably a bird-note, it yet suggested the bleating of a tiny lambkin. Presently the birds appeared—a pair of the solitary vireo. They came flitting from point to point, alighting only for a moment at a time, the male silent, but the female uttering this strange, tender note. It was a rendering into some new sylvan dialect of the human sentiment of maidenly love. It was really pathetic in its sweetness and childlike confidence and joy.

4. I soon discovered that the pair were building a nest upon a low branch a few yards from me. The male flew cautiously to the spot and adjusted something, and the twain moved on, the female calling to her mate, at intervals, *love-e, love-e,* with a cadence and tenderness in the tone that rang in the ear long afterward. The nest was suspended to the fork of a small branch, as is usual with the vireos, plentifully lined with lichens, and bound and rebound with masses of coarse spider-webs. There was no attempt at concealment except in the neutral tints, which made it look like a natural growth of the dim, gray woods.

5. Continuing my random walk, I next paused in a low part of the woods, where the larger trees began to give place to a thick second growth that covered an old barkpeeling. I was standing by a large maple, when a small bird darted quickly away from it, as if it might have come out of a hole near its base. As the bird paused a few yards from me, and began to chirp uneasily, my curiosity was at once excited. When I saw it was the female mourning ground-warbler, and remembered that the nest of this bird had not yet been seen by any naturalist—that not even Dr. Brewer had ever seen the eggs—I felt that here was something worth looking for.

6. So I carefully began the search, exploring inch by inch the ground, the base and roots of the tree, and the various shrubby growths about it, till, finding nothing, and fearing I might really put my foot in it, I bethought me to withdraw to a distance and after some delay return again, and, thus forewarned, note the exact point from which the bird flew. This I did, and, returning, had little difficulty in discovering the nest. It was placed but a few feet from the maple-tree, in a bunch of ferns, and about six inches from the ground. It was quite a massive nest, composed entirely of the stalks and leaves of dry grass, with an inner lining of fine, dark-brown roots.

The eggs, three in number, were of light flesh-color, uniformly specked with fine brown specks. The cavity of the nest was so deep that the back of the sitting bird sank below the edge.

7. In the top of a tall tree, a short distance farther on, I saw the nest of the red-tailed hawk—a large mass of twigs and dry sticks. The young had flown, but still lingered in the vicinity, and, as I approached, the mother-bird flew about over me, squealing in a very angry, savage manner. Tufts of the hair and other indigestible material of the common meadow-mouse lay around on the ground beneath the nest.

8. As I was about leaving the woods my hat almost brushed the nest of the red-eyed vireo, which hung basket-like on the end of a low, drooping branch of the beech. I should never have seen it had the bird kept her place. It contained three eggs of the bird's own, and one of the cow-bunting. The strange egg was only just perceptibly larger than the others, yet three days after, when I looked into the nest again and found all but one egg hatched, the young interloper was at least four times as large as either of the others, and with such a superabundance of bowels as to almost smother his bed-fellows beneath them. That the intruder should fare the same as the rightful occupants, and thrive with them, was more than ordinary potluck; but that it alone should thrive, devouring, as it were, all the rest, is one of those freaks of Nature in which she would seem to discourage the homely virtues of prudence and honesty. Weeds and parasites have the odds greatly against them, yet they wage a very successful war nevertheless.

John Burroughs.

HUMMING-BIRDS.

1. THE discovery of America opened up to the civilized world many new objects of interest in the animal, vegetable, and mineral kingdoms. Not the least in interest was the discovery of an extensive group of birds, consisting of several hundred species, whose diminutive size, quickness of motion, boldness of demeanor, elegance of form, and exquisite beauty of plumage attracted the attention and secured the admiration of every lover of nature.

2. The larger portion of these birds live in the West Indies and the tropical regions of America. Some occupy only a small island or district; others, a narrow belt on the side of a mountain: most do not extend their limits beyond a few degrees of latitude, while a few are migratory, and spend the summer in the temperate zone, but return to the tropical regions for the winter. Their food consists of honey and insects; and, consequently, they must live where flowers grow and insects abound.

3. The Indians gave to these interesting little creatures fanciful names that expressed the idea of sunbeams, sun-angels, sun-gems, tresses of the day-star, murmuring-birds, and the like. And naturalists have given to them names equally fanciful, expressing the same or similar ideas, such as brilliant birds, light-bearers, sun-seekers, flower-kissers, honey-suckers, living meteors, and many others of similar meaning. They derive their common name from the buzzing or humming sound which they make with their wings. These vibrate so quickly as to be visible only as a semicircular film on each side of the body. The sound made by different species varies with the velocity of their wings. That made by the vervain humming-bird resembles the sound of a large bee, while that made by the polytmus resembles the sound of a swiftly revolving wheel.

4. One of the peculiarities which first strikes a stranger, upon seeing one of these brilliant breathing gems, is the immense power of wing, shown by the quickness of his flight, also by the ease with which he balances himself in the air, whether, foraging unmolested, he is feeding at the flowers, or, attracted by curiosity, he is surveying one's person. He comes so suddenly as to give no warning to the eye; we hear a buzz, see the bird near us stationary, his form distinct, and when he leaves, so quick and sudden is his flight that the eye can scarcely trace his pathway. The muscles of his wings are more powerful and active, in proportion to his size, than those of any other bird, and the wings are very long and sharp. For this reason he can easily hover, apparently motionless, for any length of time, before a flower whose honey he wishes to obtain. He thus sips the nectar of one flower after another for hours in succession, without showing any signs of weariness, or disturbing in the least the most delicate blossom.

5. If any one wishes to observe these birds and their habits, let him, on a fine, pleasant morning, visit a cluster of gooseberry bushes when in bloom, of whose honey they are exceedingly fond, and he will probably find one or more of them quietly searching the flowers for food. If disturbed, he will frequently rise to a considerable height in an oblique direction, then dart down, almost with the velocity of a bullet, past the place of annoyance, and rise on the opposite side to an equal height; then return by reversing his course, and so repeat these sweeping movements till he sufficiently expresses his disapprobation, drives away his adversary, or retires in disgust.

6. Their bills are all very slender and sharp. Most of them are long, some are straight, many are curved downward, and a few are curved upward. They all appear to be adapted to the kind of flowers from which the birds obtain their food. Their tongue is a slender sucking-tube,

and capable of being thrust out a long distance. It appears as though composed of two minute muscular tubes, lined within by two partial tubes, of a substance resembling parchment, laid side by side, and joined together for about half of their length, but separate toward the tip, near which each partial tube becomes less curved, and apparently widened, then tapers to a point, the upper edge being irregularly notched or slit, the barbs pointing backward.

7. The tongue is constantly moistened by a glutinous saliva, by means of which it is enabled to seize and hold insects. Says Martin: "It is by a pumping or sucking action, as we have every reason to believe, that nectar or fluids are absorbed by the tubular tongue of these birds. In no other vertebrate animals, as far as we know, is the tongue constructed as a tubular sucking-pump: so far, the humming-birds stand alone; and this circumstance in itself, considering it with reference to organic structure, might be adduced as a reason for regarding these birds as a distinct order."

8. Mr. Thomas Belt, author of "The Naturalist in Nicaragua," indicates another function performed by the curious cleft tongue of the humming-bird—viz., the capture of insects. This organ is, for one half its length, made up of a substance like rather stiff parchment, or horn, and split in two. When at rest, the two halves are laid flat against each other, but they can be separated at the will of the bird, and form a pair of forceps, admirably adapted for picking out minute insects from among the stamens of flowers.

9. We may admire the elegance of form and the quickness of motion of these birds, but the dazzling splendor of their plumage, resembling that of burnished metal or polished gems, changing with every change of position, has a charm for the dullest observer, and a fascination for the more sensitive. The wonderful change in color that takes

place, according to the position of the light, from brilliant green, through the brightest golden tints, to intense velvety black, or from black to emerald, or ruby, or crimson, or flame-color, reminds one of fairy-land, or the tales of the genii. Where a metallic luster prevails, the plumage is always composed of feathers so shaped as to appear to have the form of scales. The birds vary in respect to the parts that have these feathers. While most have them on the throat, many have them on the breast and head; others have them also on the back; some have them on the wing-coverts or tail; and a few have them on nearly all parts, except the long wing-feathers, which are generally of a purplish brown.

10. It may here be asked, What causes the gorgeous metallic luster of their plumage, and the rich, changing tints of the various colors, representing every hue of the rainbow, purple, amethyst, fiery crimson, brilliant ruby, radiant topaz, emerald green, resplendent blue, and glossy violet, which, in certain lights, often gleam with a refulgence that almost dazzles the eye? They have been attributed to various causes, but it appears to be the condition of the surface of the feathers that produces the iridescence. The surface is striated, or has minute furrows, like the nacre, or mother-of-pearl of the *Haliotis*, and other sea-shells, which decompose the light—absorbing part, and reflecting part; the color of the reflected light depends upon the angle of the incident ray to the surface, and varies as the angle varies. In one direction of the incident ray the light will be wholly absorbed, and none being reflected, the surface will appear intensely black. It will readily be perceived that every movement of the bird produces more or less a change of color. Even the heaving of the breast, in breathing, sometimes produces perceptible changes.

James H. Partridge.

MY AËRIAL VISITOR.

1. To-day, Estelle, your special messenger, the humming-bird, comes darting to our oriel, my Orient. As I sat sewing, his sudden, unexpected whirr made me look up. How did he know that the very first Japan pear-bud opened this morning? Flower and bird came together by some wise prescience.

2. He has been sipping honey from your passion-flowers, and now has come to taste my blossoms. What bright-winged thought of yours sent him so straight to me, across that wide space of sea and land? Did he dart like a sunbeam all the way? There were many of them voyaged together; a little line of wavering light pierced the dark that night.

3. A large, brave heart has our bold sailor of the upper deep. Old Pindar never saw our little pet, this darling of the New World; yet he says:

"Were it the will of Heaven, an osier-bough
Were vessel safe enough the seas to plow."

Here he is, safe enough, not one tiny feather ruffled—all the intense life of the tropics condensed into this one live jewel—the glance of the sun on emeralds and rubies. Is it soft, downy feathers that take this rich metallic glow, changing their hue with every rapid turn?

4. Other birds fly: he darts quick as the glance of the eye; sudden as thought, he is here, he is there. No floating, balancing motion, like the lazy butterfly, who fans the air with her broad sails. To the point, always to the point, he turns in straight lines. How stumbling and heavy is the flight of the "burly, dozing bumble-bee" beside this quick intelligence! Our knight of the ruby throat, with lance in rest, makes wild and rapid sallies on this "little mundane bird"—this bumble-bee—this rolling sailor, never

off his sea-legs, always spinning his long homespun yarns. This rich bed of golden and crimson flowers is a handsome

Humming-Birds.

field of tournament. What invisible circle sits round to adjudge the prize?

5. What secret does he bring me under those misty wings—that busy, birring sound, like neighbor Clark's spinning-wheel? Is he busy as well—this bit of pure light and heat? Yes! he too has got a little home down in the swamp over there—that bit of a knot on the young oak sapling. Last year we found a nest lined with the floss of willow-catkin stuck all over with lichens, deep enough to secure the two pure round pearls from being thrown out, strongly fastened to the forked branch—a home so snug, so warm, so soft!—a home "contrived for fairy needs."

6. Who but the fairies or Mr. Fine-Ear himself ever heard the tiny tap of the young bird when he breaks the imprisoning shell? The mother-bird knows well the fine sound. Hours? Days? No, weeks she has sat, to hear at last that least wave of sound. What! this tiny bit of restless motion sit there still? Minutes must be long hours to her quick, panting heart. I will just whisper it in your ear, that the meek-looking mother-bird only comes out between daylight and dark—just like other busy mothers I have known, who take a little run out after tea.

7. Can it be that Mr. Ruby-Throat keeps all the sunshiny hours for himself, that he may enjoy to the full his own gay flight? Ah! you know nothing, hear nothing of woman's rights up there in that well-ordered household. Were it not well if we too could give up our royal right of choice—if we could fall back on our strong earth-born instincts—to be, to know, to do, one thing?

8. See how closely our darling curls up his slender black feet and legs, that we may not see this one bit of mortality about him! No, my little immortal does not touch the earth; he hangs suspended by that long bill which just tethers him to its flowers. Now and then he will let down the little black tendrils of legs and feet on

some bare twig, and there he rests and presses those already smooth plumules with the long, slender bodkin. Now, just now, he darts into my room, coquets with my basket of flowers, "a kiss, a touch, and then away." I heard the whirr of those gauzy wings; it was not to the flowers alone he told his story.

9. I have heard of a lady who reared these little birds from the nest; they would suck honey from her lips, and fly in and out of her chamber. Only think of seeing these callow fledglings! It is as if the winged thought could be domesticated, could learn to make its nest with us and rear its young. Bountiful nature has spared to our cold North this one compact bit from the tropics.

10. Let me, then, go on my bird's-egging, and tell you one more fact about our fairy—our humming-bird. Audubon says that "an all-wise Providence has made this little hero an exception to a rule which prevails almost universally through nature—namely, that the smallest species of a tribe are the most prolific. The eagle lays one, sometimes two eggs; the small European wren fifteen; the humming-bird two; and yet this latter is abundantly more numerous in America than the wren in Europe." All on account of his wonderful courage, admirable instinct, or whatever it is that guards and guides him so unerringly. You see we may well love him who Nature herself loves so dearly.

Atlantic Monthly.

RARE AND BEAUTIFUL NESTS.

1. THE woods hold not such another gem as the nest of the humming-bird. The finding of one is an event to date from. It is the next best thing to finding an eagle's nest. I have met with but two, both by chance. One was placed on the horizontal branch of a chestnut-tree, with a solitary

green leaf, forming a complete canopy, about an inch and a half above it. The repeated spiteful dartings of the bird past my ears, as I stood under the tree, caused me to suspect that I was intruding upon some one's privacy; and, following it with my eye, I soon saw the nest, which was in process of construction. Adopting my usual tactics of secreting myself near by, I had the satisfaction of seeing the tiny artist at work. It was the female, unassisted by her mate. At intervals of two or three minutes she would appear with a small tuft of some cottony substance in her beak, dart a few times through and around the tree, and, alighting quickly in the nest, arrange the material she had brought, using her breast as the model.

2. The other nest I discovered in a dense forest on the side of a mountain. The sitting bird was disturbed as I passed beneath her. The whirring of her wings arrested my attention, when, after a short pause, I had the good luck to see, through an opening in the leaves, the bird return to her nest, which appeared like a mere wart or excrescence on a small branch. The humming-bird, unlike all others, does not alight upon the nest, but flies into it. She enters it as quick as a flash, but as light as any feather. Two eggs are the complement. They are perfectly white, and so frail that only a woman's fingers may touch them. Incubation lasts about ten days. In a week the young have flown.

3. But the nest of nests, the ideal nest, after we have left the deep woods, is unquestionably that of the Baltimore oriole. It is the only perfectly pensile nest we have. The nest of the orchard oriole is indeed mainly so, but this bird generally builds lower and shallower, more after the manner of the vireos.

4. The Baltimore oriole loves to attach its nest to the swaying branches of the tallest elms, making no attempt at concealment, but satisfied if the position be high and the

branch pendent. This nest would seem to cost more time and skill than any other bird-structure. A peculiar flax-like substance seems to be always sought after and always found. The nest, when completed, assumes the form of a large, suspended, gourd-shaped drop. The walls are thin but firm, and proof against the most driving rain. The mouth is hemmed or overhanded with horse-hair, and the sides are usually sewed through and through with the same.

5. Not particular as to the matter of secrecy, the bird is not particular as to material, so that it be of the nature of strings or threads. A lady friend once told me that, while working by an open window, one of these birds approached during her momentary absence, and, seizing a skein of some kind of thread or yarn, made off with it to its half-finished nest. But the perverse yarn caught fast in the branches, and, in the bird's efforts to extricate it, got hopelessly tangled. She tugged away at it all day, but was finally obliged to content herself with a few detached portions. The fluttering strings were an eyesore to her ever after, and, passing and repassing, she would pause to give them a spiteful jerk, as much as to say, "There is that confounded yarn that gave me so much trouble."

John Burroughs.

BIRD-WAYS.

1. I BELIEVE we allow that birds are very highly organized creatures—next to man, they say. We, with our weary feet plodding always on the earth, our heavy arms pinioned close to our sides, look at this live creature with thinnest wing cutting the fine air! We, slow in word, slow in thought, look at this quivering flame, kindled by some more passionate glance of Nature! Next to man? Yes, we

might say, next above. Had it not been for that fire we stole one day, that Promethean spark, hidden in the ashes, kept alight ever since, it had gone hard with us. Nature might have kept her pet, her darling, high, high above us —almost out of reach of our dull senses.

2. What is our boasted speech, with its harsh, rude sounds, to their gushing melody? We learn music, certainly, with much pains and care. The bird can not tell whether it be A sharp or B flat, but he sings. Our old friend—the friend of our childhood—Mr. White of Selborne (who had attended much to the life and conversation of birds), says: "Their language is very elliptical; little is said, and much is meant and understood." Something like a lady's letter, is it not?

3. How wise we might grow if only we could "the bird language rightly spell"! In the olden times we are told the caliphs and viziers always listened to what the birds said about it before they undertook any new enterprise. I have often thought I heard wise old folk discoursing when a company of hens were busy on the side-hill scratching and clucking together. Perchance some day we shall pick up a leaf of that herb which shall open our ears to these our inarticulate sounds.

4. Why may we not (just for this summer) believe in transmigrations, and find some elder civilization embodied in this community of birds—all those lost arts taken wings, not to fly away, but to come flitting and building in our trees, picking crumbs from our door-steps?

5. Do they say birds are limited? Who are we that set bounds to this direct knowledge, this instinct? Mathematically constructive they certainly are. What bold architect has builded so snug, so airy a house—well concealed, and yet with a good outlook? We make our dwellings conspicuous; they hide their pretty art.

6. We wiseacres, who stay at home instead of following

the seasons round the globe, should learn the art of making happy homes; yet what housekeeper will not hang her head in shame and despair to see this nice adaptation of use to wants, shown each year in multitudes of nests? Now, only look at it! always just room enough—none to spare. First, the four or five eggs lie comfortably in the small round at the bottom of the nest, with room enough for the mother-robin to give them the whole warmth of her broad, red breast, her sloping back and wings making a rain-proof roof over her jewels. Then the callow younglings raise a little higher into the wider circle. Next the fledglings brim the cup; at last it runs over; four large, clumsy robins flutter to the ground with much noise, much anxious calling from papa and mamma—much good advice, no doubt.

7. They are fairly turned out to shift for themselves; with the same wise, unfathomable eyes which have mirrored the round world for so many years, which know all things, say nothing older than time, lively and quick as to-day; with the same touching melody in their long, monotonous call; soon with the same power of wing; next year to build a nest with the same wise economy, each young robin carrying in his own swelling, bulging breast the model of the hollow circle, the cradle of other young robins. So you see it is a nest within a nest—a whole nest of nests. Like Vishnu Saima's fables, or Scheherazade's stories, you can never find where one leaves off and another begins, they shut so one into the other. No wonder the children and philosophers are they who ask whether the egg comes from the bird, or the bird from the egg. Yes, it is a world-circle, a home-circle—this nest.

8. You remember that little, old, withered man who used to bring us eggs. The boys, you know, called him Egg-Pop. When the thrifty housewife complained of the small size of his ware, he always said, "Yes, marm, they

be small, but they be monstrous full." Yes, the packing of the nest is close, but closer is the packing of the egg. "As full as an egg of meat" is a wise proverb.

9. Let us look at these first-fruits which the bountiful spring hangs on our trees. "To break the egg-shell after the meat is out we are taught in our childhood, and practice in all our lives; which, nevertheless, is but a superstitious relic, according to the judgment of Pliny, and the intent hereof was to prevent witchcraft (to keep the fairies out); for, lest witches should draw or prick their names therein, and veneficiously mischief their persons, they broke the shell, as Dalecampius has observed." This is what Sir Thomas Browne tells us about egg-shells, and Dr. Wren adds: "Lest they (the witches), perchance, might use them for boates to sayle in by night." But I, who have no fear of witches, would not break them—rather use them; try what an untold variety of forms we may make out of this delicate oval.

10. By a little skillful turning and reversing, putting on a handle, a lip here, a foot there, always following the sacred oval, we shall get a countless array of pitchers and vases of perfect finished form, handsome enough to be the oval for a king's name. Should they attempt to copy our rare vases—in finest parian, alabaster, or jasper—their art would fail to hit the delicate tints and smoothness of this fine shell; and then those dots and dashes, careless as put on by a master's hand!

11. Are not these rare lines? They look to me as wise as hieroglyphics. Who knows what rhyme and reason are written there — what subtile wisdom rounded into this small curve—repeated on the breasts and backs of the birds —their own notes, it may be, photographed on their swelling breasts like the musical notes on the harp-shell—written in bright, almost audible colors, on the petals of the flowers—harmonies, melodies for ear and eye? Has this

language—older than Erse, older than Sanscrit—ever got translated? I am afraid, dear, the key has been turned in the lock and thrown into the well.

12. The ornithologists tell us that some birds build nicer nests, sing sweeter songs, than their companions of the same species. Can experience add wisdom to instinct? or is it the right of the elder-born—the birthright of the young robin who first breaks the shell? Who has rightly looked into these things?

13. I half remember the story of a beautiful princess who had all imaginable wealth in her stately palace, itself built up of rare and costly jewels. She had everything that heart could desire—everything but a roc's egg. Her mind was contracted with sorrow till she could procure this one ornament more to her splendors. I think it turned out that the palace itself was built within the roc's egg. These birds are immense, and take up three elephants at a time in their powerful talons (almost as many as Gordon Cummings himself on a good day's hunt), and their eggs are like domes.

14. Now, do not you be like the foolish princess, and desire a roc's egg; it will prove a stone—the egg of a rock indeed. Be content, rather, with the ostrich-egg I send you. With your own slender fingers lift the lid; pretty, is it not, the tea-service I send you? The tidy warblers threw out the emptied shells; one by one I picked them up, and have made cups and saucers, bowls and pitchers for you. A roc's egg never held anything one half so fine.

Atlantic Monthly.

THE BANK-SWALLOW.

1. THE bird which is the subject of this sketch is familiar to all who walk in green pastures and beside still waters; for in such haunts do the bank-swallows congregate in merry companies, making up for their want of companionship with man by a large sociability among themselves. Conservator of ancient ways, it is almost the only swallow which has not attached itself to humanity, as soon as it had an opportunity, and changed from a savage to a civilized bird. Perhaps, too, it has tried it long ago, for our bank-swallow is a cosmopolite, and has watched the rise and fall of all the dynasties and nationalities that have grouped the centuries into eras from Nineveh to San Francisco.

2. They are at present inhabitants of both continents nearly throughout their whole extent, in summer peopling the banks of Alaskan rivers, and in winter sporting themselves in the tropical regions of Mexico and Central America. So this modest little band is entitled to our respect as a traveler at least; and to compare the habits and appearance of the representatives in different portions of the globe becomes a most interesting study.

3. Under the name of bank-swallow, sand-swallow, sand-martin, it is found throughout the northern hemisphere wherever the localities are favorable for building their nests. In this distribution they seem to have been influenced by man, though owing him no other favors than the incidental help of railroad cuttings and sand-pits, which have increased the sites suitable for excavating, and have enabled them to spread inland.

4. Where these and other swallows spend the winter was a hotly debated question among ornithologists at the beginning of the present century, some affirming that they

migrated with the sun, while others, believing it impossible that such small and delicate birds could endure the great fatigue and temperatures incident to such a migration,

Bank-Swallows and their Nests.

held that they regularly hibernated, during the cold weather, sinking into the mud at the bottom of ponds, like frogs, or curling up in deep, warm crannies, like bats, and remaining torpid until revived by the warmth of spring.

5. Of this latter opinion was White, of Selborne, who alludes to it again and again, and Sir Thomas Forster wrote a "Monograph of British Swallows," apparently with no other object than to present the arguments for and against the theory of their annual submersion and torpidity. One of the difficulties which the submersionists put in the way of the migrationists was the frequent accidental and isolated appearance of the swallow before its usual time—a fact that has, in nearly every language, given rise to the proverb, "One swallow does not make a summer." The story is well known of a thin brass plate having been fixed on a swallow with this inscription : "Prithee, swallow, whither goest thou in winter?" The bird returned next spring with the answer subjoined : "To Anthony, of Athens. Why dost thou inquire?"

6. Out of this controversy, evidence of their sudden autumnal adjournment to Africa accumulated in England. Wilson, in this country, showed that their advance could be traced in the spring from New Orleans to Lake Superior and back again, and their regular migration soon came to be acknowledged. Then attention was turned to the season, manner, and limits of their migrations, and it was found that, taking advantage of favorable winds, immense flocks of swallows—and many other birds of passage as well—flying very high, passed each fall from the coast of England to the coast of Africa, and from Continental Europe across the Mediterranean direct, whence they spread southward almost to the Cape of Good Hope. No sooner had the spring fairly opened than they were suddenly back again, very much exhausted at first with their long-sustained effort, but speedily recuperated and "diligent in business." Our own migrants winter in Central America and the West Indies, or still farther south.

7. Their flight is rapid, but unsteady, "with odd jerks and vacillations not unlike the motions of a butterfly," as

White describes it; and continues: "Doubtless the flight of all hirundines is influenced by and adapted to the peculiar sort of insects which furnish their food. Hence it would be worth inquiry to examine what particular genus of insects affords the principal food of each respective species of swallow." They are constantly on the wing, skimming low over land and loch, pausing not even to drink or bathe, but simply dropping into some limpid lake as they sweep by to sip a taste of water, or cleanse their dirty coats. It seems strange, then, that birds who sustain the unremitting exertion of a flight scarcely less than a hundred miles an hour in speed, during the whole of a long summer's day, should not be thought capable of a transition from England to Africa.

8. The secret of the local distribution of the bank-swallow is the presence or absence of vertical banks suitable for them to penetrate for their burrows in which their nests are placed. Firm sand, with no admixture of pebbles, is preferred, and in such a bank, be it on sea-shore, river-bank, sand-pit, or railroad-cutting, the face will be fairly honey-combed with burrows, and here this charming and graceful bird may be seen in hundreds and thousands. Their domiciles are usually very close together, and the wonder is how the birds can distinguish their own doors. If mistakes do occur, I imagine they are very polite about it, for I know of no more peaceable bird than they.

9. In digging out their burrows they use their hard and sharp beaks, like a pickaxe, to loosen the earth, after which they remove it with their claws. Their burrows usually slope slightly upward, to avoid trouble from the rain, and they extend back from two to ten feet, depending upon the nature of the soil. The burrows will be placed high or low upon the cliff, as the birds have to fear enemies from above or below. The time employed to complete their burrows is from four days to two weeks.

10. The nests are at the extremities of the burrows. When the mother-bird is sitting, you may thrust your arm in and seize her, and she will scarcely struggle or show a sign of life. The young do not leave their nests until able to get their own living. Sometimes they are pushed off by their parents to make room for a new brood. As they pass out into the great world upon inexperienced wings, many of them fall a prey to the crows and hawks which are constantly on the lookout for them. Those who escape collect in small companies and roost at night among the river-reeds, until the time comes for their migration, when they join the elder companies and are off over land and sea.

11. But not the young alone are exposed to enemies. It would seem as though the situation of the nest precluded invasion, yet if they are near the haunts of the house-sparrow they are sure to be dispossessed of their homes by that buccaneer. Snakes, too, can sometimes reach their holes; weasels, like that one Mr. Hewitson tells us of, are often sharp enough to make their *entrée* from above; school-boys regard the pink-white eggs a fine prize; and, last and worst of all, the bank-swallows are many times utterly worried out of their galleries by fleas and young horse-flies, which swarm and increase in their nests until the bird finds endurance no longer a virtue, and digs a new burrow.

Ernest Ingersoll.

JAYS AND THEIR MISSION.

1. "THE mission of birds" has been a favorite study of mine nearly seventy years, and loses none of its interest with the advancement of age. Before I knew anything of ornithology as a science, or had access to the first edition of Wilson in 1813–'14, I had become familiar with the common names and habits of very many of the birds of

Connecticut, and the summer and autumn of 1810, spent in northern Ohio, furnished me with a starting-point to note the wonderful changes in the animal and vegetable kingdoms, incidental to the conversion of this State from a wilderness into a land of cities, villages, and cultivated farms — changes as great and numerous as those which mark the transition of one period into another in geological history.

2. In the year 1840 I located on my farm, bordering on Lake Erie, five miles west of Cleveland. Every apple and wild-cherry tree in the vicinity was then extensively impaired, disfigured, and denuded of its leaves by the bagworm, called in New England the tent-caterpillar, which annually appeared in numerous colonies. The evil was so extensive that even the most thorough farmers ceased, in despair, to attempt its counteraction. At that period I began to set out evergreen-trees of many species extensively, both for the shelter and the ornament of my grounds— an example soon followed by several of my neighbors. Favorable soil and cultivation rapidly developed stately growths, forest-like, in dense clumps.

3. While these were progressing, extensive ranges of native hemlocks and pines, bordering the precipitous banks of Rocky River, were as rapidly falling before the axe and cultivation. These ranges are from two to seven miles west from my locality, and had long been a favorite resort of the jay, as well as numerous other birds, not to mention quadrupeds and reptiles.

4. When my Norway spruces had attained to the height of some ten or twelve feet, I was pleased to find them occupied one spring by colonies of these jays, apparently migrating from the perishing evergreen forests along the river, and during the ensuing winter the new tenants, augmented in numbers, made these incipient forests their places of abode. Each successive year found them still

more numerous and exempt from the interruption of their enemies, the red squirrel, blue racer, and idle gunners, all of whom were abundant and destructive in their former resorts. They soon became so familiar as to feed about our yards and corn-cribs.

5. At the dawn of every pleasant day throughout the year, the nesting season excepted, a stranger in my house might well suppose that all the axles in the county were screeching aloud for lubrication, hearing the harsh and discordant utterances of these birds. During the day the poultry might be frequently seen running into their hiding-places, and the gobbler with his upturned eye searching the heavens for the enemy, all excited and alarmed by the mimic utterances of the adept ventriloquists, the jays simulating the cries of the red-shouldered and the red-tailed hawks.

6. The domestic circle of the barn-yard evidently never gained any insight into the deception by experience; for, though the trick was repeated every few hours, the excitement would always be re-enacted.

7. During the period of incubation silence reigned; not a note or utterance was heard; and it required close scrutiny to discover the numerous individual jays concealed in the dense clumps of limbs and foliage. If, however, a stranger, a dog, cat, hawk, or owl chanced to invade these evergreen groups, the scene rapidly changed.

8. With my person they became so familiar that I could closely approach them, and sit for hours under the shade of these trees without exciting their fears. A family cemetery occupies a place beneath the evergreens. On one occasion a lady, pensively bent over the grave of a departed friend, strewing flowers, received a smart blow upon the head. Alarmed, she arose, expecting to discover some evil-disposed person in the vicinity. Her eye could not ascertain the source of the blow, and she resumed her oc-

cupation, when the blow was renewed, and she soon saw her assailant perched on a limb just overhead, threatening to renew the contest. Near by was a female bird, brooding over a nest of young, and angrily watching the intruder.

9. Soon after they had emigrated to my evergreens, I once noticed one of the birds engaged in tearing open a nest of the bag-worm on an apple-tree. Thinking the act was a mere destructive impulse, I was about walking away, when the bird, with its bill apparently filled with several living and contorting larvæ, changed its position to a tree close by where I was standing. After several nervous and angry bows of the head and flirts of the wings, it eyed me sternly, and seemed to say, "You are inquisitive and meddling with that which is none of your business. We wish to be let alone." Its next removal was to an adjacent black-spruce-tree, where I could plainly see it distributing the captive bag-worms to sundry open and uplifted mouths.

10. From this hint I was led closely to watch the further proceedings of the community. Before the young birds had passed from the care of the parents, most of the worms' nests had been broken into, many were torn into threads, and the number of occupants evidently diminished. Two or three years afterward not a worm was to be seen in that neighborhood, and more recently I have searched for it in vain, in order to rear some cabinet specimens of the moth. In several adjacent townships it is said to be still common.

11. Early in the month of April, two years since, my attention was awakened by a commotion among the birds in my evergreens. It involved not only jays and crow-blackbirds, but robins and bluebirds. Combatants seemed to have gathered from the whole country around. At times half a dozen of these several species would engage in

a contest, screaming, biting, and pulling out feathers; and at length, in many instances, the birds, lost in rage, would actually fall to the ground. For two days this fight continued. At length the jays disappeared, and I have not seen half a dozen individuals on my farm since that period. A numerous colony of crow-blackbirds have reared their young there during the two past seasons, and have been equally assiduous in collecting worms of different species. Whether the abandoning of the locality by the jays was owing exclusively to the intrusion of the blackbirds, or in part to the scarcity of their favorite bag-worms, I can not well determine.

Jared P. Kirtland.

SUMMARY JUSTICE.

1. In his later years the celebrated Cuvier loved to recount the incident which first turned his attention to the study of natural history. While young, and in want, he was engaged as tutor, and with his pupils inhabited an old chateau in the country. Cuvier's room looked toward the garden, and early each morning he was accustomed to open his window and breathe the fresh air before commencing the instruction of his somewhat undisciplined pupils. One morning he remarked two swallows building a nest in the outer angle of his small casement. The male bird brought moist clay in his beak, which the hen, as it were, kneaded together, and, with the addition of straws and bits of hay, formed their future home. Once the frame-work was completed, both birds hastened to line the interior with feathers, wool, and dried leaves; and then taking flight together into a neighboring wood, they did not return to their nest until after the lapse of several days.

2. Meantime, some important events had happened.

While the two swallows were so busily employed in constructing their home, Cuvier had remarked two sparrows perched on a neighboring chimney, who seemed to watch the progress of affairs with much curiosity. The treacherous object of this surveillance speedily became apparent, for no sooner had the poor swallows left the coast clear than the pair of sparrows took possession of the nest, and established themselves in it as comfortably as though it had been their own property. Cuvier remarked that they never absented themselves together from the nest; one always remained on the watch, with its sturdy bill protruded through the entrance, prepared to exclude every visitor except its mate.

3. At the end of the honeymoon the rightful owners returned. What was their surprise to find their nest preoccupied! The cock flew indignantly against his dwelling, to expel the intruders, but was met by the formidable beak of the male sparrow, which quickly repulsed the unlucky proprietor with a bleeding head and ruffled feathers. Trembling with rage and shame, and his bright eye darting fire, he returned to his bride, perched on a green bough, and seemed for some moments to hold an anxious colloquy with her. Then they took flight together, and soon disappeared.

4. Presently the hen-sparrow returned, and her husband began, as Cuvier conjectured, to give her an animated account of his adventure, accompanying the recital with certain curious little cries, which might well pass for derisive laughter. Be that as it may, the prudent pair did not waste much time in chattering, but hastened out in turns to collect and store up a quantity of provisions. This accomplished, they both remained within, and now *two* stout beaks were placed ready to defend the entrance. Cries resounded in the air; crowds of swallows began to assemble on the roof. Cuvier recognized in the midst of

them the expelled householders making their wrongs known to each fresh arrival.

5. Ere long there were assembled in full conclave upward of two hundred swallows. While they were chattering in a style that fully rivaled the performances of many speakers in more ambitious and celebrated meetings, a cry of distress was heard from one of the window-sills. A young swallow, tired, no doubt, of the long parliamentary debate, had betaken himself to the pursuit of some flies who were buzzing about the window. Cuvier's pupils had placed a snare on the sill, and the poor little bird found one of its slender legs entangled by the cruel horse-hair.

6. At the cry of the captive, about twenty of his brethren flew toward him, and tried to set him free ; but in vain. Each effort only served to tighten his bonds, and so increase his pain. Suddenly the swallows, as if with one consent, took flight, and, wheeling in the air, came one by one and gave a sharp peck at the snare, which, after repeated pulls, snapped in two, and the free bird flew joyously away with his kind companions. During this scene, which passed within a few yards of Cuvier, and at about the same distance as the usurped nest, the tutor remained motionless, and the two sparrows never once stirred their threatening, protruded beaks.

7. Suddenly, and swift as thought, flew a host of swallows against the nest : each had his bill filled with mud, which he discharged against the entrance, and then gave place to another, who repeated the same manoeuvre. This they managed to accomplish while two inches distant from the nest, so as to keep out of reach of the beleaguered sparrows. Indeed, the latter were so effectually blinded by the first discharge of mud that they no longer thought of defending themselves. Meantime, the swallows continued to heap mud on the nest, until it was completely covered : the opening would have been quite choked up

but for the desperate efforts made by the sparrows, who by several convulsive shocks contrived to shake off some of the pellets. But a detachment of the implacable swallows perched on the nest, and with their beaks and claws smoothed and pressed down the tough clay over the opening, and at length succeeded in closing it hermetically. Then were heard from hundreds of little throats cries of vengeance and of victory!

8. But the swallows did not end their work here. They hastened to bring from all directions materials for a second nest, which they constructed over the blocked-up entrance of the first one; and, in two hours after the execution of the sparrows, the new nest was inhabited by the ejected swallows. Inexorable justice was now satisfied. Not only were the unfortunate sparrows doomed to expiate their crime by a lingering death, but they were forced during their torments to listen to the joyful song of the two swallows, the cause of their execution.

Chambers's Journal.

THE BIRD OF NIGHT.

1. THE owls are rapacious birds, and, in company with all the true birds of prey, belong to the great order *Raptores*. The order branches into two large groups, known, respectively, as the diurnal and the nocturnal birds of prey. To the *Diurnes* belong the vultures, hawks, and eagles; to the *Nocturnes* belong the owls.

2. If Mrs. Malaprop can not see why the owl is a "rapturous bird," she can admit its claim to openness of countenance. Once seen, the owl can never be mistaken; its flat, pussy face, and large, brassy cat-eyes, set square in front of the head, are so unbird-like. It was a London

holiday ; a shop-woman and her daughter stood before the cage of nocturnal *Raptores* at the " Zoo." Said the elder : "See these heagles!" to which the younger replied : "Them isn't heagles, they're 'awks." " If you please," interposed a servant standing near, " them isn't heagles nor 'awks, they're howls. My maister's son once kept one."

3. The owls are found nearly the whole world over. The books mention about two hundred species, as species are yet understood, and queer specimens are they, every one. As a rule, how trim, spruce, compact, and graceful are the falcons, the typical birds of prey! How fluffy, squatty, and dowdyish is the typical owl! Whether it means little or much, it is thus with the diurnal and the nocturnal *Lepidoptera*. As the elder naturalist said : " If any analogy is allowable between different tribes of animals, the owls might be said to resemble moths " (the night-fliers), "and to differ from the diurnal birds of prey as these do from the butterflies " (the day-fliers). These birds have been called "feathered cats," for the owl, cat-like, prowls at night, and steals upon its victim by a quick, fluffy, still swoop or spring. With the silent movements of a spirit, and a voice so supernatural, and with certain associations of time and place, the effect is appalling.

4. The owls are intensely carnivorous. The diminutive ones will feed largely upon insects, and some of the large kinds will eat them occasionally. But nature has made them for prowlers, and as such we find them fond of flesh, fowl, and fish. So immense is their destruction of the smaller rodents that they are worth millions to the agriculture of our country. They are the feathered Nimrods of the night. Even the American hare, the rabbit wrongly called, falls an easy victim.

5. Some of the owls can fish, too. But whether hunting, fowling, or fishing, they lack the style of doing it which belongs to the falcon tribe ; and when out bugging

A Group of Owls.

it is but a bungling business compared with the professional *rôle* of the insectivorous birds. Their angling, too, is simply upon quiet waters. They can not brave "the mutinous winds 'twixt the green sea and the azured vault." In common with all the *Raptores*, they catch their prey with the talons, not with the beak. In eating birds, the owl prefers to tear his prey in piecemeal, but a small rodent is swallowed entire, being usually tossed into the air to adjust its position, so that it may fall head first into the bird's mouth. It disappears in one astonishing gulp. A second gulp is usually needed, as the tail is often after the first left hanging from one side of the mouth.

6. The great horned owl has usually a white collar around its neck. It is truly a magnificent bird, of indomitable spirit and large size, being about two feet in length. It does not migrate, and is found pretty much all over North America. It breeds in winter and early spring, nesting in hollow trees and crevices of rocks, and is said to build also on some large branch, or in the crotch of a tree. Dr. Coues gives an interesting account of two unfledged ones, which he captured in Dakota, in the month of June. They were his pets for the whole summer, and traveled with him several hundred miles. For a while they had two different notes, the one of hunger or loneliness, a querulous, explosive syllable, and the other a harsh cry of anger, or remonstrance, when rudely handled.

7. They did not begin to hoot until they were about four months old, and then only while at liberty during the night; for, says he, they became so thoroughly tame that, as their wings grew, enabling them to take short flights, I used to release them in the evening from the tether by which they were confined. They enjoyed the liberty, and eventually would stay away all night, doubtless foraging for themselves, for their natural prey, and returning for shelter behind my tent in the morning.

8. The little horned owl is the *Scops asio*, and is variously known as the American screech-owl, the red owl, and the mottled owl. It is but ten inches long, though that is

even two inches longer than its European relative. It ranges through all the Atlantic States, even up to Greenland. Nor is it driven away by the clearing off of the woods; and now more than ever it seeks to be a winter denizen of the city parks, attracted, doubtless, by the abundance of English sparrows, which afford it food.

9. This little screech-owl, with its staring eyes and pert, ear-like tufts, has a decidedly cattish look. In truth, it wears a grave, grimalkin cast of countenance, which, in a bird, is quite uncanny and unnatural. A mounted specimen in my parlor was an object of dread to a little girl visiting us from the city. It availed nothing to tell the child that little Motley would not hurt her, while the unbird-like little thing would stare at her so.

10. To the naturalist *Scops asio* has been a provoking elf. It is to be hoped that the sage-looking little fellow did not scoff behind his gravity at these learned men, or count any of them asinine whom he so misled by his eccentric freakiness in dress. Coming before a man of science at one time wearing a suit of sober frieze, again appearing in mottled gray, and anon clad gayly in tawny red, how ludicrously easy and inviting was the trick of specie-making! Well, that controversy is over now, and to write the strife down as history would be enough to make Motley bristle to his toes.

Rev. Samuel Lockwood.

THE OWL-CRITIC.

1. "Who stuffed that white owl?" No one spoke in the shop;
The barber was busy, and he couldn't stop;
The customers, waiting their turns, were all reading
The "Daily," the "Herald," the "Post," little heeding

The young man who blurted out such a blunt question ;
Not one raised a head, or even made a suggestion ;
    And the barber kept on shaving.

2. "Don't you see, Mister Brown,"
Cried the youth, with a frown,
"How wrong the whole thing is,
How preposterous each wing is,
How flattened the head is, how jammed down the neck is—
In short, the whole owl, what an ignorant wreck 'tis ?
I make no apology ;
I've learned owl-eology.
I've passed days and nights in a hundred collections,
And can not be blinded to any deflections
Arising from unskillful fingers that fail
To stuff a bird right, from his beak to his tail.
Mister Brown ! Mister Brown !
Do take that bird down,
Or you'll soon be the laughing-stock all over town !"
    And the barber kept on shaving.

3. "I've *studied* owls,
And other night fowls,
And I tell you
What I know to be true :
An owl can not roost
With his limbs so unloosed ;
No owl in this world
Ever had his claws curled,
Ever had his legs slanted,
Ever had his bill canted,
Ever had his neck screwed
Into that attitude.
He can't *do* it, because
'Tis against all bird laws.

Anatomy teaches,
Ornithology preaches,
An owl has a toe
That *can't* turn out so !
I've made the white owl my study for years,
And to see such a job almost moves me to tears !
Mister Brown, I'm amazed
You should be so gone crazed
As to put up a bird
In that posture absurd !
To *look* at that owl really brings on a dizziness ;
The man who stuffed him don't half know his business !"
  And the barber kept on shaving.

4. "Examine those eyes.
I'm filled with surprise
Taxidermists should pass
Off on you such poor glass ;
So unnatural they seem,
They'd make Audubon scream
And John Burroughs laugh
To encounter such chaff.
Do take that bird down ;
Have him stuffed again, Brown !"
  And the barber kept on shaving.

5. "With some sawdust and bark
I could stuff in the dark
An owl better than that.
I could make an old hat
Look more like an owl
Than that horrid fowl,
Stuck up there so stiff like a side of coarse leather.
In fact, about *him* there's not one natural feather."

6. Just then, with a wink and a sly normal lurch,
   The owl, very gravely, got down from his perch,
   Walked round, and regarded his fault-finding critic
   (Who thought he was stuffed) with a glance analytic,
   And then fairly hooted, as if he should say:
   "Your learning's at fault this time, anyway;
   Don't waste it again on a live bird, I pray.
   I'm an owl; you're another. Sir Critic, good day!"
      And the barber kept on shaving.

James T. Fields.

PART X.

STRANGE BIRDS AND THEIR WAYS.

THE FLAMINGO.

1. The coasts of Florida, with semi-tropical and nearly uniform climate, are the favorite resorts of many kinds of aquatic birds which are not found in Northern waters. Conspicuous among these are numerous wading birds which have their homes along the lagoons and shallow waters of the bays. Early in the morning, or late in the afternoon, the visitor to the shore is startled by a trumpet-like noise, immediately followed by a whirr of wings, and he sees a flock of large scarlet birds rising in the air and sailing away in the shape of a triangle, after the fashion of wild geese. These are the flamingoes, and the noise was the warning note of the sentinel which is always on the lookout while the rest of the flock are feeding.

2. They are shy birds, and to obtain a near view they must be approached with great caution. Snugly ensconced in some protecting bush or tree, the observer will see scarlet flashes high in air as the birds steer toward their accustomed resort. When they alight, the triangle is straightened out into a line, the sentinel takes his place in some commanding position, and the remainder of the flock set about their search for food. At a little distance they appear like scarlet boats, with enormously long bows, floating

STRANGE BIRDS AND THEIR WAYS. 245

in the air. A closer inspection, however, reveals two long, slim legs, so entirely disproportionate to the size of the body as to give to the birds the very ludicrous appearance of walking on stilts.

3. The observer will see also that the flamingo has a small but graceful body, a finely curved and swan-like neck, and, when flying, or wading in the water, it is one of

Flamingo and Nest.

the most beautiful of all aquatic birds. It is adapted to wading, swimming, flying, and walking, and it is only on land that it appears awkward and uncomfortable. It helps itself over the ground with its long neck and bill, and its pace while running is very rapid.

4. They are web-footed, like the swimmers; not so much, however, to enable them to swim, as to walk over the

soft mud at the bottom of the water. They eat after the manner of a duck, their food consisting of such small fish as they may catch, and the mollusks, crustaceans, and marine insects which they may turn up in the mud at the bottom. Their bill is so constructed as to sort the material, and to collect the edible portion in the under mandible as in a spoon. Their tongue is thick, of a soft, oily consistence, and is covered with curved spines pointing backward; it is considered a very delicate morsel for the table.

5. Flamingoes are not entirely nocturnal birds, but they avoid the glare of the day. They fly low over the water, but high over the land. Their mode of flight is by alternately flapping their wings and sailing; and, in alighting, they generally sail round the place and come down in shallow water and wade to the shore. The neck of the bird is very flexible, and it presents an exceedingly beautiful appearance as it is bent in graceful curves to preen every part of its plumage. Its clumsy legs, which in flying are drawn to the breast so as to be nearly invisible, are well under control, for it can scratch its head with its toes as well as a canary.

6. George W. Curtis, in his "Nile Notes of Howadji," gives the following description of a flight of flamingoes which he witnessed in Egypt: "As we sat upon a green clump on the high bank of the river, we saw a dark undulating mass upon the edge of the fog-bank that was slowly moving northward away. The mass, now evidently a flight of birds, came sweeping southward toward us, high in the blue air, and veering from side to side like a ship in tacking. With every sunward sweep their snow-white bodies shone like a shower of most brilliant silver stars.

7. "There was a graceful, careless order in their flying, and as they turned from side to side the long lines undulated in musical motion. I have never seen movements so delicious to the eye as their turning sweep. The long line

throbbed and palpitated as if an electric sympathy were emitted from the fine points of their wings. There was nothing tumbling or gay in their impression, but an intense feeling of languid life. Their curves and movements were voluptuous. The southern sun flashed not in vain along their snowiness, nor were they without meaning flying to the south. There was no sound but the whirring of innumerable wings, as they passed high over our heads, a living cloud between us and the sun. Now it was a streaming whiteness in the blue, now it was as mellowly dark, as they turned to or from the sun, and so advanced, the long lines giving and trembling sometimes, like a flapping sail in a falling breeze, then bellying roundly out again as if the wind had risen.

8. "When they were directly above us, one only note was dropped from some thoughtful flamingo, to call attention to the presence of strangers below. But beyond musket-shot, even if not beyond fear, as they undoubtedly were, the fair company swept on unheeding, a beautiful boon for the south, and laden with what strange tidings from northern woods! The bodies were rosy white and the wings black, and the character of the flight imparted an air of delicacy and grace to all their movements and association; but the pageant soon passed, and the whirr of beautiful wings, and the rose-cloud of flamingoes died away deep in the south."

BIRDS-OF-PARADISE.

1. THE birds-of-paradise are a small but renowned family. They received their name from the idea, entertained at one time, that they inhabited the region of the Mosaic paradise. They live in a small locality in Australasia, including Papua or New Guinea, and a few adjacent islands.

2. In form and size they somewhat resemble our crow, or blue-jay; but some are smaller. They are usually included in the tribe of conebills, though their bills are quite slender for that group, and a little compressed. The bills are covered at the base with downy or velvety feathers, which extend over the nostrils; their wings are long and round; the tail consists of ten feathers, two of them, in some species, very long; legs and feet very long, large, and strong; outer toe longer than inner, and joined to the middle one toward the base; hind-toe very long; claws long and curved.

3. But they are chiefly remarkable for the wonderful development of various parts of their plumage, and for the metallic splendor of its rich hues. The sides of the body, and sometimes of the head, neck, breast, or tail, are ornamented with lengthened, peculiarly developed, and showy feathers. Says Wood: "In all the species, the feathers glow with resplendent radiance; in nearly all there is some strange and altogether unique arrangement of the plumage; and, in many, the feathers are modified into plumes, ribbons, and streamers, that produce the most surprising and lovely effects." The plumage of the face, breast, and throat is usually the richest in metallic tints, while other parts frequently have very beautiful and brilliant colors.

4. Their food consists of grasshoppers, butterflies, moths, and other insects; figs, the berries of various trees and shrubs; seeds, rice, and other kinds of grain. During the heat of the day they remain concealed in the woods, but in the morning and evening come forth to seek their food. Furious storms frequently bring them to the ground, when they are easily taken by the natives, who also shoot them with blunt arrows, or take them with a noose, likewise with bird-lime or other glutinous substance, placed on the branches which they frequent.

5. The greater paradise-bird (*Paradisea apoda*), fre-

quently called the Emerald Bird-of-Paradise, is smaller than the crow. Linnæus gave the specific name *apoda* to this bird, which was generally and erroneously called footless, to designate the species, not to perpetuate the error. This bird seeks the thickest foliage of the loftiest trees, in which to remain concealed during the day. The feathers on the head, throat, and neck are very short and dense. Those round the base of the bill, and on the face, are velvety and black, changing their color to green, as the direction of the light

Bird of Paradise.

changes; those on the throat, the front half of the neck, and the upper part of the breast, are of a bright, deep, emerald green; those on the head, back of the neck, and the shoulders, are of a light, golden yellow. The eye is at the common point between these colors.

6. If lines were drawn from it to the throat, to the forehead, and down the sides of the neck, and curved to a point on the breast, they would indicate very well the limits of the colors. The back, wings, tail, and belly are of a bright, reddish chestnut, the breast being a little darker, and inclining to purple. From each side beneath the wings proceed a large number of long, floating, graceful plumes, some eighteen inches in length, of exceeding delicacy of texture and appearance. These extend far beyond the tail-feathers, which are about six inches long, and their translucent golden-white vanelets produce a most superb effect, as they cross and recross each other, forming every imaginable shade of white, gold, and orange, and then deepening toward their extremities into a soft, purplish red. From the upper part of the tail proceed two black shafts or filaments, some eighteen inches long, appearing like small wires, about one sixteenth of an inch in diameter.

7. They are not easily tamed and kept confined, and few have been brought alive from their native locality. Mr. Beale had one at Macao, China, which had been in captivity nine years. In a description of this bird the writer says: "This elegant creature has a light, playful, and graceful manner, with an arch and impudent look; dances about when a visitor approaches the cage, and seems delighted at being made an object of admiration. Its notes are very peculiar, resembling the cawing of a raven, but its tones are far more varied. It washes itself regularly twice daily, and, after having performed its ablutions, throws its delicate feathers up nearly over its head, the quills of which feathers have a peculiar structure so as to enable the bird to effect this object.

8. "Its food, during confinement, is boiled rice, mixed

up with soft eggs, together with plantains, and living insects of the grasshopper tribe; these insects, when thrown to him, the bird contrives to catch in his beak with great celerity; but if, through failure to catch them, they should fall to the floor, he will not descend to them, appearing to be fearful that, in so doing, he would soil his delicate plumage. He will eat insects in a living state, but will not touch them when dead.

9. "One of the best opportunities of seeing this splendid bird, in all its beauty of actions as well as display of plumage, is early in the morning, when he makes his toilet; the beautiful sub-alar plumage is then thrown out and cleaned from any spot that may sully its purity, by being passed gently through the bill; the short, chocolate-colored wings are extended to the utmost, and he keeps them in a steady, flapping motion, as if in imitation of their use in flight, at the same time raising up the delicate, long feathers over the back, which are spread in a chaste and elegant manner, floating like films in the ambient air.

10. "In this position the bird would remain for a short time, seemingly proud of its heavenly beauty, and in raptures of delight with its most enchanting self; it will then assume various attitudes, so as to regard its plumage in every direction.

11. "Having completed his toilet, he utters the usual cawing notes, at the same time looking archly at the spectators, as if ready to receive all the admiration that it considers its elegant form and plumage demand. It then takes exercise by hopping in a rapid but graceful manner from one of the upper perches to the other, and descends suddenly upon the second perch, close to the bars of the cage, looking out for the grasshoppers which it is accustomed to receive about this time."

James H. Partridge.

TALKING BIRDS AND THEIR WAYS.

1. NEARLY all the birds that are capable of articulating words belong to the parrot family, which numbers more than three hundred species. The common gray and green parrots are too well known to need description. The family belong to the climbers, but are slow and awkward upon the ground. In climbing they use both beak and claws, and in eating they use one claw to hold the food. The beak is very strong, and capable of great destruction in either offensive or defensive warfare. They are natives of tropical climes, live in pairs, and feed upon soft, pulpy fruits, especially such as have hard kernels or seeds. When wild they are usually seen in large flocks morning and evening, active in procuring food, and exceedingly noisy and quarrelsome. In captivity they are generally capricious in temper and mischievous.

2. Innumerable anecdotes are told of them which go to show that they have not only the ability to speak, but also to attach a definite meaning to the words they utter. A few years since, I was the owner of one which we named "Poll," to distinguish her from "Polly," our other pet. She had lost her beauty by a scald on the head, and never possessed the winning ways of her companion. She would, indeed, say, when the reason of her bald pate was asked, "I've been scalded"; and whenever a bald-headed gentleman entered the room, she shouted to him, "You've been scalded!" and then, turning to her friends, and changing her grammar correctly, would cry out, to our infinite annoyance, "He's been scalded!" She could cry, "Hip, hip, hurrah! three cheers for the queen!" could sing and dance to the tune of "Polly, put the kettle on, we'll all have tea"; and would ask very peremp-

torily for her meals, "Thomas, fetch my dinner—Poll's hungry!"

3. She had one singular trait: she caught everybody's laugh. I never noticed the peculiarity of laughs in my family till "Poll" began to simulate them. From the feminine giggle to the masculine guffaw—from the boisterous laugh of the children to the titter of the house-maid, catching the gamut of every member of our household, even to the suppressed hiccough of James the footman, whose good English breeding allowed only the slightest demonstration of any sentiment whatever—"Poll" would deliver by the hour a series of idiosyncratic laughs, which, amusing enough at first, made her imitations at last an intolerable nuisance. When she once began her cachinnations, nothing would stop her. Indeed, when attacked by a gout that ended her life, her very last breath shaped itself into a giggle, so true to its original that to those who stood around her cage, mourning over her death-agonies, it was irresistibly ludicrous. Laughing herself, she died in the very odor of laughter.

4. They tell a good story in Newgate Street, London, of a parrot—or of two parrots rather, a gray and a green one—belonging to Morley, a tradesman in the Old Bailey, just opposite the prison, which is vouched for as true in the strictest sense. The man had a wonderful "bird-sense," and his power of training birds became famous throughout the metropolis. He had taught his green parrot to speak whenever a knock was heard at his street-door; but when the bell of the same door was rung, he had taught the gray parrot to answer. The house, still standing, has one of those projecting porches that prevent the second story from being seen from the pavement. One day a person knocked. "Who is there?" asked the green parrot. "The man with the leather," was the reply. The bird answered, "All right!" and then became silent. After

waiting some time, and not finding the door opened, the man knocked again. "Who is there?" again asked the green parrot. "Who's there?" cried the porter outside. "It's I, the man with the leather; why don't you open the door?" "All right!" repeated the parrot, which so enraged the man that he furiously rang the bell. "Go to the gate!" shouted a new voice, which proceeded from the gray parrot. "To the gate!" repeated the man, seeing no gate; "what gate?" "Newgate! Newgate!" responded the gray parrot. The porter was enraged; but, stepping across the street, the better to answer what he supposed to be the insolence of the house-maids, he saw that he had been outwitted and teased by a couple of parrots.

5. This same Morley had been employed by a gentleman, who had heard of his knowledge of birds, to purchase for him a white cockatoo. The price was of less importance than the health, disposition, and breeding of the bird. She was to use no bad language, be subject to no fits of passion, have been trained to be handled by women and children, and be cleanly in her habits. Morley took great pains to please his employer, and at last sent him home perhaps the most perfect specimen of the breed ever seen in London. As I saw the bird ten years ago, nothing in the way of ornithological beauty could surpass it. Of pure, snowy white from top of crown to tip of tail; without a speck of lead, gray, or crimson on a single feather; free from all sign of cross with paroquet or macaw; and in shape, attitude, bearing, and action, as distinguishable as a blooded horse—"Beauty," as she was called, stood unrivaled.

6. When she was sent home, there was perfect satisfaction; the employer was pleased, as he well might be; the family of daughters in ecstasies of admiration; and Morley richly remunerated for his trouble. But the bird would not talk. This was attributed at first to fear, then to

change of diet, and at last to absolute inability. Of course, there was great disappointment. "Beauty's" cage hung at the dining-room window; every visitor was in admiration of her spotless plumage and faultless shape; and, of course, everybody sympathized in the disappointment at her irremediable defect.

7. "What a pity it is she does not talk!" remarked a person one day at dinner; "she would be worth her weight in gold." "She almost cost it as it is," said paterfamilias. "The creature is a cheat. Fine feathers don't make fine birds, certainly not fine parrots. I paid ten guineas for her, and she can not say one word." *"Ah, but I think the more! What's the use of talking, if you have nothing to say?"* came in clear articulate sounds from the cage, to the amazement of family and guests. That settled forever "Beauty's" supremacy.

8. Whether it is possible to entirely eradicate bad habits in parrots is doubtful. Captain Simpson, well known by transatlantic passengers, used to duck his paroquet in the sea every time it swore an oath. This seemed to cure him of using profane language. The creature really connected an oath with a dowse in the water, and gave up swearing. One day, in a furious storm, a man was washed overboard, and with great difficulty was recovered. As soon as he was drawn on deck, and efforts were being made to resuscitate him, "Polly" kept hopping around the circle, shaking her head from side to side, and saying, gravely, "You've been swearing! you've been swearing!"

9. It is said that macaws are the best talkers of the whole species, providing they are reared from the nest. And not only are they able to talk, but they also sing in a peculiar, soft voice. In sweetness, though not in compass, of musical notes, they are, however, excelled by the grass or green paroquet. While the cockatoo is the hardiest of the parrot tribe, and the most easily tamed, it is, at the

same time, the most difficult to teach to talk at all well. Its disposition is more gentle, however, and its obedience more implicit, than any of the other species. The gray African parrot, from its docility and aptitude, ranks everywhere first as a favorite, though of late years the common green Amazon, from the little attention it requires, and its quick sagacity, is sharing the general favor.

10. A gentleman residing in Wilmington, Delaware, owns one of these Amazon parrots. It possesses a fluency and variety of language rarely ever equaled by the African gray. As soon as her master returns from the office for dinner, Polly begins to salute him in fondest expressions: "Papa, dear, come and kiss your pretty green beauty! Come in, come in, papa, and give us a kiss, and a thousand more!" When the footman enters the room, she says to him, but never to any one else, "Fetch my dinner, James—I'm hungry. Stupid fellow! I can't eat my head off!" To a bachelor friend, who frequently spends several weeks at the house, Polly has but one question, never put to any one else, "Oh, you gay deceiver, why did you promise to marry me, and didn't?" To a gentleman, a near neighbor, whom she had once overheard saying, at the after-dinner table, "The bird's invaluable; five hundred dollars would not buy her, if I owned her—would it, Polly?" she always addresses the salute the moment he appears, "Five hundred dollars would not buy Polly, if you owned her! Five hundred dollars! Five hundred dollars! Why, the bird's invaluable!"

11. This Wilmington parrot certainly discriminates between the sexes and between conditions in life. To a well-dressed young gentleman the remark is, "What a get-up! What a swell you are!" To a young lady, on the contrary, fondling and kissing, she says, with great deference, "Is she not nice?—so nice!" Whereas to a clergyman, who is detected by his dress, she is exceedingly

offensive, perpetually calling out, "Let us pray!" "Glory be to God!" "Amen!" She was once lost, stayed out over night, and grief and searches ruled the disconsolate household. At daybreak, however, a workman, going to his job, was hailed by Polly, from a pile of bricks, with the call, "Take me home! Take me home!" Whether the night-chilled bird did or did not attach meaning to the words, it is certain that the workman did, and that he made a good thing of bringing her home. I know of no gray parrot that has excelled this.

N. S. Dodge.

THE APTERYX.

1. ONE of the contributions which New Zealand has made to the list of queer animal forms is that of the apteryx. The name implies that it is a wingless bird, though when stripped of its covering minute rudimentary wings are discovered. This bird is another survival of the old geologic forms, of which the southern hemisphere has furnished so many specimens. In size the different species vary from that of a moderately-sized hen to that of a large turkey. It is covered with curious feathers, which are very narrow, and taper to a point at their upper extremity, giving to the bird the general appearance of a hedgehog. The covering seems to be a cross between feathers, hair, and hedgehog quills.

2. The bill of the apteryx is long and slender, and the legs are large and strong, each terminating in sharp and formidable claws. It thus possesses the characteristic organs of both scratching and wading birds, but it is exclusively a land bird, and uses its long beak to extract insects and worms from the fallen leaves and decayed wood in the forests. As it has no occasion to fly or to swim, its tail is

in the same rudimentary condition as its wings. It is called by the natives kiwi-kiwi, from its peculiar cry. Its nests are made either at the base of a hollow tree or in deep holes which it excavates in the ground. When attacked, it defends itself vigorously with its strong feet.

The Apteryx.

3. Mr. Wood, the naturalist, thus describes this bird: "The skin is tough and flexible, and the chiefs set great value upon it for the manufacture of their state mantles, permitting no inferior person to wear them, and being extremely unwilling to part with them even for a valuable consideration. The bird lives mostly among the fern; and, as it always remains concealed during the day in deep recesses of rocks, ground, or tree-roots, and is remarkably

fleet of foot, diving among the heavy fern-leaves with singular adroitness, it is not very easy of capture. It feeds upon insects of various kinds, more especially on worms, which it is said to attract to the surface by jumping and striking on the ground with its powerful feet. The natives always hunt the kiwi-kiwi at night, taking with them torches and spears. The speed of this bird is very considerable, and when running it sets its head rather back, raises its neck, and plies its legs with a vigor little inferior to that of the ostrich.

4. "The fine specimen in the Zoölogical Gardens of London has already proved a very valuable bird, as she has laid several eggs, thereby setting at rest some disputed questions on the subject, and well illustrates the natural habits of the species.

5. "Upon her box is placed, under a glass shade, the shell of one of her eggs. These eggs are indeed wonderful, for the bird weighs a little more than four pounds, and each egg weighs between fourteen and fifteen ounces, its length being four and three quarter inches and its width rather more than two inches, thus being very nearly one fourth of the weight of the parent-bird. This, next to that of the ostrich, is the largest egg known.

6. "The long, curved beak of the apteryx has the nostrils very narrow, very small, and set on at each side of the tip, so that the bird is enabled to pry out the worms and other nocturnal creatures on which it feeds, not trusting merely to the eyes. The general color of the apteryx is chestnut-brown, each feather being tipped with a darker hue, and the under parts are lighter than the upper."

THE STORK.

1. The stork appears most at home in the low lands of Holland, and by the people of that country he is held more sacred than anywhere else. In the landscapes of the old Dutch painters he forms an almost typical accessory; in every village, and in most towns even, he is at home; and in the Hague a house has been built in the middle of the market-place on purpose for him. He is of noble extraction, of high birth, as the nursery rhyme says, for his imposing nest is reared on roofs and gables. A pollard tree in the neighborhood of a house or village serves him often for a domicile; an ash, a maple, or an oak, for an elevated throne, is absolutely necessary for him, in order that he may have an extended view over his territory of meadows, fields, and morass.

2. When with the first warm March breeze the stork returns to his village, there is great rejoicing. He is greeted with song and exclamation, as one welcome back, as a faithful, long-missed friend. The old people in the village know him as the contemporary of their youth; and to the children, whose friend pre-eminently he is, he brings the assurance and the pledge that spring, for which they have so impatiently longed, is come. He has, so to say, signed Spring's passport with his *visé;* there is no longer any doubt of his arrival.

3. His very figure, how characteristic and significant! On a high wooden leg, which seems stuck into a red Russia-leather boot, is balanced his stately body, over which he has thrown his white traveling cloak, turned up with black. His tail is short and obtuse; all the more slender and elongated is his neck, which carries the peculiarly expressive head with a tranquil dignity. The plumage lies

close on the smooth forehead, like hair neatly combed back; the brown eye twinkles with clear, honest expression, in which, however, there is a touch of roguery, from out the black rings of the mark not unlike spectacles. The visor terminates very comically in a long, grotesque beak-nose,

The Stork.

which, be it observed, is a weapon also to insure respect. In gait, demeanor, manner, a pedantic pathos is expressed, reminding us of hoops and hair-powder, rapiers, high-heeled shoes, and minuets. The stork is indeed an old-fashioned figure, seemingly most in keeping with the slow paced burghers of his beloved Holland.

4. Wrapped in thoughtful silence, he stalks, like Mynheer, stiff and full of gravity, through his drains and meadows. At every step, he lifts with measured cadence the long, stocking-covered leg, as if to guard it from possible contamination; while head and neck, in a continual ticktack, nod backward and forward in comical solemnity. Thus, with ceremonious carriage, consort and spouse move along, like peripatetic philosophers, until one or the other perceives the fat, sprawling croaker in the thick sedge, and suddenly darts forward the sharp bill, like a harpoon, to impale the unhappy wretch, and bury him in the depths of the gullet. The other stork raises his head and makes a bow and a flourish.

5. It is an easy, noiseless, and yet assiduous chase; nothing interrupts them, unless it be that a curious observer comes too near them, or something unusual happens. Then they stand still; one leg is drawn up close to the body and lays hold of the other, thus to give greater firmness to the contemplative position; the neck is stretched inquiringly upward, and the eye is fixed on the object of alarm. In this attitude, which, odd as it is, never sacrifices aught of its *grandezza*, they will remain some minutes immovable, and with all the gravity of an automaton, until persuaded they may range further in safety, or that it would be wiser to take flight.

6. The large body rises with difficulty; and it is comic enough to see the worthy master of ceremonies brought so completely out of his equilibrium. He makes a few awkward jumps, then follow some heavy flaps of the wings, and the feet are stretched out like oars behind; but yet the reeling mass rises scarcely above the ground. Suddenly, with a jerk, as though it had thrown away the tardy crutch, the phlegmatic walker on stilts mounts high in the ocean of air; and now, in grandest rounds and soarings, he displays to our astonished gaze the spectacle of his

majestic flight. He will often float a long distance without a movement of the wings, as though supported by his own weight, gliding downward at last in spiral lines to the nest, where the hungry brood, in a clappering tongue, give vent to their joy.

7. As among the wandering shepherd tribes of the Steppes the chief precedes his family to look for new pastures, then returns to lead them thither, so does the male stork appear along the German rivers and the North Sea, one or two weeks before the female, in order to reconnoiter; and when he has again found the old moss-covered house-ridge with the empty nest; when he sees the fountain in the court-yard, with the wide-spreading trees beside it, and has cast a look over the country, he suddenly disappears, to return soon after with his spouse; and then, with courtly obeisances and merry clapperings, introducing her as mistress, sets about repairing the old house or building a new one. Possession is thus taken; the stork arranges his household, and paternal cares now occupy his attention.

8. Except some quarrels with his kind, growing out of jealousy, the stork is a most peaceable and tolerant character, and, just as around the baronial castle swarms of poor retainers settle and seek protection, so does he allow the sparrow and swallow to take up their abode beneath the protecting, spray-built cupola of his house. He, however, stands like an emir, in grave composure, above the noisy rabble, without allowing their boldest tricks to mislead or anger him. Indeed, the stork, above all other birds, has a feeling for home and love for domestic life. He is a watchful household chief, showing as much tenderness for his progeny as filial gratitude to parents and benefactors.

9. On this account the stork has at all times been regarded as "a bird of piety," and set up as a pattern of domestic virtue. Thus, it is said, he will carry his young upon his back when teaching them to fly, or to save them

when the nest is threatened with fire ; whence, as some suppose, he acquired the old German name of Adeboar, which literally means "luck-bringer," he being good, bringing good with him. One thing must not be forgotten, that the stork extends his love of offspring to human little ones, and that these reciprocate his love with kindness and attention.

10. Cleanliness, too, is a fundamental law of his household economy; it is a part, so to speak, of the natural character of the stork, and is, indeed, the more necessary, as on his white dress every impurity would show itself most conspicuously. The bill supplies the place of brush and comb ; and on the coat, the breast-facings, and stockings there is always a something to smooth down and order. Nor is all this a mere show of cleanliness ; he would not be satisfied with having a clean shirt-front merely, and he bathes frequently.

11. The stork, it is clear, reveals a relationship between his mode of being and action and that of man ; and hence he attaches himself to man, and man to him. Careless and confiding he walks about the court and garden of the farmer ; in seaport towns, even, he stalks on amid all the bustle of the streets, and expects every one whom he meets to make way for him ; he wanders from market to market, from fountain to fountain, examines boldly here a basket and there a dish ; in short, he feels himself at home. Despite all familiarity, he knows how to make himself respected ; and he maintains not only his perfect freedom, but even a sort of superiority.

12. When, in the height of summer, the meadows are parched and ponds and morasses are dried up, the stork resorts to the interior of the woods, with their glades, brooks, and marshes ; and when, in the beginning of autumn, the inferior animals retire into their holes and winter abodes, vast numbers, all travel-equipped, collect together and

cruise about in the air, preparing for emigration to the South. When all is ready, they depart suddenly in well-ordered ranks; but as these quickly rise to the highest regions of air, they are soon lost to sight.

13. In uninterrupted flight, and sometimes in flocks of two or three thousand, these Europe-sick birds direct their course to the Egyptian coast. Here is the stork's second home. Here, in the lowlands of the Delta, abounding in frogs and snakes, he rules as a sort of pacha, as familiar and sacred an object to the brown child of the fellah as to the fair-haired boy of the dweller among the dikes; and verily the strange bird, with his gravity and seriousness, accords well with that land of singularity and gloom. Yet even beneath the palms and the pyramids he does not forget the German village and its lime-trees; and when the glowing heat of advancing summer shines down from the brazen sky of Egypt, he returns again to his home amid the reviving verdure of our northern climate.

Hermann Masius.

THREE VIEWS OF THE EAGLE.

1. THE eagle is a well-known bird of prey, the largest and most powerful of all the birds that fly except the condor of the Andes. Its nests are usually built in the top of a lofty tree, in the midst of an inaccessible swamp or on the summit of some rocky peak. Its favorite home is on the high cliffs which border the ocean, or extend along the rapids of a river. From its lofty eyrie it watches life below, and majestically sails out into the upper air. With the keenest vision, it sees the small birds and animals afar off, and, pouncing down with a dread swoop, it seizes them in its terrible talons and bears them away to its

nest. Squirrels, rabbits, and all kinds of swimming and wading birds fall a prey to its voracity. It frequently seizes young lambs from the flock, and several instances are on record where it has snatched a baby left for a moment by its mother and carried it away to its inaccessible home.

The Eagle.

2. When live food can not be obtained, it does not disdain to feed upon dead bodies. It will attack larger animals that have been disabled, aiming furiously at their eyes.

Withal it is a determined freebooter, robbing other birds of their prey. The character ascribed to the eagle differs with the different stand-points of its observers. It has strength, keenness of sight, and a majestic poise while on the wing. It is self-reliant, and shows great attachment for its young, and exhibits great courage in their defense. All these qualities and characteristics take hold of the imagination, and give to the bird its ideal character. Viewed from the stand-point of fair play and morality, however, the eagle makes about as poor a show as the great Napoleon when judged by a similar standard.

3. We will hear first from the great ornithologist, Alexander Wilson, whose life was devoted to the observation of birds. In describing the eagle, he says: "Elevated on the high, dead limb of some gigantic tree, that commands a wide view of the neighboring shore and ocean, he seems calmly to contemplate the motions of the various feathered tribes that pursue their busy vocations below; the snow-white gulls slowly winnowing the air; the busy tringæ coursing along the sands; trains of ducks streaming over the surface; silent and watchful cranes, intent and wading; clamorous crows, and all the winged multitudes that subsist by the bounty of this vast liquid magazine of Nature. High over all these hovers one whose action instantly arrests all his attention. By the wide curvature of wing, and sudden suspension in air, he knows it to be the fish-hawk, settling over some devoted victim of the deep. His eye kindles at the sight, and, balancing himself with half-opened wings on the branch, he watches the result. Down, rapid as an arrow from heaven, descends the distant object of his attention; the roar of its wings reaches the ear as it disappears in the deep, making the surges foam around.

4. "At this moment the eager looks of the eagle are all ardor, and, leveling his neck for flight, he sees the fish-hawk once more emerge, struggling with its prey, and

mounting in the air with screams of exultation. These are the signal for the eagle, who, launching into the air, instantly gives chase and soon gains on the fish-hawk; each exerts his utmost to mount above the other, displaying in these rencontres the most elegant and sublime aërial evolutions. The unincumbered eagle rapidly advances, and is just on the point of reaching his opponent, when, with a sudden scream, probably of despair and honest execration, the latter drops his fish. The eagle, poising himself for a moment, as if to take a more certain aim, descends like a whirlwind, snatches it in his grasp ere it reaches the water, and bears his ill-gotten booty silently away to the woods."

5. We will next hear from the poet Alfred B. Street. It will be seen that here the hawk is represented as the robber, while the eagle redresses the wrong and avenges the outrages perpetrated upon the poor kingfisher. To be sure, he secures the prey in the end, but we must not expect from a poet a too close scrutiny into motives.

6. "With storm-daring pinion and sun-gazing eye,
  The gray forest eagle is king of the sky!
  Oh, little he loves the green valley of flowers,
  Where sunshine and song cheer the bright summer
      hours,
  For he hears in those haunts only music, and sees
  Only rippling of waters and waving of trees;
  There the red robin warbles, the honey-bee hums,
  The timid quail whistles, the sly partridge drums;
  And if those proud pinions, perchance, sweep along,
  There's a shrouding of plumage, a hushing of song;
  The sunlight falls stilly on leaf and on moss,
  And there's naught but his shadow black gliding across;
  But the dark, gloomy gorge, where down plunges the
      foam
  Of the fierce rock-lashed torrent, he claims as his home:

There he blends his keen shriek with the roar of the flood,
And the many-voiced sounds of the blast-smitten wood.

7. "From the crag-grasping fir-top, where morn hangs its wreath,
He views the mad waters white writhing beneath.
On a limb of that moss-bearded hemlock far down,
With bright azure mantle and gay mottled crown,
The kingfisher watches, while o'er him his foe,
The fierce hawk, sails circling, each moment more low:
Now poised are those pinions and pointed that beak,
His dread swoop is ready, when hark! with a shriek
His eye-balls red blazing, high bristling his crest,
His snake-like neck arched, talons drawn to his breast,
With the rush of the wind-gust, the glancing of light,
The gray forest eagle shoots down in his flight;
One blow of those talons, one plunge of that neck,
The strong hawk hangs lifeless, a blood-dripping wreck;
And as dives the freed kingfisher, dart-like on high
With his prey soars the eagle, and melts in the sky."

8. Lastly we will get the opinion of the shrewd and genial old philosopher, Benjamin Franklin. His remarks were made when called upon to examine a medal which had been struck off for the Cincinnati, a society formed exclusively of officers who had served in the revolutionary armies. This medal had been criticised in its execution. He says: "To me it seems tolerably done; but all such things are criticised. Some find fault with the Latin, as wanting classical elegance and correctness; and since our nine universities were not able to furnish better Latin, it was a pity, they say, that the mottoes had not been in English. Others object to the title, as not properly assumable by any but General Washington and a few others who served without pay. Others object to the bald eagle, as looking like a turkey.

9. "For my own part, I wish the bald eagle had not been chosen as the representative of our country; he is a bird of bad moral character; he does not get his living honestly. You may have seen him perched on some dead tree, where, too lazy to fish for himself, he watches the labor of the fishing-hawk; and when that diligent bird has at length taken a fish, and is bearing it to his nest for the support of his mate and young ones, the bald eagle pursues him and takes it from him. With all this injustice he is never in good case, but, like those among men who live by sharping and robbing, he is generally poor, and often very lousy.

10. "Besides, he is a rank coward; the little king-bird, not bigger than a sparrow, attacks him boldly, and drives him out of the district. He is, therefore, by no means a proper emblem for the brave and honest Cincinnati of America, who have driven all the *king*-birds from our country, though exactly fit for that order of knights which the French call *chevaliers d'industrie*. I am, on this account, not displeased that the figure is not known as a bald eagle, but looks more like a turkey. For, in truth, the turkey is, in comparison, a much more respectable bird, and withal a true original native of America. Eagles have been found in all countries, but the turkey was peculiar to ours.

11. "He is, besides (though a little vain and silly, 'tis true, but not the worse emblem for that), a bird of courage, and would not hesitate to attack a grenadier of the British Guards, who should presume to invade his farm-yard with a *red* coat on."

PART XI.

OUR FOUR-FOOTED COMPANIONS.

THE PET OF THE HOUSEHOLD.

1. WEBSTER, in an early edition of his dictionary, goes out of his way to abuse the creature, and even makes himself little less than slanderous. "The domestic cat," he says, "is a deceitful animal, and, when enraged, extremely spiteful. It is kept in houses chiefly for the purpose of catching rats and mice."

2. Would a dog have done worse? In all the sixty thousand words of the English language, which, of course, the great lexicographer knew by heart, could he not find a couple of dozen that would have been more applicable, or at least more charitable? If he had been born as weak as pussy, and had found it as hard to escape kicks and pick up a living, might he not have grown up a bit of a diplomatist? I should like to know, also, whether he was not himself subject to be "extremely spiteful when enraged."

3. Then, too, "kept in houses chiefly for the purpose of catching rats and mice"! No account taken of the gamesome ways of kittens; of the pleasure derivable from the grateful purr, the gracious movements, the furry caresses; of the affection which man, woman, and child have lavished upon the most pettable of all pets. It is enough to

make one reject Webster's derivations, and throw overboard his new orthographies.

4. As a member of the living household which man has pleased himself in collecting, the cat is useful but not slavish. The bargain which he struck with us was not submission, as was the case with the dog, but alliance. "House me," he said, "smooth my back, give me a bed for my morning naps, and I'll kill your rats and purr to you." What right have we to demand slavishness? We are too ready to suppose that everything was made for man. Perhaps the feline intellect and sense of justice have reached the conclusion that cats were made for themselves. Have they not a right to be as egotistic as we?

5. It is estimated that the rats and mice of England annually consume grain enough to feed three millions of human beings; and if it were not for the incessant exertions of the cats, these rodents might root out the present population of the island, as the Saxons rooted out the Celtic Britons. Add to this salvation the innocent and home-like pleasure furnished; the amusing pranks of say one hundred thousand kittens; the multitudinous purrings and rubbings, and grave trickeries and expositions of instinct; the old ladies and invalids and lonesome ones whose lives are cheered; the children who are provided with a living doll. True, some birds suffer; but may there not be birds enough for all? On the whole, there must be a large balance due the cats.

6. In spite of slanders to the contrary, the animal is capable of affection for persons. I had one that used to walk up and down the room with me; another that ran about after me all over the house. A third, after a separation of five months, greeted me with extravagant demonstrations of joy, leaping into my lap, down again, up again, rolling over, tremulous from head to foot, and all the while purring to split his throat. A cat belonging to a

lady who died some years since was one of the most pathetic of mourners, insisting with affectionate persistence upon sitting by the body, wailing as if his heart would break, and remaining for a long time inconsolable. Instances of this sort are by no means uncommon.

7. It is true that, in general, the cat is fonder of places than of people. He likes the old home because he knows it thoroughly ; because he has investigated its every mouse-hole and studied the advantages of its every retreat from dogs and other enemies; because he, a weak animal, feels sure that he can there feed and protect himself. Moreover, his bump of locality is prodigious, as is shown by the ease with which he finds his way back to the familiar spot, though carried blindfold a long distance from it. A friend of mine transported a cat several times five miles from home, and dismissed it into the wide liberty of earth, only to find it at his house when he returned, or very shortly afterward.

8. Do cats have intellect ? Observe the patient intelligence with which he performs his special duty of watching for prey. He loves ease and warmth ; but he will sit for hours in the cold beside a mouse-hole ; and before he commenced his siege he had examined the whole room, to see if there was any other exit for the vermin ; he had effected a reconnoissance which would have done credit to a Mohawk scalp-hunter or an experienced general. During the last summer my two youthful cats accomplished such a slaughter of birds as made my heart ache, bringing in one or two nearly every day. Now it must require no little reflection, caution, and adroitness to enable an animal who has merely legs to catch one who has both legs and wings. If the reader doubts, let him try it, and, though he take a bag of salt with him, I wager that he does not bring home a robin. It was amusing to observe the plaintive mew of annoyance with which my

hunters watched a bird who was obviously beyond their reach.

9. Champfleury tells us of a cat who used to divide her game between her master and her kittens, only she always brought her rats to the former and her mice to the latter, judging that the larger creature needed and could manage the bigger mouthfuls. My Maltese opens a door which is ajar most judiciously; he does not put nose or foot into the opening, knowing that the former might get banged and the latter pinched; he places one paw against the obstacle, braces himself sidewise on the other three legs, and so pushes; the operation is admirable for caution and for calculation of the needed power.

10. In Greenville, South Carolina, I had the honor of knowing a magnificent tom, weighing eight pounds, who opened doors by leaping up, seizing the knob forcibly between his fore-paws, and turning it, his only defect in the matter being that he could not close the door after him. Some years ago a family residing in New Haven, Connecticut, was alarmed by what the servants supposed to be a ghost, and the lady of the house a thief. An outside door was repeatedly opened, no one entering but the cat. In spite of watching, nobody was discovered, and the mystery grew to be frightful. At last the ghost was caught, and it proved to be pussy. She had observed, she had reflected, she had drawn an inference; in other words, she had performed the distinct intellectual operations. The result was, that she knew how to open doors by leaping up to the latch and pressing her paw on the thumb-piece.

11. Champfleury relates another story which shows the feline power of observation and reasoning. A German baron had noticed that his cat was much interested in the mysteries of mirrors, looking at her own reflection in them, withdrawing, approaching, and scratching at the frames.

His mirrors being all set in pieces of furniture, and an obstacle being thereby put in the way of the animal's investigations, he bought for her especial use a toilet-glass, and placed it in the middle of the room. Pussy discovered it, walked up to it, and thus assured herself that it resembled the others. Next she rushed behind it repeatedly, each time running faster than before. Not catching a cat in this manner, she went to the edge of the mirror, and looked first along the rear and then along the front.

12. Her conclusion evidently was that, as this strange creature which she had seen was neither before the glass nor behind it, it must be inside. Sitting up on her hind legs, she stretched out her fore paws, and carefully felt the thickness of the plate, until she had satisfied herself that it was too thin to contain anything of the bigness of the cat. This fact established in her mind, she seemed to come to the decision that here was a phenomenon which was beyond the circle of her ideas, and which it was therefore useless for her to investigate; and, giving it up with a common-sense promptness worthy of the imitation of many human philosophers who have got beyond their depth, she walked away from the mirror, and never after was seen to look into one.
J. W. De Forest.

OUR CANINE SERVANTS.

1. AMONG all the lower animals, the dog has ever been considered the most genuine friend and faithful servant of man. Bred in the household and fed from the family table, he has apparently absorbed many human attributes, and in his domesticated state he is more widely different from his wild progenitors than any other animal. He has shown himself capable of instruction in a very remarkable degree, and the instruction of one generation has been

transmitted to the next in the form of inherited tendencies, until we have breeds of dogs differing from each other in appearance, temper, and habits to such an extent as to make it seem impossible that they could have had a common origin.

2. The intelligence displayed by dogs in the accomplishment of their purposes, and often in adapting means to ends in a new emergency, appears to differ from human reason in degree rather than in kind. The intellectual manifestations, however, are not very wide in their scope, and are mostly confined to the field of activity which distinguishes the breed. When the idea derived from inheritance takes full possession of them, for the time being it seems that nothing can divert them from the movements which this idea prompts. A hunting-dog on the track of game can not be turned aside, and, though usually quickly obedient to his master's voice, he now seems entirely oblivious to it, overmastered by the mighty instinct derived from his long line of ancestry. The shepherd's dog will not desert his charge even to get food to save him from starvation.

3. The dog's peculiar intellectual development, however, appears to be entirely of human origin. The primal instinct which led him to seek his food by hunting has been so modified by human training as to almost lose its original character, and in its place we find the diversified characteristics which now mark the species. Dogs left to themselves could not have developed in these various ways, human companionship and direction being necessary factors in the result.

4. In other ways the dog has shown a great superiority over the whole brute creation, and these are in affection for his human associates and in faithfulness to their interests. While dogs show great fondness for each other, the depth of their emotion is shown only toward their masters

and human friends. At times they seem to almost lose their animal propensities, and to be transformed into living embodiments of virtues which are usually considered essentially human. Thus, they show gratitude for favors received, fidelity to trusts committed to them, a sensitiveness which sometimes appears almost superhuman, and an absolute devotion which proves stronger than the love of life. We can here illustrate these points only in a few directions.

5. All dogs, more or less, are susceptible of being taught, and teachability infers culture of the brain, the possibility of an enlarged intelligence. Without training, a pointer would point at any kind of vermin as readily as at the game of which the sportsman is in quest, but a well-trained pointer will make no such mistake. Without training, he would only stand pointing for a few seconds, and then run in upon the game and put it up; but a well-trained pointer waits till he receives the word of command, when his master has come near enough to use his gun.

6. It may be in part through instinct that a shepherd's dog performs many of the important services which he renders to his master in the driving and tending of sheep; but it can not be altogether through instinct, for the best shepherd's dogs are always those which have been carefully trained. Even that which the shepherd's dog does without training, and which seems natural to him from his puppyhood, is probably very much to be ascribed to what is called hereditary instinct, the fruit of the training of many successive generations. But all can not be ascribed to instinct, whether natural to the race, or acquired and become hereditary. How can any one think so who has observed a shepherd's dog at his work, and marked his prompt obedience to the command of his master—how readily he understands each word or sign, and at once hastens to do what he is bidden?—perhaps to bring in a number of sheep from a distance, which he accomplishes

very quickly, and yet without hurrying them too much, for he is very careful not to do them any harm; and his barking, although sharp, is not angry, nor do the sheep seem to think so, or to be in the least degree alarmed, for they also have profited by experience, and they know him and his ways.

7. Let the object of the shepherd be to get sheep through a gate: the dog evidently perceives it at once, and knows what to do—to bark behind the sheep, to run before them and bark, to drive them to the gate, and to prevent their passing it. More remarkable still, and most decidedly an evidence of the possession of reason, is the fact that a good shepherd's dog will assist a sheep to rise when it has fallen, rolled over on its back, and can not get up again, because, in consequence of its thick fleece, it can not get a foot to the ground. This often happens, especially on hill-pastures, in the latter part of spring and beginning of summer, before the sheep-shearing time, and the shepherd must visit his flock several times a day, lest the sheep that have rolled over on their backs should die. But his dog saves him much walking and fatigue, scouring over the hill for him, and, as soon as he finds a sheep on its back, proceeding to turn it over with his muzzle, till it gets its feet to the ground so that it is able to rise.

8. The shepherd's dog, or, at all events, the *collie* of the south of Scotland, which I take to be the most refined and cultivated breed of shepherd's dog, shows himself also very sensible of affront, and vexed by it. He has a ready appetite for oat-cakes—oatmeal in one form or other, but mostly in that of porridge, being a chief part of his food, as it is of his master's; and he will at any time gladly receive a little bit of oat-cake; but let any one hold out to him a very large piece, and he evidently thinks it a cruel jest, feels himself insulted, turns away his head, and will not look at the cake, far less accept it. We know of no

other kind of dog that so generally shows his fastidiousness. We have tried the experiment with collies, and always with one result: they would have nothing to do with a very large piece of bread.

9. No wonder that the sheep-dog is a favorite of his master, and is treated as a kind of humble friend. He is not turned into a kennel nor into an outhouse when he comes home from his work; his place is at the fireside, where he often wags his tail and puts on a very intelligent look, as if he understood some part of the conversation that takes place. Certainly "Collie" knows well enough when he is spoken of, and dogs of some other kinds evidently do so too. They know when they are alluded to in terms of praise and when with blame; in the former case, giving unmistakable signs of delight; in the latter, hanging their heads and looking ashamed.

10. It is worthy to be observed concerning the shepherd's dog that no severity is ever used in his training. The shepherd has no dog-whip. A single punishment, such as a gamekeeper often finds or thinks it necessary to inflict on a pointer, would spoil a collie altogether and make him worthless for life. He would not resent it by turning savagely on his master, but he would at once become broken-spirited and inert. Words of commendation or of censure are all that he needs, all that suits his nature. The same thing may be observed in animals of some other kinds—as in the elephant and in the finest breeds of horses.

11. The fine feelings of the Scottish shepherd's dog, and his capability of having his feelings deeply wounded, are sometimes very strikingly illustrated. The grandfather of the present writer had an excellent collie, by name Wattie, which was a great favorite, and greatly attached to him and to all the family. When the dog grew old and feeble, it was thought necessary to get another one; but, on the new dog's arrival, poor old Wattie left his

place at the fireside and went out to a green bank beside a pond, where he lay down, and no persuasions could induce him to return to the house. He wagged his tail a little when kindly spoken to, but he continued to lie in the same spot, and would not rise. He refused food, and in two days he was dead. He seems to have felt that his day was over, that his services were no longer valued, and his old place no longer his, and took it all to signify that his time was come to die. His death, however, seems not to have been the result of mere old age, but to have been hastened by his wounded feelings.

12. The Ettrick shepherd gives the following graphic account of his dog Sirrah : " He was, beyond all comparison, the best dog I ever saw. He was of a surly, unsocial temper, disdaining all flattery ; he refused to be caressed, but his attentions to my commands and interests will never again, perhaps, be equaled by any of the canine race. When I first saw him a drover was leading him by a rope ; he was both lean and hungry, and far from being a beautiful animal, for he was almost all black, and had a grim face, striped with dark brown. The man had bought him of a boy somewhere on the border for three shillings, and had fed him very ill on the journey. I thought I discovered a sort of sullen intelligence in his countenance, notwithstanding his dejected and forlorn appearance. I gave the drover a guinea for him, and I believe there was never a guinea so well laid out, at least I am satisfied I never laid one out to so good a purpose.

13. "He was scarcely a year old, and knew so little of herding that he had never turned a sheep in his life ; but, as soon as he discovered that it was his duty to do so, and that it obliged me, I can never forget with what anxiety and eagerness he learned his different evolutions. He would try every way deliberately, till he found out what I wanted him to do, and when once I made him understand

a direction, he never forgot or mistook it again. Well as I knew him, he often astonished me; for, when hard pressed in accomplishing the task that he was put to, he had expedients of the moment that bespoke a great share of the reasoning faculty.

14. "On one occasion about seven hundred lambs, which were under his care at weaning time, broke away at midnight and scampered, in three divisions, across the hills, in spite of all I and my assistant could do to keep them together. The night was so dark that we could not see Sirrah, but he heard me lament their absence in words which of all others were sure to set him most on the alert, and, without more ado, he silently set off in quest of the recreant flock. We spent the whole night in scouring the hills for miles around, but neither of the lambs or Sirrah could we obtain the slightest trace. It was the most extraordinary circumstance that ever happened in the annals of pastoral life. At dawn we set out on our return, with the comforting assurance that the whole flock of lambs was lost, and that we did not know what had become of one of them.

15. "On our way home, however, we discovered a lot of lambs at the bottom of a deep ravine, and the indefatigable Sirrah, standing in front of them, looking around for some relief, but still true to his charge. The sun was then up, and, when we first came in view, we concluded that it was one of the divisions which Sirrah had been unable to manage until he came to that cómmanding situation. But what was our astonishment when we discovered that not one lamb of the whole flock was missing. The charge was left entirely to himself from midnight until the rising sun; and if all the shepherds in the forest had been there to assist him, they could not have effected it with greater propriety. All that I can say further is that I never felt so grateful to any creature under the sun as I did to my honest Sirrah that morning.

16. "It is a curious fact in the history of these animals that the most useless of the breed have often the greatest degree of sagacity in trifling and useless matters. An exceedingly good sheep-dog attends to nothing else but that particular branch of business to which he is bred. His whole capacity is exerted and exhausted upon it, and he is of little avail in miscellaneous matters; whereas a very indifferent cur, bred about the house and accustomed to assist in everything, will often put the more noble breed to disgrace in these services. If one calls out, for instance, that the cows are in the corn, or the hens are in the garden, the house-collie needs no other hint, but runs and turns them out. The shepherd's dog knows not what is astir, and, if he is called out in a hurry for such work, all that he will do is to break to the hill and rear himself up on end to see if no sheep are running away.

17. "A well-bred sheep-dog, if coming hungry from the hills, and getting into the milk-house, would, most likely, think of nothing else than filling himself with cream. Not so his lowly brother; he has been bred at home to form higher principles of honor. I have known such to lie, night and day, among from ten to twenty pans full of milk, and never once break the cream of one of them with the tip of his tongue, nor would he suffer cat, rat, or any other creature to touch it. This latter sort, too, are far more acute in taking up what is said in a family."

18. Sir Walter Scott says: "The wisest dog I ever had was what is called the bull-dog terrier. I taught him to understand a great many words, insomuch that I am positive that the communication between the canine species and ourselves might be greatly enlarged. Camp one day bit the baker who was bringing bread to the family. I beat him, and explained the enormity of his offense, after which, to the last moment of his life, he never heard the least allusion to the story, in whatever voice or tone it was

mentioned, without getting up and retiring into the darkest corner of the room with the greatest appearance of distress. Then if you said, 'The baker was well paid,' or 'The baker was not hurt after all,' Camp came forth from his hiding-place, capered, and barked and rejoiced."

Chambers's Journal.

CONSCIENCE IN ANIMALS.

1. ONE of the prevailing theories in regard to conscience is that it is the resultant of intelligence combined with the instinct of sociability and the emotion of sympathy, and that its germs may be found in the lower animals. If this be true, we must look for its manifestations in the three groups of dogs, elephants, and monkeys, where alone we find the conditions essential to any considerable development of the moral sense.

2. I need not say anything about the intelligence or the sociability of these animals, for it is proverbial that there are no animals so intelligent or more social. It is necessary, however, to say a few words about sympathy. In the case of dogs, sympathy exists in an extraordinary degree. I have myself seen the life of a terrier saved by another dog which staid in the same house with him, and with which he had always lived in a state of bitter enmity. Yet, when the terrier was one day attacked by a large dog, which shook him by the back, and would certainly have killed him, his habitual enemy rushed to the rescue, and, after saving the terrier, had great difficulty in getting away himself.

3. Dr. Hooker informs me that an elephant, which he was riding in India, became so deeply bogged that he remained stuck fast until next day, when he was extracted

by means of ropes. Under such circumstances elephants seize with their trunks any object, dead or alive, to place under their knees, to prevent their sinking deeper in the mud; and the driver was dreadfully afraid lest the animal should have seized Dr. Hooker and crushed him to death. But the driver himself, as Dr. Hooker was assured, ran no risk. This forbearance, under an emergency so dreadful for a heavy animal, is a wonderful proof of noble fidelity.

4. Many cases of sympathy in monkeys might be given, but I shall confine myself to stating one which I myself witnessed at the Zoölogical Gardens. A year or two ago there was an Arabian baboon and an Anubis baboon confined in one cage, adjoining that which contained a dog-headed baboon. The Anubis baboon passed its hand through the wires of the partition in order to purloin a nut which the large dog-headed baboon had left within reach—expressly, I believe, that it might act as a bait. The Anubis baboon very well knew the danger he ran, for he waited until his bulky neighbor had turned his back upon the nut with the appearance of having forgotten all about it. The dog-headed baboon, however, was all the time slyly looking round with the corner of his eye, and no sooner was the arm of his victim well within his cage than he sprang with astonishing rapidity and caught the retreating hand in his mouth. The cries of the Anubis baboon quickly brought the keeper to the rescue, when, by dint of a good deal of physical persuasion, the dog-headed baboon was induced to let go his hold. The Anubis baboon then retired to the middle of his cage, moaning piteously, and holding the injured hand against his chest while he rubbed it with the other one.

5. The Arabian baboon now approached him from the top part of the cage, and, while making a soothing sound, very expressive of sympathy, folded the sufferer in its arms —exactly as a mother would her child under similar cir-

cumstances. It must be stated, also, that this expression of sympathy had a decidedly quieting effect upon the sufferer, his moans becoming less piteous so soon as he was infolded in the arms of his comforter; and the manner in which he laid his cheek upon the bosom of his friend was as expressive as anything could be of sympathy appreciated. This really affecting spectacle lasted a considerable time, and, while watching it, I felt that, even had it stood alone, it would in itself have been sufficient to prove the essential identity of some of the noblest among human emotions with those of the lower animals.

6. I have a setter just now which has been made a pet of since a puppy. As he has a very fine nose, and is at liberty to go wherever he pleases, he often finds bits of food which he very well knows he has no right to take. If the food he finds happens to be of a dainty description, his conscientious scruples are overcome by the temptations of appetite; but if the food should be of a less palatable kind, he generally carries it to me in order to obtain my permission to eat it. Now, as no one ever beats or even scolds this dog for stealing, his only object in thus asking permission to eat what he finds must be that of quieting his conscience. It should be added that when he brings stolen property to me it does not always follow that he is allowed to keep it.

7. One other curious fact may here be mentioned about this dog. Although naturally a very vivacious animal, and, when out for a walk with myself or any other young person, perpetually ranging about in search of game, yet if taken out for a walk by an elderly person he keeps close to heel all the time—pacing along with a slow step and sedate manner, as different as possible from that which is natural to him. This curious behavior is quite spontaneous on his part, and appears to rise from his sense of the respect that is due to age.

8. A terrier I once owned used to be very fond of catch-

ing flies upon the window-panes, and if ridiculed when unsuccessful, was evidently much annoyed. On one occasion, in order to see what he would do, I purposely laughed immoderately every time he failed. It so happened that he did so several times in succession—partly, I believe, in consequence of my laughing—and eventually he became so distressed that he positively *pretended* to catch the fly, going through all the appropriate actions with his lips and tongue, and afterward rubbing the ground with his neck as if to kill the victim; he then looked up at me with a triumphant air of success. So well was the whole process simulated that I should have been quite deceived had I not seen that the fly was still upon the window. Accordingly, I drew his attention to this fact, as well as to the absence of anything upon the floor; and, when he saw that his hypocrisy had been detected, he slunk away under some furniture, evidently very much ashamed of himself.

9. The terrier in question far surpassed any animal I ever knew in the keen sensitiveness of his feelings, and he was never beaten in his life. One day he was shut up in a room by himself while everybody in the house went out. Seeing his friends from the window as they departed, he appears to have been overcome by a paroxysm of rage, for, when I returned, I found that he had torn all the bottom of the window-curtains to shreds. When I first opened the door, he jumped about as dogs do under similar circumstances, having, in his joy to see me, apparently forgotten the damage he had done. But when, without speaking, I picked up one of the torn shreds of the curtains, the terrier gave a howl, and, rushing out of the room, ran upstairs screaming as loudly as he was able.

10. It is remarkable, also, that this animal's sensitiveness was not only of a selfish kind, but extended itself in sympathy for others. Whenever he saw a man striking a dog, whether in the house or outside, near at hand or at a

distance, he used to rush to the protection of his fellow, snarling and snapping in a most threatening way. Again, when driving with me in a dog-cart, he always used to seize the sleeve of my coat every time I touched the horse with the whip.

11. I had had this dog for several years, and had never —even in his puppyhood—known him to steal. On the contrary, he used to make an excellent guard to protect property from other animals, servants, etc., even though these were his best friends. Nevertheless, on one occasion he was very hungry, and in the room where I was reading and he was sitting there was, within easy reach, a savory mutton-chop. I was greatly surprised to see him stealthily remove this chop and take it under a sofa. However, I pretended not to observe what had occurred, and waited to see what would happen next. For fully a quarter of an hour this terrier remained under the sofa without making a sound, but doubtless enduring an agony of contending feelings. Eventually, however, conscience came off victorious, for, emerging from his place of concealment and carrying in his mouth the stolen chop, he came across the room and laid the tempting morsel at my feet. The moment he dropped the stolen property he bolted again under the sofa, and from this retreat no coaxing could charm him for several hours afterward. Moreover, when during that time he was spoken to or patted, he always turned away his head in a ludicrously conscience-stricken manner.

12. I have seen this dog escort a donkey which had baskets on its back filled with apples. Although the dog did not know that he was being observed by anybody, he did his duty with the utmost faithfulness, for every time the donkey turned back its head to take an apple out of the baskets, the dog snapped at its nose; and such was his watchfulness that, although his companion was keenly

desirous of tasting some of the fruit, he never allowed him to get a single apple during the half hour they were left together. I have also seen this terrier protecting meat from other terriers (his sons), which lived in the same house with him, and with which he was on the very best of terms. More curious still, I have seen him seize my wristbands while they were being worn by a friend to whom I temporarily lent them.

G. J. Romanes.

PUSS WITH A MISSION.

1. ONE of the greatest satisfactions of my boyhood consisted in watching the warfare carried on against the canine race by a little and lissome black tabby who abode in the principal store in the village. She seemed to be crazy to avenge the wrongs of her kind. She went at every dog-skin on four legs the moment she saw it; disparity of size or numbers was a matter of no consideration.

2. On one occasion a cur rolled howling out of the store in agony. Two other canines, who had heard the noise of the conflict, arrived simultaneously, whereupon the black paws struck out right, left, and forward, one, two, three, with the quickness of rapiers, the result being a victorious cat in the middle and three yelping fugitives taking three different roads for safety. The miller's black and tan terrier, having been once pitched bleeding down a staircase, conceived such a terror of this fierce avenger of centuries of wrong that, when his master came to the store for groceries, he could not be wheedled nearer than the blacksmith's shop, an eighth of a mile away, but remained there, barking anxiously, until the imprudent human should return.

3. As for the postmaster's dog—a long, lean, and frowzy

spaniel, much given to pointing and setting at stray bones and swill-pails—scarcely a week passed that he was not caught in the store-keeper's garden and soundly scratched for his poachings. Hurry-scurry through the squash-vines and green corn; dog "a leetle ahead," but pussy close on his bushy tail; now the fugitive reaches the board fence and squats for a leap; in that moment a streak of furry lightning mounts his back and draws a yelp; away now to another hopeful corner, and another, and another; a lucky bound at last, and then a straight race for life; of course the longest legs win it.

4. This feline fencer was tremendous on eyes; she lunged right at them and held on like a tiger. I have seen a short-legged, stout-bodied, obstinate cur whirl her three times around his head, with her claws fastened in the skin of his stolid physiognomy. She was pitched a couple of yards at last, and with great violence; but the moment she struck earth she was up like Antæus, and at him again. Of all the dogs in the neighboring country, only big Pomp Wheeler was ever known to make Pussy Lewis turn her tail. Both these heroic combatants are now with Hector and Julius Cæsar. Peace to their *manes*, such as they had!

J. W. De Forest.

CANINE JUSTICE.

1. A CASE which occurred at a fashionable watering-place on the east coast of Ireland some years ago exhibits the remarkable sagacity displayed by a dog in devising and administering justice. The jetty which stretched along the small harbor was at that time used as a promenade by the *élite* among the sojourners on the coast, where, after the heat of the long summer days, they regaled themselves with the fresh evening breezes wafted in from the sea.

2. Among the frequenters of this fashionable resort was a gentleman of some position, who was the owner of a fine Newfoundland dog which inherited the time-honored possessions of that noble breed—very great power and facility in swimming; and, at the period of the evening when the jetty was most crowded with promenaders, his master delighted to put this animal through a series of aquatic performances for the entertainment of the assembled spectators. Amusement being at a premium on the coast, these nightly performances grew into something like an "institution," and the brave "Captain"—for such was his name—speedily became a universal favorite on the jetty.

3. It happened, however, that among the new arrivals on the coast there came a certain major in her majesty's army, accompanied by two bull-dogs of unusual size and strength, and of great value; but, value in a bull-dog being inversely proportionate to its beauty, the appearance of the major and his dogs excited no very enthusiastic pleasure among the æsthetic strollers on the jetty. On the first night on which the major presented himself nothing unusual occurred, and Captain dived and swam as before. But on the second evening the brave old favorite was walking quietly behind his master down the jetty, when, as they were passing by the major and his dogs, one of these ugly brutes flew at Captain and caught him by the neck in such a way as to render his great size utterly useless for his defense. A violent struggle ensued, but the bull-dog came off the victor, for he stuck to his foe like a leech, and could only be forced to release his hold by the insertion of a bar of iron between his teeth.

4. The indignation of the by-standers against the major was, of course, very great; and its fervor was not a little increased when they saw the poor Captain wending his way homeward bleeding, and bearing all the marks of defeat. Some two or three evenings after this occurrence,

when Captain again made his appearance on the jetty, he looked quite crestfallen, bore his tail between his legs, and stuck closely to the heels of his master. That evening passed away quietly, and the next, and the next, and so on for about a week—Captain still bearing the aspect of mourning.

5. But one evening about eight or ten days after the above encounter, as the major was marching in his usual pompous manner along the jetty, accompanied by his dogs, something attracted his attention in the water, and, walking to the very edge of the jetty, he stood for a moment looking down into the sea. Scarcely had the two bull-dogs taken up their stand beside their master when Captain, seizing the opportunity for which he had so long looked, rushed at his former conqueror, and, catching him by the back of the neck, jumped off the jetty, with his foe in his mouth, down some twenty feet or more into the sea. Once in the water, the power of his enemy was crippled, while Captain was altogether in his own element; and, easily overcoming all efforts at resistance, he succeeded in resolutely keeping the bull-dog's head under water.

6. The excitement on the shore was, of course, intense. The major shouted, and called out: "My dog! my beautiful dog! Will no one save him?" But no one seemed at all inclined to interfere, or to risk his life for the ugly dog. At length the major called out: "I'll give fifty pounds to any one who will save my dog!" and soon afterward a boat which lay at some little distance pulled up to the rescue. Even then, however, it was only by striking Captain on the head with the oars that he could be forced to release his victim, which was taken into the boat quite senseless from exhaustion and suffocation, and was with difficulty brought to itself again. Captain, on the other hand, swam in triumph to the shore, amid the plaudits of the spectators, who shared, in sympathy at least, his well-earned honors of revenge.

Chambers's Journal.

HELPING A FRIEND.

1. A GENTLEMAN of wealth and position in London had, some years ago, a country-house and farm about sixty miles from the metropolis. At this country residence he kept a number of dogs, and among them a very large mastiff and a Scotch terrier; and, at the close of one of his summer residences in the country, he resolved to bring this terrier with him to London for the winter season. There being no railway to that particular part of the country, the dog traveled with the servants in a post-carriage, and, on his arrival at the town-house, was brought out to the stable, where a large Newfoundland dog was kept as a watch-dog. This latter individual looked with anything but pleasure on the arrival of the little intruder from the country; and, consequently, the Scotch terrier had not been very long in his new home when this canine master of the stable attacked him, and, in the language of human beings, gave him a sound thrashing.

2. The little animal could, of course, never hope by himself to chastise his host for this inhospitable welcome, but he determined that by some agency chastisement should come. Accordingly, he lay very quiet that night in a remote corner of the stable, but when morning had fully shone forth he was nowhere to be found. Search was made for him, as the phrase says, high and low, but without success; and the conclusion reluctantly arrived at was, that he had been stolen. On the third morning after his disappearance, however, he again showed himself in London, but this time not alone; for, to the amazement of every one, he entered the stable attended by the big mastiff from Kent.

3. This great brute had no sooner arrived than he flew at the Newfoundland dog, who had so badly treated his

little terrier friend, and a severe contest ensued, which the little terrier himself, seated at a short distance, viewed with the utmost dignity and satisfaction. The result of the battle was, that the mastiff came off the conqueror, and gave his opponent a tremendous beating. When he had quite satisfied himself as to the result, this great avenger from Kent scarcely waited to receive the recognition of his master, who had been sent for immediately on the dog's arrival, but at once marched out of the stable, to the door of which the little terrier accompanied him, and was seen no more.

4. Some few days afterward, however, the gentleman received a letter from his steward in the country, informing him of the sudden appearance of the terrier there, and his as sudden disappearance along with the large mastiff; and stating that the latter had remained away three or four days, during which they had searched in vain for him, but had just then returned home again. It then, of course, became quite clear that the little dog, finding himself unable to punish the town bully, had thought of his "big brother" in the country, had traveled over the sixty miles which separated them in order to gain his assistance, and had recounted to him his grievance; it was plain, also, that the mastiff had consented to come and avenge his old friend, had traveled with him to London, and, having fulfilled his promise, had returned home, leaving the little fellow free from annoyance in the future.

Chambers's Journal.

PIERROT THE FAITHFUL.

1. AND now, my dear readers, let me tell you a story of another friend of mine, who was a donkey, but not a *savant*. His name was Pierrot.

2. The frost was silvering the trees of the Park Monceau with dull, white powder, like the head of a marquis of the old *régime*. It was in front of the rotunda, and nine o'clock in the morning. The sun hung in the fog like a globe of fire, but cast forth no beams. The wind was cruel to the poor world. People walked rapidly along the Boulevard de Courcelles; women veiled their faces, and men drew their heads inside their collars. It was a day when a lover's sigh would have frozen in the air.

3. I was hurrying by like everybody else. A female rag-picker, pale and famished, led by the bridle a poor little donkey, which seemed a hundred years old, and which dragged a poor little cart, full of the rubbish of the street: rags, broken bottles, torn papers, worn-out skillets, crusts of bread—the thousand nothings which are the fortune of the rag-pickers. The woman had done good work since midnight, but the donkey was ready to drop. He stopped short, as if he had made up his mind to go no farther. His legs trembled and threatened a fall. He hung his head with resignation, as if awaiting the stroke of death.

4. The sight touched and arrested me. A man would have cursed and beaten the poor beast to rouse him; the woman looked at him with an eye of motherly pity. The donkey returned the look, as if saying, "You see it is all over. I have done my best for you, night after night, because I saw your misery was greater than mine. You have treated me well, sharing your bread with me, and your neighbors' oats when you could get them; but I am dying at last."

5. The woman looked at him and said, gently, "Come, come, dear Pierrot, do not leave me here." She lightened the load by taking out a basket of broken bottles. "Come, now," she said, as if talking to a child. "You can get along nicely now." She put her shoulder to the wheel, but the donkey did not move. He knew that he had not

strength to walk to St. Ouen, his wretched home. She still coaxed him. "How do you think we can get along this way, Pierrot? To be sure, I could drag the cart. But I can't put you in it, and you would be ashamed to be

Pierrot the Faithful.

dragged after it." The donkey raised his ears, but no move.

6. I was going to speak to her, when she ran into the nearest wine-shop. The donkey followed her with anxious eyes; he seemed fearful that he would die without his mis-

tress. He was so little you would have taken him at a distance for a Pyrenean dog. He had grown gray in the harness. A few tufts of gray hair remained here and there on his emaciated body. He looked like a mountain burned bare in many places. His resigned air showed a mind free from worldly vanities. He was far past the age when one strikes attitudes. He was almost transparent in his leanness. But his face was all the more expressive. It had something almost human in its intelligence and goodness. Why had he been condemned to such suffering? Was it the expiation of a former life passed in luxurious orgies?

7. The rag-picker soon returned, bringing a piece of bread and a lump of sugar. The donkey turned and showed his teeth, like old piano-keys. But, although it was his breakfast-time, he had no more strength in his mouth than in his legs. She gave him the sugar. He took it as if to oblige her, but dropped it again, and the same with the bread.

8. "Ah! what shall I do?" said the rag-picker. She thought no more of her cart. She was full of anxiety for her friend Pierrot. "Pierrot!" she cried again. Two great tears came to her eyes. She took his head in her arms and kissed him like a child. The caress did what nothing else could do. The donkey roused himself, and brayed as in his best days. I feared it was only his swan-song. I approached, and said to the woman: "You seem to be in trouble."

9. "Oh!" she said, crying, "if you knew how I love this beast. I saved him from the butchers four years ago. In those days I had only a hod. I have raised seven children with my hook. The father is gone and one other, and my eldest daughter was taken a fortnight ago. My worst grief was that I had to take one to the Foundlings. I had eleven in all; four of them died. It's no use; you can't take good care of them when you work in the streets

all night. This little donkey has been my only consolation. He was better company than my husband. He never got drunk, and never beat me; and I never beat him. Did I, Pierrot?"

10. The poor little beast seemed to share in the conversation. He half raised his ears and assented. One of my friends passed by, and asked me what I was doing. "I am making a new friend."—"He may be witty, but he is not handsome."—"I find him admirable, and I would like to see you in his place. He has been out since midnight. Here, you want to help me in a work of charity?"—"With all my heart."—"Very well; let us buy this donkey and put him on the retired list. This good woman will take care of him."

11. The rag-picker looked at us severely, fearing we were laughing at her. But when she saw the shine of the louis-d'or she smiled. "How much did Pierrot cost?"—"Ten francs."—"Well, you go back to the abattoir and buy another donkey, and take care of this one." I gave my card to the woman, and said good-by to her and the donkey. The miracle was complete. The donkey started off in high spirits, the woman pushing the cart from behind.

12. That evening the woman came to me in tears. I understood at once. "Oh! sir, he is gone."—"Poor Pierrot!"—"Yes, sir, we got to St. Ouen one way or another; but when he came in sight of our hut he fell on his knees. I tried to raise him, but this time it was all over. My children came running and crying. They talked to him and kissed him. He looked at them so sadly as to break our hearts. I tell you there are lots of people in the world not worth half so much as poor Pierrot. Think of it: he wanted to die at home after finishing his day's work." Like a soldier who dies after firing his last cartridge.

13. The rag-picker opened her hand, and I saw the money I had given her in the morning. "Here is your

hundred francs, sir." I do not know whether I most admired her or the donkey—the donkey who did his duty to death, or the woman more delicate than our charity.

Arsene Houssaye.

EMOTIONAL EXPRESSION.

1. THE first principle upon which the emotional expression of animals depends is, that the muscular movement which gives the expression is serviceable to the animal at the time it is made. Among the carnivora, some crouch to remain concealed until the game is within reach of their spring; others crouch to get out of sight altogether; some boldly advance to the attack, every muscle and nerve connected with their organs of attack in extreme tension; and others await the attack, the nerves and muscles connected with the organs of defense in equal tension. The various attitudes assumed are necessary for the best performance of the act which is to succeed, and the attitude becomes the expression of the mood of the animal at the time.

2. The second principle of expression is that of antithesis. Certain states of mind lead to certain movements which are of service. When a directly opposite state of mind is induced, there is a strong and involuntary tendency to make movements of a directly opposite nature, though these have never been of any service. We can best illustrate these principles by referring to the actions of the dog and cat, which can be observed by all.

3. When a dog approaches a strange dog or man in a hostile frame of mind, he walks upright and very stiffly; his head is slightly raised, or not much lowered; the tail is held erect and quite rigid; the hairs bristle, especially along the neck and back; the pricked ears are directed forward, and the eyes have a fixed stare. These actions fol-

low from the dog's intention to attack his enemy, and are thus intelligible. As he prepares to spring upon his enemy he utters a savage growl, the canine teeth are uncovered, and the ears are pressed close backward on the head.

4. Let us now suppose that the dog suddenly discovers that the man whom he is approaching is not a stranger, but his master; and let it be observed how completely and instantaneously his whole bearing is reversed. In-

A Fierce Dog.

stead of walking upright, the body sinks downward, or even crouches, and is thrown into flexuous movements; his tail, instead of being held stiff and upright, is lowered and wagged from side to side; his hair instantly becomes smooth; his ears are depressed and drawn backward, but not closely to the head: and his lips hang loosely. From the drawing back of the ears, the eyelids become elongated, and the eyes no longer appear round and staring. It should be added that the animal is at such times in an excited condition of joy, and the nerve-force will be generated in excess, which naturally leads to actions of some kind.

5. Not one of the above movements, so clearly expressive of affection, is of the least service to the animal. They are explicable, as far as I can see, solely from being in complete opposition or antithesis to the attitude and movements which, from intelligible causes, are assumed when a dog intends to fight, and which, consequently, are expressive of

An Affectionate Dog.

anger. It is not a little difficult to represent by pictures affection in a dog while caressing its master, for the very essence of the expression lies in the wagging of the tail and in the continuous flexuous movements of the body.

6. I will here give one instance of this antithesis in expression. I formerly possessed a large dog, who, like every other dog, was much pleased to go out walking. He showed his pleasure by trotting gravely before me with high steps, head much raised, moderately erected ears, and a tail carried aloft, but not stiffly. Not far from my house a

path branches off to the right, leading to the hot-house which I used often to visit for a few moments to look at my experimental plants. This was always a great disappointment to the dog, as he did not know whether I would continue my walk; and the instantaneous and complete change of expression which came over him as soon as my body swerved in the least toward the path—and I sometimes tried this as an experiment—was laughable.

7. His look of dejection was known to every member of the family, and was called his hot-house face. This consisted in the head drooping much, the whole body sinking a little and remaining motionless, the ears and tail falling suddenly down; but the tail was by no means wagged. With the falling of his ears and of his great chaps, the eyes became much changed in appearance, and I fancied they looked less bright. His aspect was that of piteous, hopeless dejection; and it was the more laughable as the cause was so slight. Every detail in his attitude was in complete opposition to his former joyful yet dignified bearing, and I can explain it in no other way except through this principle of antithesis.

8. We will now turn to the cat. When this animal is threatened by a dog, it arches its back in a surprising manner, erects its hair, opens its mouth and spits. We are not here concerned with this well-known attitude, expressive of terror and anger combined; we wish to observe that which expresses anger alone. This is not often seen, but may be observed when two cats are fighting; and I have seen it well exhibited by a savage cat when plagued by a boy. The attitude is almost exactly the same as that of the tiger disturbed and growling over his food, which every one must have beheld in menageries.

9. The animal assumes a crouching position, with the body extended; and the whole tail, or the tip alone, is lashed or curled from side to side. The hair is not in the

least erect. Thus far, the attitude and movements are nearly the same as when the animal is prepared to spring on its prey, and when, no doubt, it feels savage. But when preparing to fight there is this difference: the ears are closely pressed backward; the mouth is partially opened, showing the teeth; the forefeet are occasionally struck out with protruded claws; and the animal occasionally utters a fierce growl. These actions naturally express the intent of attacking the enemy.

A Cat, Savage, and ready to Fight.

10. Let us now look at a cat in a directly opposite frame of mind, while feeling affectionate and caressing her master, and mark how opposite her attitude is in every respect. She now stands upright, with her back slightly arched, which makes her hair appear rather rough, but it does not bristle; her tail, instead of being extended and lashed from side to side, is held quite stiff, and perpendicularly upward; her ears are erect and pointed; her mouth is closed; and she rubs against her master with a purr instead of a growl.

11. Let it further be observed how widely different is the whole bearing of an affectionate cat from that of a dog when, with his body crouching and flexuous, and ears depressed, he caresses his master. This contrast in the attitudes of these two carnivorous animals, under the same pleased and affectionate frame of mind, can be explained, as it appears to me, solely by their movements standing in complete antithesis to those which are naturally assumed when these animals feel savage and are prepared either to fight or to seize their prey.

An Affectionate Cat.

12. In these cases of the cat and the dog there is every reason to believe that the gestures, both of hostility and affection, are innate or inherited; for they are almost identically the same in the different races of the species, and in all the individuals of the same race both young and old. *Charles Darwin.*

TO FLUSH, MY DOG.

1. Loving friend, the gift of one
Who her own true faith hath run

Through thy lower nature ; *
Be my benediction said
With my hand upon thy head,
    Gentle fellow-creature !

2. Underneath my stroking hand,
Startled eyes of hazel bland,
    Kindling, growing larger,
Up thou leapest with a spring,
Full of prank and curveting,
    Leaping like a charger.

3. Leap ! thy broad tail waves a light ;
Leap ! thy slender feet are bright,
    Canopied in fringes.
Leap ! those tasseled ears of thine
Flicker strangely, fair and fine,
    Down their golden inches.

4. Yes, my pretty, sportive friend,
Little is 't to such an end
    That I praise thy rareness !
Other dogs may be thy peers,
Haply in those drooping ears
    And this glossy fairness.

5. But of thee it shall be said,
This dog watched beside a bed
    Day and night unweary—
Watched within a curtained room,
Where no sunbeam broke the gloom
    Round the sick and dreary.

6. Other dogs in thymy dew
Tracked the hares, and followed through

---

* This dog was the gift of my dear and admired friend, Miss Mitford.

Sunny moor or meadow ;
This dog only crept and crept,
Next a languid cheek that slept,
  Sharing in the shadow.

7. Other dogs of loyal cheer
Bounded at the whistle clear,
  Up the woodside hieing ;
This dog only watched, in reach
Of a faintly uttered speech,
  Or a louder sighing.

8. And if one or two quick tears
Dropped upon his glossy ears,
  Or a sigh came double—
Up he sprang in eager haste,
Fawning, fondling, breathing fast,
  In a tender trouble.

9. And this dog was satisfied
If a pale, thin hand would glide
  Down his dewlaps sloping,
Which he pushed his nose within,
After platforming his chin
  On the palm left open.

10. This dog, if a friendly voice
Called him now to blither choice
  Than such a chamber keeping,
"Come out," praying from the door,
Presseth backward as before,
  Up against me leaping.

11. Therefore to this dog will I,
Tenderly, not scornfully,
  Render praise and favor :
With my hand upon his head,
Is my benediction said,
  Therefore, and for ever.

Mrs. Browning.

PART XII.

OUR FOUR-FOOTED NEIGHBORS.

HOW RATS MANAGE.

1. It is easy to show that the rat is one of the wisest of animals. Just think how closely he sticks to man, though man tries day and night to get rid of him. Rats always stay with us, never are stained, always look sleek and comfortable, and always seem to feel more at home in our houses than we ourselves feel. What seems more hopeless than a rat on board a ship, with the ocean all around him, and not a friend to protect him, and every human being in the vessel ready to kill him if he shows his head? And yet rats thrive on board ship better than men do, and they increase so fast that, when the vessel reaches port, it may have to be deserted for a time by all on board in order to drive out the rats by smoke or steam.

2. On the return of the English man-of-war Valiant from Havana, in 1766, the rats were found to have so increased that they ate a hundred pounds of biscuit in a day; so the ship was smoked out, and for days together they collected daily six basketfuls of rats. In the Arctic regions, where Dr. Kane and his crew could hardly keep themselves alive, the rats constantly multiplied, and the dogs were afraid to go into the hold of the vessel. The crew stayed on deck one terribly cold night and tried to

smoke out the rats, but in vain. Then Dr. Hayes burned charcoal till he nearly set the ship on fire, but it did very little good, and at last the men got used to sleeping with rats among their blankets, and Dr. Kane made rat-soup for dinner.

3. But on land, when rats find themselves in danger, a whole colony of them will sometimes remove from a building, of their own accord, and set up housekeeping in some safer place. Mr. Buckland tells a story of some men who had made great preparations for destroying all the rats in a certain barn in England. When the morning came the men entered the barn with dogs and ferrets and big sticks, but not a rat could they find. The ferrets ran into the holes, the dogs got under the straw, and the men poked with their sticks, but not a rat could they find. Afterward a laborer came and said that he had seen a whole regiment of rats, on that very morning, as they marched away from that barn to another.

4. One reason why rats are able to live and thrive in spite of everything is that they show such sagacity in obtaining food. A lady of my acquaintance found that the eggs in her kitchen disappeared very fast, and she and her husband, after patient watching, saw the rats at work upon them. She saw one rat lie upon its back and take an egg or two between its paws, with the help of the others. Thus it became a sort of live sled, or wheelbarrow without wheels; and another rat, taking in its mouth the tail of the first one, dragged the load of eggs to their hole. Other observers have seen parties of rats pushing eggs up or down stairs, two being busy with each egg; sometimes they have been seen formed in a line, and passing along the eggs from one to another, as firemen pass buckets of water at a fire. This shows the same intelligence that beavers show when they unite in their engineering work.

5. The same lady told me that she had discovered how

the rats drink sweet-oil. Her husband was an apothecary, and had a number of bottles of sweet-oil, some of which were found nearly empty. They watched, and saw two rats at work upon the bottle. They pulled out the cork, or nibbled through it, and then one of them let his tail down into the bottle, and, soon drawing it out, let his comrade lick it. Then the comrade took his turn, and dipped in his tail, and the first rat licked that, and so they were as happy as you may see poor little children on wharves around a cask of molasses. The same thing has been described in the books, but it seems very hard to believe. Naturalists say that these stories "lack confirmation"; but they would hardly be repeated so often if they were not true, and I believe my old friend's account, at any rate.

6. There is a story of a good woman in England who heard for two nights a terrible hubbub in her cellar, so that she collected her neighbors to defend her. On the third night her maid found that a barrel of sweet wine had been entirely emptied by rats. They had first gnawed through the bung, to drink the wine, and then, as it sunk lower and lower, they had eaten away the whole side of the barrel. The servant-girls declared that "the ghost had taken the wine"; but, if so, the ghost's teeth made marks exactly like rats' teeth; and Mr. Buckland still keeps the remains of the cask to show what these little animals can do.

7. Rats certainly use their tails a great deal, whether they dip them into bottles or not. If you observe a rat climbing, or springing, or rising on his hind legs, you will see that his tail helps him very much. It is thick and strong, and the naturalist Cuvier says that it has as many muscles as the human hand. It seems very surprising that rats should be so clean when they live on such dirty food and in such dirty places. Cats seem to lose some of their instinct of cleanliness when they have to live as rats live; but rats clean themselves after eating as carefully as the

most domestic cats; and no fleas or other insects are ever found upon them. Our rats are commonly of the gray species, which has gradually driven out the black rat.

8. But sometimes white rats are kept as pets, and sometimes a variety of colors may be seen among wild rats. A lady of my acquaintance once lived in a house in Boston, with a stable behind it, from which a great many large rats used to come into the kitchen and coal-shed. They were so familiar that the cook once declared that she heard a knock at the kitchen door, and, on opening it, saw a large rat standing on his hind legs and looking at her, "so impudent," as she said. Be that as it may, this lady was once looking out into the yard and saw several rats drinking by the pump. In their midst was lying (as she thought) a beautiful piece of reddish fur. As she wondered how it came there, it suddenly took to its heels and ran away into the stable with the other rats, and she never saw it again.

9. Rats are not easy to tame, and yet they have sometimes made excellent pets. The driver of a London omnibus once found in his hay-loft a young rat of a piebald color, which he brought home for his children to play with. The little thing soon grew tame, and was a great favorite, the children naming him "Ikey," after their eldest brother. He would lie before the fire at full length, or run round and round after his own tail like a cat. His master often carried him in his pocket, or put him in his dinner-basket to guard the dinner. Ikey was always honest except when there was plum-pudding in the basket, and then he had not moral courage enough to resist nibbling at the plums. But if others touched the basket, Ikey flew at them and drove them away. In return, his master taught him to sit on his hind legs and beg, to jump through a hoop, to drag a little cart, and to carry money in his mouth. *T. W. Higginson.*

THE CHIPMUNK AT HOME.

1. WITH the first sweet blossoms of the *Epigæa*, and long before the foremost warbler greets his old-time home with gleesome songs, our little chipmunk has roused himself from his long winter's nap, and, sniffing the south wind as it whirls the dead leaves about, scampers to and fro while the sun shines, and dives into his winter quarters, it may be for a whole week, if the north wind whispers to the tall beech-trees. But the blustering days of March give way in due time to showery April, and then, with more courage, "chip" faces the music of the winds, blow they from whatever quarter, and, darting along the top rail of our zigzag fences, chatters, scolds, and calls at and to his equally noisy companions. They know full well that they have the summer before them, and, while determined to enjoy it, begin early and in good earnest to make arrangements for its coming duties. We watched several pairs of them from March to November, during the last year (1874), and our sketch is based on numerous notes made at different times.

2. Until the weather became fairly settled, and really spring-like in temperature, these little chipmunks did not frequently show themselves, and then only in the middle of the day. The occurrence of a cold storm they appeared to foretell by twenty-four hours, and resumed their hibernating sleep, becoming lethargic, and very difficult to restore to consciousness. A pair that we dug out in March, having two days before re-entered their winter quarters and become again torpid, were apparently lifeless when first taken up in the hands, and not until after several hours' warming did they become lively and altogether themselves again. This seemed to us the more curious, in that they can respond to a favorable change in the weather in a short

time, even when the thermometric change is really but a few degrees.

3. On the 3d of May a pair made their appearance in the yard of our residence, and took up their abode in a

American Chipmunk.

stone wall having a southern outlook, and on the edge of a steep descent of seventy feet, which hill-side is thickly wooded, and harbors scores of these little chipmunks, or "ground-squirrels," as they are more commonly called. From the fact of these little animals living wholly underground, and it being stated that their underground homes were quite elaborate in structure, we determined to wait until the pair in our yard had completed their excavations in and under the stone wall and arranged their nest, which time we judged by their actions, and then seeking out the home of another couple, which was readily accessible, we undertook to expose the nest and its approaches. This we did on May 29th.

4. The nest contained five young, not more than forty-eight hours old. The two entrances were at the foot of a large beech-tree standing about six feet from the brow of the hill. The grass alone grew about the tree, and the holes on the surface of the ground were very conspicuous. No attempt at concealment had been made; but this was evidently because there is here almost a total absence of their particular enemies. Animals soon learn this fact, and their homes and habits vary with the knowledge. From the right-hand entrance to the nest was an intervening space of nine feet traversed by a cylindrical passage somewhat serpentine in its course, which made the distance really about twelve feet. The nest itself was oval, about twenty inches in length and ten inches in height. It was lined with very fine grass. We had hoped to find several passages leading from the nest, and two or more "extra" nests, or magazines for storing away food, but no trace of them was to be found.

5. On the 23d of June six young chipmunks made their appearance about the stone wall in the yard, and to these, with their parents, we will now confine our attention. It puzzles us now, when we think of it, to imagine when this company of eight chipmunks took any rest. Very frequently during the summer we were astir at sunrise, but the chipmunks were already on the go, and

throughout July they appeared to do little but play, which sporting, by the way, is very animated. They seem to be playing at what children know as "tag," i. e., they chase each other to and fro, and try not simply to touch, we should judge, but to bite each other's tail.

6. The way in which they scamper along the tapering points of a paling fence is simply astonishing; but however mad may be their galloping, let a hawk come near, and in a moment every one is motionless. If on a fence, they simply squat wherever they may be at the time, and trust to remaining unnoticed. If on the ground, and not too far from their burrows, which is not often the case, they will dart to their nests with an incredible celerity, going, we believe, the whole length of their passage-way to the nest, turning about, and retracing their steps to the entrance, from which they will peer out, and, when the danger is over, reappear and recommence their sports.

7. About August 15th they commenced to work in real earnest. Instead of playful, careless creatures, that lived from hand to mouth, they became very sober and busy indeed. Instead of keeping comparatively near home, they wandered to quite a distance, for them, and, filling both cheek-pouches full of corn, chincapins (dwarf chestnuts), and small acorns, home they would hurry, looking, in the face, like children with the mumps. This storing away of food was continued until the first heavy white frosts, when the chipmunks, as a member of Congress once said, went "into a state of retiracy."

8. The food gathered, we believe, is consumed in part on their going into winter quarters, they spending some time in their retreats before commencing their hibernating sleep. This belief, on our part, is based on the result of digging out a third nest on the 3d of November. The last time we noted down seeing a chipmunk belonging to a certain nest was October 22d. Twelve days after we very

carefully closed the three passages that led to the nest and dug down. We found four chipmunks very cozily fixed for winter, in a roomy nest, and all of them thoroughly wide awake.

9. Their store of provisions was wholly chestnuts and acorns, and the shells of these nuts were all pushed into one of the passages, so that there should be no litter mingled with the soft hay that lined the nest. How long this underground life lasts before hibernation really commences, it is difficult to determine; but as this torpid state does not continue until their food-supply is again obtainable out of doors, the chipmunks, no doubt, store away sufficient for their needs throughout the early spring, and perhaps until berries are ripe.

Charles C. Abbott.

AN EXCAVATOR.

1. WALKING through the fields one May morning, I surprised a mole above ground—a very large specimen, one of the giants of this kind. It was an unwonted spectacle, something I had never seen before—this purblind, shovel-footed, subterranean dweller, this metaphysician of the earth, groping his way along in the open daylight. Had he grown tired, then, of the darkness, of the endless burrowings that lead nowhither, of undermining the paths and the garden, and culling off the tender rootlets of the plants?

2. He was ill-equipped for traveling above ground; he was like a stranded fish; the soil was his element, and he knew it as well as I did. The moment I disturbed him he began to go into the ground as a diver into the water. When he moved, his tendency was downward, like a plow. It was amusing to see his broad, muscular, naked front

feet, while turned outward and upward instead of downward, shovel their way through the grass into the turf. In less than half a minute he would nearly bury himself from view. Then by the tail I would draw him forth, and see him repeat the attempt. He did not look or feel about for a hole or for a soft place, but assaulted the turf wherever he touched it, his slender, sensitive nose feeling the way, and his huge, fleshy hands opening the passage. He was indeed a giant in these members; they were to him what the wings of a bird are to the bird; all his powers and speed lay here; his hind legs were small and feeble, and often trailed behind him, as if helpless or broken.

3. Fancy a race of savages by some peculiar manual occupation developing an enormous hand—a hand as long and broad as a scoop-shovel, usurping the wrist and the forearm, with the legs and feet proportionately small, and you have a type of the mole. This creature was a cripple at the surface, but a most successful traveler a few inches below. His fur was like silk plush, finer and softer than that of any other creature known to me, excepting, perhaps, the bat. Why should these creatures of darkness have such delicate vestments? Probably because they *are* creatures of darkness. The owl is softer clad than the hawk, the hare than the squirrel, the moth than the butterfly.

4. I looked in vain for the mole's eyes. I blew open the fur and explored the place with the point of a pin, but no eyes, or semblance to eyes, could I find, and I began to think that Aristotle was right in saying the mole is blind. Then I dispatched him and stripped off his skin, and the eyes were revealed—two minute black specks, that adhered to the tissues of the head after the skin was removed. It was only by the aid of a pocket-glass that I was able to determine that they really were eyes. There was no eye-socket, and I wondered that they had not come away with the skin. Probably the only use the mole has for eyes is

to distinguish daylight from darkness, and for this purpose these microscopic dots may suffice; but as regards any other and more specific visual powers, he is practically blind.

John Burroughs.

FOREST ENGINEERS.

1. THE beaver is at once an engineer, a carpenter, and a mason. As we shall see, it prepares the place for its habitations with all the skill of an experienced engineer, and in its building it uses the materials and methods of both the carpenter and mason. The beaver was once an inhabitant of all the northern part of the United States, but is now met with only in the remote parts of the Northwest and in Canada. Its nearest relation now among us is the musquash, or musk-rat, which ought to be called the musk-beaver, as it is no rat at all. And if you want to know about the beaver, the best thing you can do is to observe the habits of the musquash. His house is very much like the beaver's house, only smaller, and he can do almost everything that his cousin does, except make dams and canals. And even the beaver does not build those, except when they are really needed, as I shall show.

2. A beaver is two or three times as large as a musquash; indeed, sometimes he is as heavy as a stout boy, weighing seventy or eighty pounds. His tail is flattened, like that of the musquash, only much more so, and the edges are horizontal instead of vertical. It was once thought that he used this broad, flat tail as a spade or trowel, but this is not now generally believed. At any rate, the tail is the most curious part of the animal, it is so long and large, and covered with rough scales instead of fur. The beaver sculls his way with it in the water, as you can scull a boat

by one oar in the stern. And he supports himself by it when he rears on his hind legs to cut down a tree. I suspect a beaver who had lost his tail would find it hard to get a living.

Beaver Dam.

3. I said that the beaver does not always build dams. That is one thing which shows his intelligence. If he lives beside a lake, with plenty of water, why should he need a dam? In such a case he has a hole in the bank, and a hut

in front of it, and keeps house just as a musquash would. But if he has to live by a stream where there is not water enough to surround his hut, he then goes to work, just as a man would, to make an artificial pond by means of a dam.

4. In the first place, he and his family cut down small trees, and then divide them into shorter lengths, such as they can carry in their mouths. Sometimes the trees are as much as two feet thick. They are really cut, not merely nibbled or hacked. The beaver's front teeth are sharp like chisels, and his work looks as if done with a chisel, in long cuts. It is smoother than a boy's hatchet-cutting is apt to be, and looks at a distance as if done with an axe. Many specimens of these cuttings are now preserved in museums, and they are very curious.

5. Then the beaver drags these cuttings to the place where he is to build his dam. He brings branches in his mouth, and pushes earth with his paws, and rolls stones along, and sometimes has been seen swimming with hay and brush upon his head—all to be piled together and made into a dam. At first the dam is rough and loose, like the mound of a musquash. But, when once made, it lasts for years and even centuries, and the beavers keep constantly at work on it, smoothing it and pressing it down and stopping all the gaps, so that at last it is a solid dam, that will bear the weight of many men. These old dams are neatly finished with earth-work on the upper side and with rough stick-work on the lower side, and gradually they are overgrown with grass and bushes, and look as if they were natural banks. A millwright in Michigan told me that the beaver-dams were as solid as any that he could build, and that he built his upon just the same plan—filling the stream with boughs, and gradually pressing these down with stones and gravel and logs.

6. The beavers keep these dams constantly in repair, and may sometimes be seen by night at work on them,

when the trappers have made holes in them. There are sometimes several dams on the same stream, one below another, so that the water of each flows back nearly to the foot of that above. Sometimes they seem to protect a large dam by a smaller one below, so that the pressure of the water from below may resist the pressure at the bottom of the principal dam. In one case seven dams were found on the same stream within a distance of one hundred and sixty feet.

7. But I do not think that even the dams made by beavers show so much thought or ingenuity as their canals. It is much easier and safer for them to carry their food and building material by water than by land. So sometimes they cut a canal across the bend of a stream to shorten the distance. Sometimes, again, it is cut through the mud until they reach firm ground for their burrows. These canals are usually about three feet wide and three deep, and they are sometimes five hundred feet long. Any engineer will tell you that it needs a good deal of skill and ingenuity to decide where to lay out such a canal as that, and then to cut it regularly, so that the water shall flow smoothly through. And the most remarkable thing of all is, that they know how to combine the principles of the canal and the dam, so that when they come to an obstruction, such as a rock in the bed of their stream, they immediately make a dam to secure the necessary flow of water. Successive generations evidently work for many years upon these canals, and I can hardly think of anything else done by an animal that shows so much contrivance.

8. The house or lodge is always separate from the dam, and it looks like that of the musquash, only that it is much larger, and built of stronger materials. Sometimes a cord of wood is used in building one house. There is an entrance under water like that of the musquash, and sometimes two. These openings are very neatly made. The

beavers drag their branches and pieces of bark into the water, and then take them into the dining-room by the hidden entrance. Indeed, I believe the house is all dining-room, but it is always very neatly swept.

9. There are not often more than eight or ten beavers, old and young, in a single house. Hearne, an old traveler, once found thirty-seven under a single roof. But I suppose that was a kind of "tenement-house" with several families. Besides the houses, they like to have burrows in the banks, and spend part of their time in each. The young beavers live at home for about two years before they go to housekeeping for themselves. They are queer little things, and their cry is like that of a young child. Mr. Morgan once saw a little beaver in an Indian's house, and it was lapping milk out of a saucer, like a kitten, and an Indian baby was pulling its fur. Then there was a little cry, and Mr. Morgan thought it was the Indian baby, till he found it was the baby beaver.

10. It has always been an interesting question for naturalists how the beaver learns to build. Does he learn it by observing his parents, or would he know how to do it if he were brought up alone? Buffon, a great naturalist, thought that it was all learned by observation. So Cuvier, another great naturalist, took a very young beaver and brought him up by hand, apart from all his kind. He was fed with branches of willow. He ate the bark, then cut the branches in pieces and piled them up in the corner of the cage. Then they gave him earth, straw, and other branches. They saw him form the earth into lumps with his forefeet. Then he pushed these lumps together with his mouth and chin, and piled them, with the straw and branches, into a solid mass. This shows that an instinct taught the little beaver to build, even without any other beaver to set the example.

11. Now, there are several remarkable things about the

instinct of beavers. First, the way they act together in so large a family. Most quadrupeds act singly or in pairs. Then the way they use their judgment in their own affairs. This is what makes it so hard to tell the difference between what we call instinct and what we call reason. Animals, like beavers, seem really to think and decide, for instance, whether they need a dam, instead of going on blindly and building one whether they need it or not. If the water is already wide and deep enough, they save themselves the trouble, and live comfortably in their houses, like musquashes.

12. Then, again, when they are placed in wholly new positions they are said to change their habits altogether. When very hard pressed, they not only do without a dam, but they do without a house, and they live almost alone. On the river Elbe, in Europe, they have ceased to build houses within the last fifty years, and live in holes in the cliffs along the banks of the stream. On the banks of the Rhone, where they are still found, they make holes in the dikes which keep the river from overflowing. So they can not be hunted without destroying the dikes.

T. W. Higginson.

ELEPHANTS, AND HOW THEY ARE CAUGHT.

1. ELEPHANTS, like dogs, show the most intelligence when tamed. Indeed, it is said that out of all the animal world these are the only two creatures that will work in the absence of a master. You know how a dog will carry home a basket or a bundle, and go trotting along without anybody to watch him. It is just so with the elephant. When he has been trained to do a certain work, he will keep at it by himself, and will seem to take as much interest in it, and do it as intelligently, as any man would

do. For instance, when elephants are taught to pile logs in a timber-yard, in the East Indies, they will go on piling without any command from their masters; and they are taught, when the pile grows high, to lean two logs against it and roll the remaining logs to the top.

2. I remember a story told by Sir James Tennent which shows this independence of action in the elephant. He says: "One evening, when riding in the vicinity of Kandy, my horse showed some excitement at a noise which approached us in the thick jungle, and which consisted of the ejaculation *urmph! urmph!* in a hoarse and dissatisfied tone. A turn in the forest explained the mystery, by bringing me face to face with a tame elephant, unaccompanied by any attendant. He was laboring painfully to carry a heavy beam of timber, which he balanced across his tusks; but, the pathway being narrow, he was forced to bend his head to one side to permit it to pass endways, and the exertion and inconvenience combined led him to utter the dissatisfied sounds. On seeing us halt, the elephant raised his head, reconnoitered us a moment, then flung down the timber and forced himself backward among the brushwood so as to leave a passage, of which he expected us to avail ourselves.

3. "My horse still hesitated; the elephant observed it, and impatiently thrust himself still deeper into the jungle, repeating his cry of *urmph!* but in a voice evidently meant to encourage us to come on. Still the horse trembled, and being anxious to observe the instinct of the two sagacious creatures, I forbore any interference. Again the elephant wedged himself farther in among the trees, and waited impatiently for us to pass him; and after the horse had done so, tremblingly and timidly, I saw the wise creature stoop and take up his heavy burden, trim and balance it on his tusks, and resume his route, hoarsely snorting as before."

4. Now, almost any trained animal, if left alone to decide for himself in such a case, would have put down his load, if he could, and walked away. But how like a faithful and industrious man this elephant acted! As there was no room to pass, he made way, waited for the horse, encouraged him to come on, and then, when he had passed, took up his load again and went along.

5. But I think the most wonderful manner in which the Asiatic elephants show their intelligence and fidelity is the way the tame animals help to ensnare the wild ones. But for their skill and ingenuity very few elephants would be captured alive. This is the way they do it. When a herd of elephants is to be caught, in Ceylon, the people build an inclosure called a *corral*. It is made of small trees stuck in the ground and secured by cross-beams. It is an inclosure perhaps five hundred feet long by half that width; it has only a small opening at one end.

6. At the opening there is a gate, and from each angle of the end by which the elephants are to approach, two lines of the same strong fencing are continued on each side and cautiously concealed among the trees. Then men go beating through the woods for many miles, driving the elephants toward this inclosure, which is easily done, for they are very shy and gentle so long as they are not excited. Sometimes it takes more than a month to bring together forty or fifty elephants in this way, and sometimes two hundred have been caught. At last, when the hunters have them all within the projecting fences, they choose a favorable night and suddenly light a great many fires and torches, discharge guns, beat drums and *tom-toms*, and try to drive the elephants into the *corral*. Sometimes the whole herd will break through the fences and get away; but commonly they are driven by degrees into the *corral*.

7. The moment they get inside, the gate is shut, and the hunters immediately surround the *corral* with torches,

which they push through the fence at the elephants, if they approach, so that the great creatures are frightened and gradually collect in the middle of the inclosure, forming a circle, with their young in the center. Then it is that the wonderful skill and intelligence of the trained elephants are called into use. I will give you an account of this scene, drawn from a description by Sir James Tennent, who watched the whole of one of these hunts from a platform built in a tree overlooking the inclosure.

8. After the herd was all in, the bars which secured the entrance to the *corral* were cautiously withdrawn, and two trained elephants passed stealthily in, each ridden by his *mahout* (or driver) and one attendant, and carrying a strong collar formed by coils of rope, made of cocoa-nut fiber, from which hung on either side cords of elk's hide, prepared with a ready noose. With them, and concealed behind them, the head man of the "noosers" crept in, eager to secure the honor of taking the first elephant.

9. One of the two decoy elephants was of prodigious age, having been in the service of the Dutch and English governments in succession for upward of a century. The other, called by her keeper "Siribeddi," was about fifty years old, and distinguished for her gentleness and docility. She was a most accomplished decoy, and showed the utmost relish for the sport. Having entered the *corral* noiselessly, she moved along with a sly composure and an assumed air of easy indifference, sauntering leisurely in the direction of the captives, and halting now and then to pluck a bunch of grass or a few leaves as she passed.

10. As she approached the herd, they put themselves in motion to receive her, and the leader, having advanced in front and passed his trunk gently over her head, turned and paced slowly back to his dejected companion. Siribeddi followed with the same listless step, and drew herself up close behind him, thus affording the nooser an op-

portunity to stoop under her and slip the noose over the hind foot of the wild one. The latter instantly perceived his danger, shook off the rope, and turned to attack the man. He would have suffered for his temerity had not Siribeddi protected him by raising her trunk and driving the assailant into the midst of the herd, when the old man, being slightly wounded, was helped out of the *corral*, and his son Ranghanie took his place.

11. The herd again collected in a circle, with their heads toward the center. The largest male was singled out, and two tame ones pushed boldly in, one on either side of him, till the three stood nearly abreast. He made no resistance, but betrayed his uneasiness by shifting restlessly from foot to foot. Ranghanie now crept up, and, holding the rope open with both hands (its other extremity being made fast to Siribeddi's collar), and watching the instant when the wild elephant lifted his hind foot, he succeeded in passing the noose over its leg, drew it close, and fled to the rear. The two tame elephants instantly fell back, Siribeddi stretched the rope to its full length, and, while she dragged out the captive, her companion placed himself between her and the herd, to prevent any interference.

12. In order to secure him to a tree, he had to be drawn backward some twenty or thirty yards, making furious resistance, bellowing in terror, plunging on all sides and crushing the smaller timber, which bent like reeds beneath his clumsy struggles. Siribeddi drew him steadily after her and wound the rope round the proper tree, holding it all the time at its full tension, and stepping cautiously across it when, in order to give it a second turn, it was necessary to pass between the tree and the elephant. With a coil round the stem, however, it was beyond her strength to haul the prisoner close up, which was, nevertheless, necessary in order to make him perfectly fast; but the second

tame one, perceiving the difficulty, returned from the herd, confronted the struggling prisoner, pushed him shoulder to shoulder and head to head, and forced him backward, while at every step Siribeddi hauled in the slackened rope till she brought him fairly up to the foot of the tree, where he was made fast. A second noose was then passed over the other hind leg and secured like the first, both legs being afterward "hobbled" together by ropes.

13. The second elephant singled out from the herd was secured in the same manner as the first. It was a female. When the noose was placed upon her forefoot she seized it with her trunk and succeeded in carrying it to her mouth, where she would speedily have severed it had not a tame elephant interfered, and, placing his foot on the rope, pressed it downward out of her jaws. It is strange that in these encounters the wild elephants made no attempt to attack or dislodge the *mahouts* who rode on the tame ones.

14. The conduct of the tame elephants during all these proceedings was truly wonderful. They seemed to understand every movement, both the object to be attained and the means of accomplishing it. They showed the utmost enjoyment in what was going on. Their caution was as remarkable as their sagacity; there was no hurrying, no confusion, they never ran foul of the ropes, were never in the way of those noosed, and, amid the most violent struggles, when the tame ones had frequently to step across the captives, they in no instance trampled on them, or occasioned the slightest accident or annoyance. So far from that, they saw for themselves a difficulty or a danger, and tried at once to remove it. In tying up one of the larger elephants, he contrived, before he could be hauled close up to the tree, to walk once or twice round it, carrying the rope with him; the decoy, perceiving the advantage he had thus gained over the nooser, walked up of her own

accord and pushed him backward with her head till she made him unwind himself again, when the rope was hauled tight and made fast. More than once, when a wild one was extending his trunk, and would have intercepted the rope about to be placed over his leg, Siribeddi, by a sudden motion of her own trunk, pushed his aside and prevented him; and on one occasion, when successive efforts had failed to put the noose over the leg of an elephant which was already secured by one foot, but which wisely put the other to the ground as often as it was attempted to pass the noose under it, the decoy watched her opportunity, and, when his foot was again raised, suddenly pushed in her own leg underneath it and held it up till the noose was attached and drawn tight.

15. Now, I do not know where you can find such an exhibition of skill as this in any other animal. Of course, the elephants have been trained, in some degree, by their drivers; but all accounts agree that the chief skill is shown by the animals themselves. They set their brains at work, in order to outwit the brains of the wild elephants. They observe what is needed, and act promptly for themselves, without orders. Think of that great creature, with his heavy foot pushing the rope quickly from the trunk of the other elephant, for fear he should break it in two. Horses and dogs can be trained to do very difficult things, but they do nothing which requires such quickness and foresight as this.

J. W. Higginson.

THE FORCE OF INSTINCT.

1. A PRETTY little fawn had been brought in very young from the woods, and nursed and petted by a lady in the village until it had become as tame as possible. It was graceful, as those little creatures always are, and so gentle

and playful that it became a great favorite, following the different members of the family about, caressed by the neighbors, and welcome everywhere.

2. One morning, after gamboling about as usual until weary, it threw itself down in the sunshine, at the feet of one of its friends, upon the steps of a store. There came along a countryman who for several years had been a hunter by pursuit, and who still kept several dogs; one of the hounds came with him to the village on this occasion. The dog, as it approached the spot where the fawn lay, suddenly stopped; the little animal saw him and darted to its feet. It had lived more than half its life among the dogs of the village, and had apparently lost all fear of them; but it seemed now to know instinctively that an enemy was at hand. In an instant a change came over it; and the gentleman who related the incident, and who was standing by at the moment, observed that he had never in his life seen a finer sight than the sudden arousing of instinct in that beautiful creature.

3. In a second its whole character and appearance seemed changed, all its past habits were forgotten, every wild impulse was awake; its head erect, its nostrils dilated, its eye flashing. In another instant, before the spectators had thought of the danger, before its friends could secure it, the fawn was leaping wildly through the street, and the hound in full pursuit. The by-standers were eager to save it; several persons instantly followed its track, the friends who had long fed and fondled it calling the name it had hitherto known, but in vain.

4. The hunter endeavored to whistle back his dog, but with no better success. In half a minute the fawn had turned the first corner, dashed onward toward the lake, and thrown itself into the water. But if for a moment the startled creature believed itself safe in the cool bosom of the lake, it was soon undeceived; the hound followed in

hot and eager chase, while a dozen village dogs joined blindly in the pursuit.

5. Quite a crowd collected on the bank—men, women, and children—anxious for the fate of the little animal known to them all; some threw themselves into boats, hoping to intercept the hound before he reached his prey; but the plashing of the oars, the eager voices of the men and boys, and the barking of the dogs, must have filled the beating heart of the poor fawn with terror and anguish, as though every creature on the spot where it had once been caressed and fondled had suddenly turned into a deadly foe.

6. It was soon seen that the little animal was directing its course across a bay toward the nearest borders of the forest, and immediately the owner of the hound crossed the bridge, running at full speed in the same direction, hoping to stop his dog as he landed. On the fawn swam, as it never swam before, its delicate head scarcely seen above the water, but leaving a disturbed track, which betrayed its course alike to anxious friends and fierce enemies. As it approached the land the exciting interest became intense. The hunter was already on the same line of shore, calling loudly and angrily to his dog, but the animal seemed to have quite forgotten his master's voice in the pitiless pursuit. The fawn touched the land; in one leap it had crossed the narrow line of beach, and in another instant it would reach the cover of the woods. The hound followed true to the scent, aiming at the same spot on the shore; his master, anxious to meet him, had run at full speed, and was now coming up at the most critical moment; would the dog hearken to his voice, or could the hunter reach him in time to seize and control him? A shout from the village bank proclaimed that the fawn had passed out of sight into the forest; at the same instant, the hound, as he touched the land, felt the hunter's strong arm clutching his neck.

7. The worst was believed to be over; the fawn was leaping up the mountain-side, and its enemy under restraint. The other dogs, seeing their leader cowed, were easily managed. A number of persons, men and boys, dispersed themselves through the wood in search of the little creature, but without success; they all returned to the village, reporting that the animal had not been seen by them. Some persons thought that, after its fright had passed over, it would return of its own accord. It had worn a pretty collar, with its owner's name engraved upon it, so that it could be easily known from any other fawn that might be straying about the woods.

8. Before many hours had passed, a hunter presented himself to the lady whose pet the little creature had been, and, showing a collar with her name upon it, said that he had been out in the woods, and saw a fawn in the distance; the little animal, instead of bounding away as he had expected, moved toward him; he took aim, fired, and shot it to the heart. When he found the collar about its neck he was very sorry that he had killed it. And so the poor little thing died. One would have thought that terrible chase would have made it afraid of man; but no, it forgot the evil and remembered the kindness only, and came to meet as a friend the hunter who shot it. It was long mourned by its best friend. *Miss Cooper.*

CURIOUS FRIENDSHIPS.

1. WHY married folk, so ill-mated as to agree only to differ, should be said to lead a cat-and-dog life, is not very clear, since those household pets, being intelligent, affectionate, cheerful, and sociable creatures, very frequently contrive to live harmoniously enough together. The Aston

Hall cat, that ate, associated, and slept with a huge bloodhound, only did what innumerable cats have done. Such companionships are too common to be reckoned among strange animal friendships, such as that most singular instance of attachment between two animals of opposite natures and habits, related to Mr. Jesse by a person on whose veracity he could depend. The narrator boasted the proprietorship of an alligator which had become so **tame** that it would follow him up and down stairs; while it was so fond of his cat's society that, when she lay down before the fire, the alligator followed suit, made a pillow of puss, and went off to sleep; and, when awake, the reptile was only happy so long as puss was somewhere near, turning morose and ill-tempered whenever she left it to its own devices.

2. Many equine celebrities have delighted in feline companions, following in this the example of their notable ancestor, the Godolphin Arab, between whom and a black cat an intimate friendship existed for years—a friendship that came to a touching end; for when that famous steed died, his old companion would not leave the body, and, when it had seen it put underground, crawled slowly away to a hay-loft, and, refusing to be comforted, pined away and died.

3. Mr. Huntington, of East Bloomfield, New York, owns a thorough-bred horse named Narragansett and a white cat. The latter was wont to pay a daily visit to Narragansett's stall, to hunt up the mice and then enjoy a quiet nap. Mr. Huntington removed to Rochester with his family, leaving the cat behind; but she complained so loudly and so unceasingly that she was sent on to the new abode. Her first object was now to get somebody to interpret her desires. At last her master divined them, and started off with her to the barn. As soon as they were inside, the cat went to the horse's stall, made herself a bed near his head,

and curled herself up contentedly. When Mr. Huntington visited the pair next morning, there was puss close to Narragansett's feet, with a family of five beside her. The horse evidently knew all about it, and that it behooved him to take heed how he moved his feet. Puss afterward would go out, leaving her little ones to the care of her friend, who would every now and then look to see how they were getting on. When these inspections took place in the mother's presence, she was not at all uneasy, although she showed the greatest fear and anxiety if any children or strangers intruded upon her privacy.

4. A gentleman in Sussex had a cat which showed the greatest affection for a young blackbird, which was given to her by a stable-boy for food a day or two after she had been deprived of her kittens. She tended it with the greatest care; they became inseparable companions, and no mother could show a greater fondness for her offspring than she did for the bird.

5. A pair of carriage-horses taken to water at a stone trough, then standing at one end of the Manchester Exchange, were followed by a dog who was in the habit of lying in the stall of one of them. As he gamboled on in front, the creature was suddenly attacked by a mastiff far too strong for his power of resistance, and it would have gone hard with him but for the unlooked-for intervention of his stable-companion, which, breaking loose from the man who was leading it, made for the battling dogs, and with one well-delivered kick sent the mastiff into a cooper's cellar, and then quietly returned to the trough and finished his drink.

6. In very sensible fashion, too, did Mrs. Bland's half-Danish dog Traveler show his affection for his mistress's pet pony. The latter had been badly hurt, and, when well enough to be turned into a field, was visited there by its fair owner and regaled with carrots and other delicacies;

Traveler, for his part, never failing to fetch one or two windfall apples from the garden, laying them on the grass before the pony, and hailing its enjoyment of them with the liveliest demonstrations of delight.

7. That such relations should exist between the horse and the dog seems natural enough; but that a horse should be hail-fellow with a hen appears too absurd to be true; yet we have Gilbert White's word for it that a horse, lacking more suitable companions, struck up a great friendship with a hen, and displayed immense gratification when she rubbed against his legs and clucked a greeting, while he moved about with the greatest caution lest he might trample on his "little, little friend."

8. Colonel Montagu tells of a pointer which, after being well beaten for killing a Chinese goose, was further punished by having the murdered bird tied to his neck—a penance that entailed his being constantly attended by the defunct's relict. Whether he satisfied her that he repented the cruel deed is more than we know; but after a little while the pointer and the goose were on the best of terms, living under the same roof, feeding out of one trough, occupying the same straw bed; and, when the dog went on duty in the field, the goose filled the air with her lamentations for his absence.

9. A New Zealand paper says: "There is a dog at Taupo, and also a young pig, and these two afford a curious example of animal sagacity and confidence in the friendship of each other. These two animals live at the native *pah* on the opposite side of Tapuaeharuru, and the dog discovered some happy hunting-grounds on the other side, and informed the pig. The pig, being only two months old, informed the dog that he could not swim across the river, which at that spot debouches from the lake, but that in time he hoped to share the adventures of his canine friend. The dog settled the difficulty. He went into the

river, standing up to his neck in water, and crouched down; the pig got on his back, clasping his neck with his fore legs. The dog then swam across, thus carrying his chum over. Regularly every morning the two would in this way go across and forage around Tapuaeharuru, returning to the *pah* at night; and, if the dog was ready to go home before the pig, he would wait till his friend came down to be ferried over. The truth of this story is vouched for by several who have watched the movements of the pair for some weeks past."

10. Frank Buckland relates: "A gentleman, traveling through Mecklenburg, was witness to a very singular circumstance in a village post-house. After dinner the landlord placed on the floor a large dish of soup, and gave a loud whistle. Immediately there came into the room a mastiff, a fine Angora cat, an old raven, and a remarkably large rat with a bell about its neck. They all four went to the dish, and, without disturbing each other, fed together, after which the dog, cat, and rat lay before the fire, while the raven hopped about the room. The landlord, after accounting for the familiarity which existed among these animals, informed his guest that the rat was the most useful of the four, for the noise he made had completely freed the house from the other rats and mice with which it had previously been infested."

11. In 1822 some white rats were trapped in Colonel Berkeley's stables. Mr. Samuel Moss, of Cheltenham, took a fancy to a youngster, and determined to make a pet of him. He was soon tamed, and christened Scugg. Then he was formally introduced to a rat-killing terrier, a ceremony so well understood by Flora that she not only refrained from assaulting the new-comer, but actually constituted herself his protectress, mounting guard over Scugg whenever a stranger came into the room, growling, snarling, and showing her teeth, until convinced he had no evil

intentions toward her *protégé*. These two strangely assorted friends lapped from the same saucer, played together in the garden, and, when Flora indulged in a snooze on the rug, Scugg ensconced himself snugly between her legs. He would mount the dinner-table and carry off sugar, pastry, or cheese, while Flora waited below to share in the plunder.

12. One day a man brought Mr. Moss another white rat, while the terrier and Scugg were racing about the room. The stranger was shaken out of the trap, and presently two white rats were scampering across the floor, pursued by Flora. The chase did not last long, one of them quickly falling a victim to the terrier's teeth, much to the experimentalist's alarm, as his eyes could not distinguish one rat from the other. Looking around, however, his mind was relieved, for there in his corner was Scugg, with Flora standing sentry before him—a position she held until the man and the dead rat were out of the room. When his master took a wife to himself, a new home was found for Scugg; but the poor fellow died within a month of his removal, and it is not improbable that the separation from his canine friend was the primary cause of the rat's untimely decease.

13. Not long ago, an ailing lioness in the Dublin Zoological Gardens was so tormented by the rats nibbling her toes that a little terrier was introduced into the cage. His entrance elicited a sulky growl from the invalid; but, seeing the visitor toss a rat in the air and catch it with a killing snap as it came down, she at once came to the sensible conclusion that the dog's acquaintance was worth cultivating. Coaxing the terrier to her side, she folded her paw round him and took him to her breast; and there he rested every night afterward, ready to pounce upon any rat daring to disturb the slumbers of the lioness.

14. The last time we visited the lion-house of the Re-

gent's Park Zoölogical Gardens we watched with no little amusement the antics of a dog, who was evidently quite at home in a cage occupied by a tiger and tigress. The noble pair of beasts were reclining side by side, the tiger's tail hanging over the side of their couch. The dog, unable to resist the temptation, laid hold of it with his teeth and pulled with a will; and, spite of sundry gentle remonstrances on the part of the owner of the tail, persisted until he elicited a very deep growl of disapproval. Then he let go, sprang upon the tiger's back, curled himself up, and went off to sleep. *Chambers's Journal.*

THE LION AND THE SPANIEL.

1. In the afternoon our company went again to the Tower, to see as well as to hear the recent story of the great lion and the little dog. They found the place thronged, and all were obliged to pay treble prices, on account of the unprecedented novelty of the show; so that the keeper, in a short space, acquired a little fortune.

2. The great cage in the front was occupied by a beast who, by way of pre-eminence, was called the king's lion; and, while he traversed the limits of his straitened dominions, he was attended by a small and very beautiful black spaniel, who frisked and gamboled about him, and at times would pretend to snarl and bite at him; and again the noble animal, with an air of fond complaisance, would hold down his head, while the little creature licked his formidable chaps. Their history, as the keeper related, was this:

3. It was customary for all, who were unable or unwilling to pay their sixpence, to bring a dog or cat as an oblation to the beast in lieu of money to the keeper. Among others, a fellow had caught up this pretty black

spaniel in the streets, and he was accordingly thrown into the cage of the great lion. Immediately the little animal trembled and shivered, and crouched, and threw itself on its back, and put forth its tongue, and held up its paws, in supplicatory attitudes, as an acknowledgment of superior power, and praying for mercy. In the mean time the lordly brute, instead of devouring it, beheld it with an eye of philosophic inspection. He turned it over with one paw, and then turned it with the other; smelled of it, and seemed desirous of courting a further acquaintance.

4. The keeper, on seeing this, brought a large mess of his own family dinner; but the lion kept aloof and refused to eat, keeping his eye on the dog, and inviting him, as it were, to be his taster. At length, the little animal's fears being something abated, and his appetite quickened by the smell of the victuals, he approached slowly, and, with trembling, ventured to eat. The lion then advanced gently and began to partake, and they finished their meal very lovingly together.

5. From this day the strictest friendship commenced between them—a friendship consisting of all possible affection and tenderness on the part of the lion, and of the utmost confidence and boldness on the part of the dog; insomuch that he would lay himself down to sleep within the fangs and under the jaws of his terrible patron. A gentleman who had lost the spaniel, and had advertised a reward of two guineas to the finder, at length heard of the adventure, and went to reclaim his dog. You see, sir, said the keeper, it would be a great pity to part such loving friends; however, if you insist upon your property, you must even be pleased to take him yourself; it is a task that I would not engage in for five hundred guineas. The gentleman rose into great wrath, but finally chose to acquiesce rather than have a personal dispute with the lion.

6. As Mr. Felton had a curiosity to see the two friends

eat together, he sent for twenty pounds of beef, which was accordingly cut in pieces and given into the cage; when immediately the little brute, whose appetite happened to be eager at the time, was desirous of making a monopoly of the whole, and, putting his paws upon the meat, and grumbling and barking, he audaciously flew into the face of the lion. But the generous creature, instead of being offended with his impotent companion, started back, and seemed terrified at the fury of his attack; neither attempted to eat a bit till his favorite had tacitly given permission.

7. When they were both gorged, the lion stretched and turned himself and lay down in an evident posture for repose, but this his sportive companion would not admit. He frisked and gamboled about him, barked at him, would now scrape and tear at his head with his claws, and again seize him by the ear and bite and pull away, while the noble beast appeared affected by no other sentiment save that of pleasure and complacence.

Henry Brooke.

HOME LIFE OF SCOTTISH DEER.

1. NEAR Slui, on the Findhorn, there is a range of precipices and wooded steeps crowned with pine, and washed by the clear and rippling stream of the river, through which there is an excellent ford very well known to the roe for escaping to the woods when pressed by the hounds. In this reach is a remarkable crag, a sheer, naked, even wall of limestone, lying in horizontal strata, eighty or ninety feet high. At the eastern extremity of this rock there is a great division, partly separated from the main curtain by a deep, woody slope, which dips into the precipice with little more inclination from the perpendicular than to admit of a careful footing. In the face of the di-

vided crag, the decomposition of the softer stone between the courses of the strata has wasted it away into narrow galleries, which, passing behind the tall pillars of the pines growing from the rifts and ledges, extend along the face of the precipice, veiled by a deep tapestry of ivy, which spreads over the mighty wall of rock and hangs from shelf to shelf over the covered ways.

2. Beyond the crags, the bank of the forest, an abrupt steep, covered with oak and copsewood, slopes down to the river, its brow darkened with a deep-blue cloud of pines, and its descent carpeted with moss, primroses, and pyrolas, here and there hollowed into quaint "cuachs," filled with hazels, thorns, and giant pines. Along this woody scarp, and through its thick copse, the roe had made narrow galleries, which communicated with the ivy corridors on the face of the crag, to which there were corresponding ways upon the opposite side. In that fortress of the rock, for shelter from the sun and flies, and seclusion from the stir of the world during the day in the heat of summer, the red deer and roe made their secret haunt, concealed behind the deep, dim veil of leaves, unseen and unsuspected in the cool hollows of the cliff. The prying eye might search the crag from below, and the beaters or the woodmen might whistle and whoop and shout above, but nothing appeared or moved except the gray falcon, which rose channering out of the rifts.

3. Above the crag the wooded bank was so abrupt that to the front view there was no indication of a slope, and any one who passed quickly over the brow was immediately out of sight. At each descent beyond the extremities of the whole range of rocks there was a common roe's run and pass, which was supposed to be "deadly sure" if the deer took the path, since the precipice below was believed to be an infallible barrier against any intermediate escape. Often, however, when pressed upon the terrace above, the deer

neither went through the passes nor turned against the beaters, but vanished as if by magic—nobody could tell where; and it was the common opinion of the drivers and fishermen that, when forced near the river, they threw themselves over the crags "for spite." The truth was that those which disappeared dashed down the sudden dip of the bank between the precipices, and, turning through the ivy corridors, went out through the copse-galleries upon the other side, and either descended to the water or skirted below the pass, and went back into the forest.

4. In the same mysterious passages which gave concealment and escape to the stags and bucks the does were used to lie with their fawns, and from thence at morning and evening they brought them out to pluck the tender grass upon the green banks beyond. Often from the brow above, or from behind the ivy screen, we have watched their "red garment" stealing through the boughs, followed by the little pair drawing their slender legs daintily through the wet dew, and turning their large velvet ears to catch every passing sound upon the breeze as it brought the hum of the water, or the crow of the distant cock—now trotting before, now lingering behind their dam, now nestling together, now starting off as the gale suddenly rustled the leaves behind them—then listening and reuniting in a timorous plump, pricking their ears and bobbing their little black noses in the wind—then, as the doe dropped on her knees in the moss, and laid her side on the warm spot where the morning sun glanced in through the branches, they gamboled about her, leaping over her back, and running round in little circles, uttering that soft, wild, plaintive cry like the treble note of an accordion, till, weary of their sport, they lay down at her side and slept while she watched as only a mother can.

5. No marvel it was that they loved that safe and fair retreat, with all its songs and flowers, its plenty and repose.

All around was sweet and beautiful and abundant, such as the poetical imagination of the painter can rarely compose, and *never* unless, like Salvator, he has lived in the wilderness with its free denizens. Upon the summit above the crag there was a broad and verdant terrace surrounded by ivied pines and feathering birches, and upon a little green glade in the midst grew two of the most beautiful objects ever produced by art or nature. These were a pair of twin thorns exactly similar in size, age, and form, and standing about three yards from each other, their stems as straight as shafts, and their round and even heads like vast bushes of wild thyme, but each so overgrown with ivy and woodbine that their slender trunks appeared like fretted columns, over which the thorny foliage served as a trellis to suspend the heavy plumes of the ivy and the golden tassels of the woodbine. Many a "ladye's bower" we have seen, and many a rich and costly plant reared by the care of man, but none so beautiful as those lonely sisters of the forest, planted by His hand in His great garden, where none beheld but those for whom He made it lovely—the ravens of the rock, the deer who couched under its shade by night, and the birds who sang their matins and their even-song out of its sweet boughs.

6. In these lonely thickets the doe secretes her young, and covers them so carefully that they are very rarely found. There was a solitary doe that I had frequently seen on the hillside, but I was careful not to disturb her haunt. Accordingly, when at evening and morning she came out to pick the sweet herbs at the foot of the brae, or by the little green well in its face, I trod softly out of her sight, and, if I passed at noon, made a circuit from the black willows and thick junipers where she reposed during the heat of the day.

7. One fine sunny morning I saw her come tripping out from her bower of young birches as light as a fairy,

and very gay and canty. For various mornings afterward I saw her on the bank, but she was always restless and anxious, listening and searching the wind, trotting up and down, picking a leaf here and a leaf there; and, after her short and unsettled meal, she would take a frisk, round leap into the air, and dart down into her secret bower and appear no more until the twilight. In a few days, however, her excursions became a little more extended, generally to the terrace above the bank, but never out of sight of the thicket below.

8. At length she ventured to a greater distance, and one day I stole down the brae among the birches. In the middle of the thicket there was a group of young trees growing out of a carpet of deep moss which yielded like a down pillow. The prints of the doe's slender, forked feet were thickly tracked about the hollow, and in the center there was a bed of the velvet "fog," which seemed a little higher than the rest, but so natural that it would not have been noticed by any unaccustomed eye. I carefully lifted the green cushion, and under its veil, rolled close together, the head of each resting upon the flank of the other, nestled two beautiful little fawns, their large velvet ears laid smooth on their dappled necks, their spotted sides sleek and shining as satin, and their little, delicate legs as slender as hazel wands, shod with tiny, glossy shoes, as smooth and black as ebony, while their large, dark eyes looked at me out of the corners with a full, mild, quiet gaze, which had not yet learned to fear the hand of man; still, they had a nameless doubt which followed every motion of mine, their little limbs shrank from my touch, and their velvet fur rose and fell quickly; but as I was about to replace the moss, one turned its head, lifted its sleek ears toward me, and licked my hand as I laid their soft mantle over them.

9. I often saw them afterward when they grew strong, and came abroad upon the brae, and frequently called off

old Dreadnought when he crossed their warm track. Upon these occasions he would stand and look at me in wonder, turn his head from side to side, sniff the ground again to see if it was possible that he could be mistaken, and, when he found that there was no disputing the scent, cock one ear at me with a keener inquiry, and, seeing that I was in earnest, trot heavily onward with a sigh.

Charles Edward Stuart.

DEER-STALKING IN THE SCOTTISH HIGHLANDS.

1. ONE beautiful day in early September the old keeper MacLellan and I started for a day's sport in the hills. After about an hour's stalking we came upon the shoulder of a long slope, which looks into the gorges of two or three short glens, opening to a narrow plain, on which we saw a noble sight—a herd of four or five hundred deer, among which were many fine stags. After having feasted my eyes with this splendid sight—the illustrious cavalry of the hill, the crowned and regal array of the wilderness—I began to calculate how to make the approach, how to slip between the chain of vedette hinds and numerous pickets of small stags which commanded almost every knoll and hollow. In the center of the main body, with a large plump of hinds—which he herded within a wide vacant circle—there was a mighty black hart, with a head like a blasted pine, and a cluster of points in each crown. Though each stag of the surrounding circle had not less than ten points, there was none which approached his size, and they all kept at a respectful distance, while he marched round and round the central group of hinds. "He will have them all in the ring before long," said MacLellan; "yon's one of the old heroes; he has not been four-

and-twenty hours in the forest." I looked with an eager and longing eye at his gigantic stature, but there was no apparent possibility of approaching even the outward circle of stags.

2. The herd was scattered over all the ground between the hills, and every little knoll and eminence had its restless pickets, and plumps of discomfited stags, which had been beaten by the great hart, and were chafing about, driving off and prodding the buttocks of all the inferior stags that came in their way, then returning and staring with jealous disgust at the mighty stranger, who gave them no notice, except when one or two more audacious, or less severely beaten, made a few steps before his companions, upon which he immediately charged, drove them before him, and scattered the nearest in every direction. Upon these occasions some hind of greater levity than the rest took the opportunity of extending her pasture, or paying her compliments to her companions, for which she immediately received a good prod in the haunch, and was turned back again into the center.

3. "There is no doing anything there," said I. "'Deed no," replied MacLellan, shutting up his glass, "we be to go down to the foot of the burn." This was a stream which runs through the middle of the narrow plain and empties itself into the Fidich, about four miles below, at the east end of the forest. Before resolving upon this, however, we made an attempt to cross the little glen to the northwest; but, after passing round one hill, and nearly to the top of another, we fell in with a small herd of insignificant stags, but none among them being worth the disturbance of the great herd; and, being unable to pass them unobserved, we were obliged to adopt the last alternative and descend to the Fidich. In about an hour and a half we performed this retrogration, and, having crossed at the forester's house, ascended the burn till we again approached

the deer, and, stealing from knoll to knoll, again came in sight of the herd. The outskirts of its wide circle had been much broken and deranged by the jousts and expulsions during our absence; and we saw that it was impossible to get near the better stags without taking the channel of the stream.

4. We immediately descended into the water and crept up the middle, sometimes compelled to crouch so low that the pools reached our hips, and, as the stones were round and slippery, it was very difficult to proceed without floundering and splashing. At length, however, we were within the circle of the deer; there was not a breath of wind, and the least sound was audible in the profound stillness. We slipped through the water like eels, till we came to a little rock, which, crossing the burn, made a shelving fall, which there was no means of passing but by drawing ourselves up the shoot of the stream. With some difficulty I pushed my rifle before me along the edge of the bank, and then, while the water ran down our breasts, we glided up through the gush of the stream and reached the ledge above.

5. The return of the water, which I had obstructed, made, however, a rush and plash different from its accustomed monotonous hum, and I had scarce time to lay flat in the burn when a hind sprang up within a few yards and trotted briskly away, then another, and another. I thought that all was over, and that, in the next moment, we should hear all the clattering hoofs going over the turf like a squadron of cavalry. All remained still, however, and, in a few seconds, I saw the first hind wheel about and look back steadily toward the fall. I was rejoiced to observe that she had not seen us, and had only been disturbed by the unusual sound of the water. She continued, however, anxious and suspicious; watched and listened; picked off the tops of the heather; then walked on, with her ears

laid back, and her neck and step stilting away as stiff as if she had been hung up in the larder for a week. This, however, was not the worst; all the surrounding hinds which noticed her gait gathered here and there, and stood on the tops of the little knolls, like statues, as straight as pucks, with nothing visible but their narrow necks and two peg-legs, and their broad ears perked immovably toward us, like long-eared bats.

6. MacLellan gave me a rueful look. "Never mind," said I, "we shall see who will be tired first." The forester gave a glance of satisfaction, slid up his glass on the dry bank, and we lay still as the stones around us, till the little trouts, which had been disturbed by our convulsion, became so accustomed to our shapes that they again emerged from under the flat pebbles and returned to their station in the middle of the stream, skulking their little tails between my legs with no more concern than if I had been a forked tree. At length the immobility of the hinds began to give way: first one ear turned back, then another, then they became sensible of the flies, and began to flirt and jerk as usual, and finally one applied her slender toe to her ear, and another rubbed her velvet nose upon her knee; it was more than half an hour, however, before, one by one, they began to steal away, perking and snuffing, and turning to gaze at the least air that whiffed about them.

7. At length they all disappeared except one gray, lean, haggard old grandmother of hinds, who had no teeth, and limped with one leg, probably from a wound which she received fifty or perhaps a hundred years before I was born. Her vigilance, however, was only sharpened by age; time, and the experience of many generations, had made her acquainted with all the wiles and crafts of the hill; her eyes and ears were as active as a kid's, and I have no doubt she could smell like Tobit's devil. MacLellan looked at her through his glass, spit into the burn, and grinned

against the sun—as if he was lying in the bilboes instead of cold water. The old sorceress continued to watch us without relaxation, and at last lay down on the brow of the knoll and employed her rumination in obstinate contemplation of the bank under which we were ambushed.

8. There was now no alternative but to recommence our progress up the burn; and, as I was determined to circumvent the hind, I prepared for every inconvenience which could be inflicted by the opposite vexations of a sharp, rough, slippery, and gravelly stream. Fortunately, at the place where we then were, it was so narrow that we could hold by the heather on both sides, and thus drag ourselves forward through the water, between each of which advances I pushed my rifle on before me. In this manner we reached the turn of the brook, where I concluded that we should be round the shoulder of the knoll and out of sight of the hind, who lay upon its east brow. This was effected so successfully that, when we looked behind, we only saw her back, and her head and ears still pointing at the spot which we had left.

9. One hundred yards more would bring us within sight of the great hart. The general position of the herd had not changed, and I hoped to find him near the central knoll of the flat, at the base of which the burn circled. We were almost surrounded by deer; but the greater number were small, vigilant hinds, the abomination and curse of a stalker. At length, however, we reached the knoll, and rested to take breath at its foot. I examined my rifle, to see that the lock was clean and dry. We took a view of all around us, and, drawing ourselves cautiously out of the burn, slid up through the heather on the south side of the eminence. Scarce, however, had our legs cleared the stream when we discovered a pair of ears not above fifteen yards from the other side. "My curse upon you," whispered MacLellan. She had not discovered us, however,

and we glided round the base of the knoll—but on the other side lay three hinds and a calf, and I could see no trace of the great hart.

10. On the edge of the burn, however, farther up, there were five very good stags, and a herd of about thirty deer, on the slope of the north brae. All round us the ground was covered with hinds, for the prevalence of the westerly wind during the last few days had drawn the deer to that end of the forest. Upon the spot where I lay, though I could only see a portion of the field, I counted four hundred and seventy; and it was evident that no movement could be made upon that side. We tried again the opposite side of the knoll; the hind which we had first seen was still in the same place, but she had lain down her head, and showed only the gray line of her back over the heather. We drew ourselves cautiously up the slope and looked over the summit. On the other side there was a small, flat moss, about seventy yards in breadth; then another hillock; and to the left two more, with little levels, and wet, grassy hollows between them. Upon the side of the first knoll there were two young stags and some hinds; but the points of some good horns showed above the crest. The intervening ground was spotted with straggling hinds, and we might lay where we were till to-morrow morning without a chance of getting near any of the good deer.

11. While we deliberated, MacLellan thought that, by crawling with extreme caution up a wet hollow to the left, we might have a chance to approach the stags whose horns we had seen behind the other knoll, and, as nothing better could be done, we decided upon this attempt. The sun was going down from the old towers of Auchandùn, and we had no more time than would give light for this venture. We slid away toward the hollow, and, drawing ourselves inch by inch through the heather and tall, thin grass, had reached the middle of the level between the hillocks,

when we heard a stamp and a short grunt close beside us. I had scarce time to turn my head and catch a glimpse of a base little gray hind, who, in crossing the hollow, had stumbled upon us. It was but a moment; a rapid wheel

The Stag.

and rush through the long grass, and I heard the career of a hundred feet going through the hollow. I sprang on my knee, and scare a dozen small stags and hinds which came upon us at full speed; for those behind, not knowing from whence came the alarm, made straight for the hill. The herd was now gathering in all directions, charging, flying, reuniting, dispersing, and reassembling in utter disorder, like a rout of cavalry.

12. I made a run for the middle knoll; two stags with pretty good heads met me right in the face. I did not stop to look at them, but rushed up the brae. What a sight was seen from its top! Upward of six hundred deer were charging past, before, behind, around, in all directions. The stately figure which I sought, the mighty black hart, was slowly ascending an eminence about three hundred yards off, from whence he reconnoitered the ground below, while the disarray of stags and hinds gathered round him, like rallying masses of hussars in the rear of a supporting column. I was so intent looking upon the king of the forest that I saw nothing else. No other heads, forms, numbers, took any place in my senses; all my faculties were on the summit of that height.

13. At this moment I felt my kilt drawn gently; I took no notice, but a more decided pull made me look round. MacLellan motioned up the slope, and I saw the points of a good head passing behind a little ridge, about eighty yards away. I looked back at the hart; he was just moving to the hill. What would I have given to have diminished a hundred and fifty yards of the distance which divided us! He passed slowly down the back of the eminence and disappeared, and the gathering herd streamed after him. The stag whose horns I had seen had come out from behind the ridge, and stood with his broad side toward me, gazing at the herd; but as they moved away he now began to follow. The disappearance of the great hart and the disappointment of MacLellan recalled me to the last chance. I followed the retreating stag with my rifle, passed it before his shoulder, whiz went the two-ounce ball, and he rolled over headlong in the heath, on the other side

of the knoll, which the next stretch would have placed between us.

14. I looked to the hill above. The whole herd was streaming up the long, green hollow in its west shoulder, headed "by the mighty of the desert." They rounded and passed the brow, and sloped upward on the other side, till the forest of heads appeared bristling along the sky-line of the summit. In a few moments afterward, as the sun was going down upon the far western hills of Loch Duiach, the terrible wide-forked tree came out in the clear eastern sky on the top of the hill, and, crowding after, at least two hundred heads — crossing and charging and mingling — their polished points flashing in the parting sunbeams, and from many a horn the long streamers of the moss fluttering and flying like the pennons and banderoles of lances. The herd continued to file along the ridge of the hill, and, wheeling below the crest, countermarched along the sky-line till their heads and horns slowly decreased against the light.

Charles Edward Stuart.

PART XIII.

STRANGE ANIMALS AND THEIR WAYS.

MUSICAL MICE.

1. In this country we have several species of wood-mice, often called white-footed mice, that have wonderful musical powers. They are diminutive things, not so large as the house-mouse, their sides are yellowish-brown, the back considerably darker, the abdomen and feet almost snowy-white. Their home is the woods. With but little sympathy for man, they will occasionally intrude for a time into his dwelling, when, as I believe, the domestic mouse withdraws. A friend of mine at his Florida home, near St. Augustine, was disturbed at night by what he supposed to be the chirping of birds in the chimney. The mystery was cleared up in an unexpected way. A very small mouse came up from a crevice in the hearth, and, with singular boldness, took position in the middle of the sitting-room floor. Here it sat up on its hind feet, and looked around with the utmost confidence, all the time singing in a low, soft, yet really warbling style.

2. It paid the penalty of its temerity by being captured. About a month after, this prodigy was intrusted to the custody of the writer. Of course, it came introduced as a "singing house-mouse." What was our astonishment at recognizing in the little stranger a true Hesperomys, and

no house-mouse at all! It was one of the wood-mice, and among the smallest of the species. It is a female, and fully grown, yet not so large as a domestic mouse. Every pains was taken to secure the comfort and well-being of my little guest.

3. And what an ample reward I reaped! For a considerable time she caroled almost incessantly, except when she slept. Day and night she rollicked in tiny song, her best performances being usually at night. To me it was often a strange delight when, having wrought into the late hours, and the weary brain had become so needful and yet so repellent of sleep, I lay down, and gave myself up to listening to this wee songster, whose little cage I had set on a chair by my bedside. To be sure, it was a low, very low, sweet voice. But there was, with a singular weirdness, something so sweetly merry that I would listen on, and on, until I would fall asleep in the lullaby of my wingless and quadrupedal bob-o'-link.

4. The cage had a revolving cylinder or wheel, such as tame squirrels have. In this it would run for many minutes at a time, singing at its utmost strength. This revolving cage, although ample as regards room, was not over three and a half inches long and two and a half inches wide. Although I have now been entertained by these pretty little melodies for a year, yet I would not dare redescribe them. She had two especially notable performances. I called these *rôles*—one the *wheel-song*, because it was usually sung while in the revolving cylinder, and the other the *grand rôle*. A remarkable fact in the latter is the scope of the little creature's musical powers. Her soft, clear voice falls an octave with all the precision possible; then, at its wind-up, it rises again into a very quick trill on C sharp and D.

5. Though it be at the risk of taxing belief, yet I must in duty record one of Hespie's most remarkable perform-

ances. She was gamboling in the large compartment of her cage, in intense animal enjoyment. She had just woke from a long sleep, and had eaten of some favorite food, when she burst into a fullness of song very rich in its variety. While running and jumping, she caroled off what I have called her *grand rôle*; then, sitting, she went over it again, ringing out the strangest diversity of changes, by an almost whimsical transposition of the bars of the melody; then, without, for even an instant, stopping the music, she leaped into the wheel, sent it revolving at its highest speed, and, while thus running in the wheel, she went through the wheel-song in exquisite style, giving several repetitions of it. After this, without at all arresting the singing, she returned to the large compartment, sat upright, resumed again the *grand rôle*, and put into it some variations which astonished me.

6. One measure, I remember, was so silvery and soft that I said to a lady who was listening, that a canary able to execute that strain would be almost beyond price. I occasionally detected, what I am utterly unable to explain, a literal dual sound, a sort of rollicking chuckling, very like a boy whistling as he runs, and drawing a stick along the pickets of a fence. So the music went on, as I listened, watch in hand, until actually nine minutes had elapsed. Now, the wonderful fact is, that the rest between the *rôles* was never much more than a second of time; and during all this singing the muscles could be seen in vigorous action through the entire length of the abdomen. This feat would be impossible to a professional singer; and the nearest to it that I have heard was the singing of the wild mocking-bird in a grove.   *Rev. Samuel Lockwood.*

BATS AND THEIR HABITS.

1. EXCEPTING the colder regions, all parts of the world are inhabited by bats. There are many kinds, and they often occur in very large numbers. Probably there are very few persons, young or old, who have not seen a bat. Yet, aside from professed naturalists, it is equally probable that there are still fewer who, from direct observation, could give any accurate description of their appearance or their habits, their structure, or their relations with the "birds of the air," or the "beasts of the earth," to both of which bats bear more or less resemblance.

2. Nor is this strange ; for bats pass the day in caves and deserted buildings, and fly about in pursuit of prey only in the twilight. Much less rapid than that of birds, their flight is so irregular as to render it difficult to follow their course, and in the dusk they are often mistaken for somewhat eccentric members of the swallow family.

3. Their very aspect is repulsive; they often emit an unpleasant odor. When taken, they bite so fiercely that we may be thankful that they are no larger, and that, as a rule, they prefer insects to human beings as food. No tiger could be more violent in its demonstrations or more capable of using its only weapons, the sharp, almost needle-like eye-teeth.

4. We may as well state at once that a bat is really a *mammal;* that is, it agrees with moles, rats, sheep, horses, cats, monkeys, and men, in bringing forth its young alive, and nursing them by milk ; in having red blood-corpuscles, which contain no nucleus; in being clothed with hair; and in possessing a *corpus callosum*—that is, a band of fibers connecting the two cerebral hemispheres. There are other anatomical features which link the bats closely with the moles and shrews and hedgehogs. Indeed, the bat might

be described as a flying mole, or the mole as a burrowing bat.

5. When I was a boy, one of our common bats flew into the house one evening and was caught under a hat. It squeaked and snapped its little jaws so viciously that all efforts toward closer acquaintance were postponed until morning. When uncovered the next day it seemed as fierce as before, but less active in its movements, probably overpowered by the glare of daylight. When touched, its jaws opened wide, the sharp teeth were exposed, and from its little throat came the sharp steely clicks so characteristic of our bats.

6. Nor did this fierce demeanor soften in the least during the day, and when night approached I was about to let it go, but the sight of a big fly upon the window suggested an attempt to feed the captive. Held by the wings between the points of a pair of forceps, the fly had no sooner touched the bat's nose than it was seized, crunched, and swallowed. The rapidity of its disappearance accorded with the width to which the eater's jaws were opened to receive it, and, but for the dismal crackling of skin and wings, reminded one of the sudden ingulfment of beetles by a hungry young robin.

7. A second fly went the same road. The third was more deliberately masticated, and I ventured to pat the devourer's head. Instantly all was changed. The jaws gaped as if they would separate, the crushed fly dropped from the tongue, and the well-known click proclaimed a hatred and defiance which hunger could not subdue nor food appease. So at least it seemed, and I think any but a boy-naturalist would have yielded to the temptation to fling the spiteful creature out of the window. Perhaps, too, a certain obstinacy made me unwilling to so easily relinquish the newly formed hope of domesticating a bat. At any rate, another fly was presented, and, like the former,

dropped the moment my fingers touched the head of the bat. With a third I waited until the bat seemed to be actually swallowing, and unable to either discontinue that process or open its mouth to any extent.

8. Its rage and perplexity were comical to behold, and, when the fly was really down, it seemed to almost burst with the effort to express its indignation. But this did not prevent it from falling into the same trap again; and, to make a long story short, it finally learned by experience that, while chewing and swallowing were more or less interrupted by snapping at me, both operations were quite compatible with my gentle stroking of its head. And even a bat has brains enough to see the foolishness of losing a dinner in order to resent an unsolicited kindness.

9. In a few days the bat would take flies from my fingers; although, either from eagerness or because blinded by the light, it too often nipped me sharply in its efforts to seize the victim. Its voracity was almost incredible. For several weeks it devoured at least fifty house-flies in a day (it was vacation, and my playmates had to assist me), and once disposed of *eighty* between daybreak and sunset. This bat I kept for more than two months. It would shuffle across the table when I entered the room, and lift up its head for the expected fly. When traveling it was carried in my breast-pocket. In the fall it died, either from overeating or lack of exercise, for I dared not let it out of doors, and it was so apt to injure itself in the rooms that I seldom allowed it to fly. I should add that it drank frequently and greedily from the tip of a camel's-hair pencil. The following bits of bat biography are from White's "Natural History of Selborne":

10. "Having caught a lively male specimen of the common 'long-eared bat' and placed the little fellow in a wire-gauze cage, and inserted a few large flies, he was soon attracted by their buzz, and, pricking up his ears (just as a

donkey does), he pounced upon his prey. But, instead of taking it directly into his mouth, he covered it with his body and beat it by aid of its arms, etc., into the bag formed by the interfemoral membrane. He then put his head under his body, withdrew the fly from the bag, and devoured it at leisure.

11. "This appeared to be always the *modus operandi*, more or less cleverly performed. Several times, when the fly happened to be on the flat surface of the ground, the capture appeared more difficult, and my little friend was, by his exertions, thrown on his back. The tail could then be seen turned round, with its tip and the margin of the membrane pressed against the stomach, forming a capital trap, holding the fly, the captor remaining on his back till he had withdrawn the fly from the bag."

Professor Burt G. Wilder.

THE LEMMING AND ITS MIGRATIONS.

1. THE Norway rat, of which we wish to say a few words, is the lemming, a species of the mouse-tribe, somewhat smaller than the Guinea-pig, to which in form it bears a considerable resemblance, only the head and body are flatter. Its length is about six inches, of which the short stump of a tail forms half an inch. It is black in color, mottled with tawny spots, which vary in their disposition in different individuals, and the belly is white, with a slight tinge of yellow. The fore legs are short and strong, and the hind legs are nearly one half longer than the former, enabling it to run with considerable speed. The feet are armed with strong hooked claws, five in number, enabling it to burrow in the earth, and among the frozen snows of its native region.

2. Its cheeks are blanched, and it sports a pair of long, light whiskers, and its eyes, though small, are beautifully black and piercing. The lip is divided, and the ears are small and sharply pointed. As its home borders on the region of eternal snow, in the valleys of the Kolen Mountains, which separate Sweden from Nordland, its hair is both thick and soft, and becomes almost white during the long and cheerless winter of these inhospitable regions. The skin is much thinner than in any of its congeners.

The Lemming, or Norway Rat.

When enraged, it gives utterance to a sharp yelp, similar to that of a month-old terrier-whelp.

3. It is a lively little fellow, when met with in its native haunts during the short summer—now sitting on its haunches nibbling at a piece of lichen, or the catkins of the birch, which it conveys to its mouth with its fore paws, after the manner of the squirrel, or engaging in a romp with its fellows, popping in and out of its burrow in the earth, where it sleeps and rears its young, of which the female has two or three litters annually, numbering from five

to seven in each. It is a most audacious little fellow, and fears neither man nor beast, refusing to give way save on the compulsion of superior force. Travelers speak of having seen them frisking about in hundreds in their native forests, when they dispute the path even with man.

4. From the vantage-ground of the mounds of earth at the entrance to their burrows they sit on their beam-ends and scan the intruders with comical gravity. If the traveler has a dog with him, unhappily ignorant of the ways of this cool and impudent *varmint*, he will likely advance with the easy nonchalance of his tribe to smell the odd little animal—which betrays no fear at his approach—to be rewarded by a sharp and trenchant bite on the nose, a reception so sudden and unexpected that it is ten chances to one against his prosecuting his investigations further, for a dog is too well bred to attack any strange living object which awaits his approach.

5. The lemming multiplies so rapidly that in the course of ten or twelve seasons food becomes scarce, and, on the approach of some winter, when the food-question has become one of life or death, the overstocked market is relieved by an expedient unparalleled in its nature among four-footed animals. This singular little creature is so local in its habits that, unless under the circumstances we are about to narrate, it never leaves the mountain region to establish itself on the plains, where food is more abundant.

6. When the time for the settlement of the question of partial extermination for the benefit of the race, or total extermination by starvation, can no longer be delayed, they assemble in countless thousands in some of the mountain valleys leading into the plains, and, the vast army of martyrs being selected, they pour across the country in a straight line, a living stream, often exceeding a mile in length and many yards in breadth, devouring every green thing in their line of march, the country over which they

have passed looking as if it had been plowed, or burned with fire. They march principally by night, resting during the day, but never seek to settle in any particular locality, however abundant the food may be in it, for their final destination is the distant sea, and nothing animate or inanimate, if it can be surmounted, retards the straight, onward tide of their advance.

7. When the reindeer gets enveloped in the living stream, they will not even go round its limbs, but bite its legs until, in its agony and terror, it plunges madly about, crushing them to death in hundreds, and even killing them with its teeth. If a man attempts to stem the living torrent, they leap upon his legs; and, if he lay about him with a stick, they seize it with their teeth, and hold on to it with such determined pertinacity that he may swing it rapidly round his head without compelling them to loosen their hold. If a corn- or hay-rick be in the way, they eat their way through it; and, on arriving at the smooth face of a rock, they pass round it, forming up in close column again on the other side. Lakes, however broad, are boldly entered, and the passage attempted; and rivers, however deep and rapid, are forded, impediments in the water being as boldly faced as those on shore. They have been known to pass over a boat, and to climb on to the deck of a ship, passing, without stop or stay, into the water on the farther side.

8. Their natural instincts are not in abeyance during this migration, as females are frequently seen accompanied by their young, and carrying in their teeth some one which had succumbed to the fatigues of the march, which might not be stayed until the helpless one was recruited.

9. Foxes, lynxes, weasels, kites, owls, etc., hover on their line of march and destroy them in hundreds. The fish in the rivers and lakes lay a heavy toll upon them, and vast numbers are drowned, and die by other accidents in

"flood and field"; but the survivors, impelled by some irresistible instinct, press onward with no thought of stopping, until they lose themselves in the sea, sinking in its depths, as they become exhausted, in such numbers that for miles their bodies, thrown up by the tide, lie putrefying on the shore. Comparatively few ever return to their native haunts, but there can be no doubt that some do so, as they have been seen on the return, pursuing their backward journey in the same fearless and determined manner as their advance.

Temple Bar.

THE COATI-MONDI.

1. SAILORS from South America occasionally, among other pets, bring a small animal, which, because of its long nose, they invariably call an ant-eater. Thus was a little stranger introduced to our care a few years ago. A glance was enough to see that it was no ant-eater at all, but a pretty female coati-mondi. Gallant Jack Tar, her master on ship, unconscious of the incongruity, had made a namesake of her, and called her Jack. Science had already named her *Nasua*, and in a matter-of-fact way, for the word interpreted just means — Nosie. The animal was about the size of a cat, with a thick, coarse fur, of a brownish hue on the back and sides, and underneath shades from yellow to orange. The long tail was ornamented by a series of black and yellowish-brown rings.

2. Her nasal prominence reminded me of a queer Spaniard, once employed in the government service to detect spurious coin. His "counterfeit detector" was a sensitive proboscis. By sticking this organ into the glittering heaps, he literally "nosed" out the bad from the good. To that man his nose was the instrument of his profession; and to Nasua her nose was equally important. It even prompted

a nick-name and a juvenile pun—"Nosie's nose knows too much!" Inappeasably inquisitive, she was incessantly intruding that organ into everything. Having made no allowance for an extra-tropical temperature, this little South American made a failure in an attempt to lift with her nose the lid of a pot in the cook's domain.

3. The next attempt, a successful one, was on the knife-box, whose closely fitting lid was pried open and every article inspected, in happy ignorance of the proverb about edged tools. It was enough that anything was hollow to excite her curiosity, which was of a thoroughly simian type. The dinner-bell was turned over; but, unable to detach the clapper and chain, it was soon abandoned in disgust. A round sleigh-bell received more persevering attention. Unable to get her nose or paws into the little hole at the side, the clatter within set her wild with excitement, and evoked a desperate attack on the little annoyance with her teeth. She then gave it up as a bootless job.

4. A bottle of hartshorn was next made the subject of investigation. We had purposely loosened the cork, and promised ourselves a "nice sell"; and *we* got it—not Nosie. She was not in the least disconcerted by the drug. In fact, she had a strong nose for such things. A man gave her his tobacco-box. Resting it on the floor between her two paws, which possessed uncommon flexibility, she turned it over and over, round and round, exercising alternately her nose, claws, and teeth upon it with great energy, but to no avail. It seemed that the smell of its contents infatuated her, as she showed no disposition to stop. The man opened the box for her. She was in rapture. In went the nose, also both front paws. Very soon that wonderfully mobile organ had separated every fiber, so that the mass seemed trebly increased. The same man let her have his dirty pipe, when her velvety nose was instantly squeezed into the rank nicotian bowl.

5. It would be wrong to infer that Nasua's prying propensity never got her into trouble. In the following instance, speaking metaphorically, she put her foot into it: The old cat had just finished her nap, and was stretching herself, an operation which means that she stood with her four feet close together, the limbs elongated, the back rounded up like that of a camel, the head erect and drawn back, and the mouth yawning widely. Such a sight Nosie had never seen, hence it must be looked into. So in a trice, erect, and resting flatly on her hind feet like a little bear, she put her arms round Tabbie's neck, and, reeking with nicotine, down went that inquisitive nose into the depths of the feline fauces. This unwarrantable intrusion was met by a reception more feeling than felicitous, judging from the haste in which Nasua withdrew to a corner of the room to ruminate on the untoward incident. Her method of relieving the injured member was itself original. She placed it between her paws, holding it tightly, then jerked it through them, giving a violent sneeze every time it came out. That sneezing was genuine, because it was involuntary. Both hartshorn and nicotine had signally failed to get up any-

Coati-Mondi.

thing respectable in that line; but that cat-nip, pure and simple, did the business finely.

6. Quite pretty was the pattern of the animal's ears—they were so clean, trim, soft, and small. Though rather pert, they had an air about them that was really amiable, and such as the canine fancier would pronounce elegant. She was not averse to a little fondling, and I well remember the first time she climbed upon my lap. Those pretty ears suddenly quivered. The ticking of my watch had excited her. Down goes that ubiquitous utilitarian organ

Coati-Mondi asleep.

into the watch-pocket. Failing with the nose, she makes a desperate effort with that and both forefeet all at once. Still unable to evict that case of mystery, she thrusts her nose down by its side, and for several minutes, with simian quaintness, listens to the ticking of mortal Time.

7. In the same manner, though not to the same extent, the nose of the Nasua, like the same organ of the elephant, projects far beyond the mouth. At our first acquaintance with the animal, we were anxious to see if it could drink

out of a deep, narrow vessel. So a mug, containing about a gill of milk, was set before her. She instantly turned up the proboscis toward her forehead, and, in the easiest way imaginable, lapped the vessel dry. The organ was not even wet. The sight, though comical, was really pretty. It was the only time that I had ever seen the turning up of the nose at one's friends so deftly and gracefully done. And she could turn the same organ in a contrary way quite as easily.

8. Sometimes for an airing the animal was tied by a long tether to a flower-stand on the lawn. She had nearly all the appetencies of the domestic swine; and the end of her proboscis was essentially a swine's snout. I now beheld the use of this singularly tipped organ. And an interesting sight it was to see that little thing plow up the greensward with the tip of her nose—and so easily. Here appeared the veritable swinish acuteness of scent for insects and worms, and the swinish facility for rooting in the ground. With surprising rapidity furrow after furrow was made, of about the width of a man's thumb. Whenever a worm or insect was discovered, as when drinking, the nose was curved up, so that the mouth could extract the object from the furrow.

9. The tail of Nasua is quite suggestive of the raccoon; but Nasua's tail is a much handsomer affair—longer, and with rings more numerous and of gayer colors. With admirable intelligence, our pet put this beautiful appendage to a remarkable use. She was tethered by a string to a chair, and an egg was put on the floor at a tantalizing distance. She could just touch it with a paw, and that touch caused the coveted prize to roll out of reach. She then turned her hind feet toward it, pulling hard so as to stretch her neck; still, even with a hind foot she could not touch it. The logic of events was now, "Get it if you can!"

10. All this Nasua well understood, for she turned tail

on the subject altogether—not, however, as did Reynard on the grapes, but strategically. She gathered herself up, and looked at the coveted object with speculative eyes. Then she swung herself round again, pulling hard on the tether by the neck. She then curved the tip of the tail so as to make a little hook. Now she grasps the base of the tail with one paw, as with a hand, thus stiffening and steadying the organ. She next slowly and cautiously rolled the egg, by the curved tip of the tail, through a section of a circle, until it was brought within reach of one of the front feet. The egg now seized, sitting on her hind feet like a bear, she cracks it, extracts the contents, and neither spills a drop on the floor, nor so much as soils that wonderful nose; for among her many gifts is her soft and extensile tongue.

11. A word is necessary as to the peculiar temerity of this animal. From two points it was liable to give way to extreme impulsiveness—the excitement of opposition, or of inquisitiveness. If anything attacked her, whatever the object or the odds might be, she would face the assailant, and close in with her shrill little squeaks of rage, and in a wild sort of dash. If one slapped her, whatever might be her terror, she would rush upon and snap at the hand. The dog-like sagacity of running under the table or chair was not her way. Hers was the peccary instinct of running upon danger. No monkey could be a more importunate or impertinent teaser than was our coati; but Jocko shows sagacity with his jokes—for he always adroitly leaps aside of consequences.

12. I have watched our pet tease the cat with imperturbable persistency, until Tabbie, unable to tolerate matters any longer, has struck her sharp claws into that soft proboscis, then moved away, leaving her persecutor dazed with astonishment. Then, in a moment, forgetting all, she would turn her attention to the setter-dog, and, despite

his growls and menacing teeth, would keep up a systematic worrying—catching at his tail, nipping at his legs, and even poking her nose into his ears. At length the poor brute, fairly goaded to rage, seized her like a rat, and, but for my prompt interference, that would have been the last display of Nasua's rashness.

13. One morning she got into the dining-room as we were at breakfast. She took possession of madam's lap. Her first act was to poke her nose at the coffee-urn. This evoked a squeak of pain. It was supposed that she had had enough. Not quite. Her next essay was on a cup of hot coffee, with a similar result. She now smelt the contents of the sugar-bowl. This discovery so excited that "sweet will" of hers that instant removal became imperative.

14. Later in the day she tried to capture a wasp. She struck it down, and held it a second under her foot. This was met by an appeal, addressed solely to her understanding, of so pointed a nature as made her chatter with distress. Disabled in one wing, the insect could not fly away. Although still smarting from the wounded foot, the moral of the lesson is only half learned. Coati can not give "little yellow-jacket" up. So she tries the wasp again—this time with her nose. Alas, that sting! Miss Nasua now finds that other little folks besides herself can utilize their tails; for, in proof of this, she receives not a merely duplicated, but an intensified experience, such as exacts a staccato outgush of agony of truly simian expression.

15. We can recall but one lesson which she took sincerely to heart. The old cow was quietly ruminating near the house. With her usual temerity, for she was always ready to "go it blind," Coati made an attempt to climb one of Cushie's legs. The cow raised her foot to shake the annoyance off, and in setting it down she put her hoof on Nasua's tail, and there standing, gravely ruminating, held

her fast to the ground. Her rapid, chattering cry brought one of the ladies to her rescue. The tail was very badly hurt. Ever after, between Coati and Cushie a respectful distance was maintained.

Rev. Samuel Lockwood.

JEMMY.

1. As company for the monkeys and myself, for many years past I have had a "Jemmy." All my Suricates I call "Jemmys." The Latin name is *Suricata Zenick*. Jemmy is a very pretty little beast, somewhat like a small mongoose or a very large rat. His head is as like the head of a hedgehog as can be imagined. His color is light brown, with darker stripes down the sides. He is an African animal, and lives in burrows on the plains, whence he is sometimes called the African prairie-dog, or the *meercatze*. Captain Adams tells me that, when in South Africa, he has frequently come across a camp of Jemmys. The plain will appear covered with them, sitting up motionless like so many ninepins; at the least notice, they simultaneously and in an instant disappear down their holes.

2. I would like now to say something of the habits of this pretty little fellow. Jemmy the Third (for I have previously had two Jemmys) was allowed the free range of the whole house. He was full of curiosity and restlessness, running continually from one room to another. He very seldom walked; his pace, on the contrary, was a short gallop, or rather canter. When on the move he always gave tongue, like a hound on a scent. It is impossible to describe his melodious cry in words. When handled and petted he would utter a sharp bark, not unlike that of a dog; and, if in a very good humor, I could, by imitating

him, make him bark alternately with myself. His great peculiarity was his wonderfully intelligent and observing look. He had the peculiarity also of sitting up on his tail, like a kangaroo; his fore paws on this occasion were like a dog's when begging. He was very fond of warmth, and would sit up inside the fender and warm himself, occasion-

The Suricate (Jemmy).

ally leaning back against the fender and looking round with the satisfied air of an old gentleman reposing after dinner. When the morning sun came into the room, Jemmy would go and sit in the sunbeams and look out of the window at the passing cabs and omnibuses. When doing this he had a way of turning round very sharply and looking with his little pig's eyes at me and back, as much as to say, " What do you think of that ? "

3. When breakfast came up he would dance round me on his hind legs, watching for something. I often put him on the breakfast-table; if I did not put him up he would climb up uninvited. It was very amusing to see him go and smell the egg, and, in his own language, swear at it for being hot. He could not understand its being hot enough to burn his nose; raw eggs were his special favor-

ites. His great delight was to be allowed to upset the sugar-basin, and then scratch about among the lumps of sugar. He was also very fond of cream, and it was most amusing to see him try to get the little drops of cream I had left for him out of the cream-can, as left by the milk-woman. I am obliged to have my cream in this little can, as the cats, marmoset, or something else would be sure to have it before I came down. I placed the cream-can on the floor, and it was fun to see Jemmy try to force it open with his teeth, to get the cream out; he used quite to lose his patience with this metal cream-can.

4. After breakfast, Jemmy generally had a stand-up fight with the monkeys. He would inspect (from the outside) the bottom of the monkey-cage. If he discovered any portion of the monkeys' breakfast which he thought might suit him, he would immediately try to steal it by thrusting his arms through the bar. The monkeys invariably resented this indignity. The carroty, old, crippled monkey, Jane, could only make eyes and faces at him. The wicked, impudent "Little Jack" would jump up and down like an India-rubber ball, all the time well inside the cage, where Jemmy could not get at him. When Jemmy was fighting the monkeys, he would stand on his hind legs and show his lovely, white, carnivorous teeth at them, turning up his sharp, mole-like nose in a most contemptuous manner, all the time keeping up a continuous bark, into which fun the parrot generally entered and barked like Jemmy also.

5. One morning, in the middle of the fight, Jemmy forgot himself for the moment in turning round, and gave the ever-vigilant Little Jack a chance. Little Jack seized Jemmy's tail with screams of delight, and pulled him straight up to the bars. Carroty Jane then joined in, and they were getting the best of it, when suddenly Jemmy turned sharp round and made his teeth meet in Little

Jack's hand. Little Jack skirmished round the cage three or four times on three legs; then, holding up his wounded hand, gazed mournfully and piteously at it, every now and then leaving off looking to make fiercer faces, and cock his ears at Jemmy. Never since has Little Jack ventured his hands outside the bars when a Jemmy fight came on.

6. One of the funniest scenes that ever happened with Jemmy was as follows: Some sea-side specimens had been sent me, and among the sea-weed was a live shore-crab about the size of a five-shilling piece. Little "Chick-Chick," the marmoset, who will eat any quantity of meal-worms, blue-bottle flies, etc., came down at once off the mantel-piece and examined Mr. Crab, who was crawling about on the floor. None of my animals had evidently seen a live crab before. The monkeys were very much frightened, and made the same cry of alarm as when I show them a snake or the house-broom. Chick-Chick evidently thought that the crab was a huge insect. The crab put out his two nippers at full length and gave the marmoset such a pinch that he retreated to the mantel-piece, and from this safe height gazed down upon the still threatening crab, uttering loud cries of "Chick, chick, chick!" alternated with his plaintive, bat-like, shrill note.

7. Presently round the corner comes Mrs. Cat. The cat evidently thought that the crab, which was gently crawling about, was a mouse. She instantly crouched, head, eyes, and ears all intent, as if trying to make up her mind whether the crab was a mouse on which she ought to pounce or not. Hearing the row caused by the crab and marmoset fight, up comes Jemmy in full cry, with tail cocked well in the air. He also attacked the crab, but could not make head or tail of him. He did not like the smell, still less did he like the sundry nips in the nose that he received from the crab's claws. A grand crab and Jemmy fight, which lasted nearly half an hour, then took place, ending

in the discomfiture of the crab, whose carcass the marmoset and the cat, both coming forward, evidently desired to share. Although it was apparent that the taste of the crab was not agreeable to Jemmy's palate, yet he gradually ate him up—claws, shells, and all—simply to prevent the other animals from getting a single bit.

8. Jemmy has teeth half carnivorous, half insectivorous. When he is at home in Africa he lives upon mice, beetles, etc. He probably digs these creatures out of the ground, for, whenever he sees a crack in the floor, or a hole in a board, he will scratch away at it, as though much depended upon his exertions. When he is fed, it is curious to observe how he always pretends to kill his food before eating it. He invariably retreats backward while he is scratching and biting at his supposed lively food. The living food evidently is in the habit of escaping forward. Mr. Jemmy takes good care that he shall not do so, by scratching incessantly in a backward direction.

9. The cat's-meat man comes punctually every day at half-past one; when the cats hear the cry "meat," they rush down into the area, and Master Jemmy, seeing them bolt, would run also, his object being to steal the ration of meat from one of the cats. By instinct or experience he had somehow found out that the cat's claws are very sharp, and whereas his mode of attack upon the monkey was face to face, the monkeys being clawless, he attacked the cats by ruffing his hair up and pushing himself backward.

10. The cat, annoyed by being disturbed at dinner, would leave off eating and strike sharply at Jemmy with her paw; that was his opportunity. In a moment he would seize the cat's meat and bolt with it, but by a most peculiar method, for when within striking distance of the cat's paw he would turn round and back up to the cat's face, and, directly she struck at him, he caught the blow on the back; then he would put his nose down through his

fore legs, and through the hinder ones, and have the meat in a moment, leaving the cat wondering where it was gone. Jemmy had by this time taken it into a place of safety. Under the table in Mr. Searle's office there is just room for him to crawl; here the angry cat could not, of course, follow him. In this retreat he would finish up what he had stolen, and then emerge licking his lips, and probably laughing to himself at the disappointed face of the cat.

11. Jemmy was always fond of getting under anything or in any kind of hole, and his great delight was to get into a boot, and when he got to the end, scratching it as though he wanted to get farther into the burrow. Frequently I found my boots going round the room, propelled, apparently, by some internal machinery. This machinery was Master Jemmy. Jemmy was a greedy little fellow. John could not bring up any kind of food into my room without Jemmy. He would watch the cook broiling the chop down stairs, and, when John brought it up, would follow close to his heels, and what between Jemmy's pretty, begging manner, the monkey's plaintive cries, and the parrot's demand, it often happens that I get very little of the chop.

Frank Buckland.

THE AARD-VARK.

1. THIS animal, known in science as the orycteropus, belongs to the order *Edentata*, or insect-eaters. It is a native of South Africa, and is called by the Dutch settlers the aard-vark, or earth-hog. It is of heavy build, with arched back, like a pig, which animal it further resembles in that its skin is sparsely strewed with hairs. But its very long ears, instead of being pendent like those of the pig, rise like horns on both sides of the head. Neither is the tail slender or twisted into a corkscrew curl; on the

contrary, it is of conical shape, and very thick at the base. Finally, the rather elongated head, terminating in a regular snout, has at its extremity a buccal opening rather larger than in the ant-eater, but yet far smaller than in swine.

2. The teeth, numbering five or six pairs in the lower jaw and six or seven in the upper, increase in size from the first to the one before the last on each side. Their structure is peculiar, being far less dense than in most mammalia, and having no coating of enamel. The grinding surface is flattened, and the single root is pierced with a number of holes in its periphery. The slender, protractile tongue is, as in nearly all of the *Edentata*, covered with a viscous substance, designed to secure the small insects on which the animal lives. The short, heavy feet terminate, the anterior in four digits, the posterior in five, all armed with strong, hoof-like claws. In the posterior feet, as in the anterior, the external lateral digits are a little shorter than the others.

3. It will be seen that the body is swollen like a full skin-bottle, and furrowed with creases which radiate from the abdominal region between the paws. The latter are of enormous size, and the tail, which is soft and flabby, falls to the ground by its own weight. The general appearance of the animal is at once mean and grotesque. Looked at from behind, it resembles a bag, the long ears projecting on each side being the ends of the string by which the mouth of the bag is tied.

4. This orycteropus lives in pairs in the plains of Kordofan, where it is called by the Arabs *abudelatif*, i. e., "the father that owns claws." In the daytime it lies hidden and doubled up in a deep hole, which it digs in the loose soil of the plain by means of its broad, sharp claws. Toward evening it quits this hiding-place and begins to move about, advancing either by leaps, or else with an unsteady gait, walking nearly always on the extremities of its

digits. Whatever may have been written heretofore by naturalists, the orycteropus is in fact digitigrade rather than plantigrade. When the animal is walking, the head is inclined, the snout nearly touching the ground, the ears laid half-way back, and the tail trailing. From time to time the animal stops to listen; it is guided principally by hearing and smell, and by the same means contrives to escape from its enemies.

5. On finding a path that has been traveled over by ants or termites, it follows it up to the ant-hill; having reached the latter, it attacks the structure with its paws, making the dust fly all around, and digging rapidly till it

The Aard-Vark.

comes to the center, or at least to one of the principal streets. Then, alternately exserting and retracting its viscous tongue, it devours the ants by the thousands. Having made an end of one nest, it attacks another, and so on till its hunger is appeased. When we consider the alarming rate at which ants and termites multiply, and the damage they cause, we must recognize in the orycteropus one of the most efficient of man's auxiliaries in tropical regions.

6. The orycteropi are extremely timid: at the slightest noise they try to get under ground. If they find no suitable hole or crevice, then they quickly dig for themselves a hiding-place. The late J. Verreaux, who had many a time

observed orycteropi at the Cape, has told me of how, having once seized by the tail one of them when it had got but half of its body under ground, he could not get the animal out except by having the ground dug to a considerable depth. In eastern Africa the negroes, approaching cautiously, kill the orycteropus by a sudden thrust of a lance before it has time to disappear. In Senegal, on the other hand, the animal is caught in iron traps, or hunted with dogs by night. The skin of the animal is thick, and makes good, strong leather. The flesh is by some travelers described as juicy, with a taste like that of pork; according to others it is disgusting, being strongly impregnated with ant-odor.

From the French of Oustalet.

THE ORNITHORHYNCHUS.

1. THE discoverers of Australia and New Zealand, and the early voyagers who visited those regions, brought back marvelous accounts of the curious plants, animals, and birds which they found there. The objects described so differed from those known in the northern hemisphere that the stories were usually regarded as of the Munchausen order, resulting from an imperfect observation united with a very lively imagination, or from a deliberate effort to deceive. As these regions have become better known, the veracity of the old navigators has been completely vindicated, and it has been found that the half was not told. Most of living organisms, both vegetable and animal, seem constructed upon a different plan from those we are accustomed to see, and science shows that they are more nearly akin to the extinct forms of the old geological ages than to the present flora and fauna of the great continents.

2. In some specimens of animal life there is such a

strange mixture of different species, and sometimes of different orders—a mixture of beast, bird, reptile, and fish—that it would seem as if Nature, in a jocose mood and with a broad grin upon her countenance, had purposely formed living conundrums to excite curiosity and prove the despair of science. Some of these strange forms are ranked as beasts and some as birds, as the mixed characteristics predominate in one direction or the other.

3. One of these creatures is ranked as a mammal, and is familiarly called the duck-bill. In science it is known as

The Ornithorhynchus.

the ornithorhynchus, or the beast with a bill, and it is certainly a marvel in structure and habits. It has a broad, flat body, with four short legs, the feet terminating in five toes armed with sharp claws, and is about the size of a woodchuck. It is clothed with a coat of fine fur, dark brown above and whitish below. Its young are born blind, like puppies, and are nourished with milk. It burrows in the river-banks and forms nests of the roots of trees, and it can walk and run rapidly on the land and climb trees. So far, it is quite like many of the mammals.

4. Its toes are webbed, and, when spread out, the membrane reaches beyond their extremities. Its tail is broad and flat, serving as a rudder in the water. But its most peculiar feature is a broad, flat bill, which gives to it its popular name of duck-bill. Its bony structure is a cross between a reptile and a bird, and its internal organs are mostly those of a bird. It swims and dives readily, and feeds upon the worms and insects which it turns up at the bottom after the manner of a duck. When standing upon its hind legs, with its short fore legs drawn in toward its breast, it resembles the penguin. In these particulars it is most like a bird.

5. It is cleanly, and is fond of warmth and dryness. It is nocturnal in its habits, lying in its nest rolled up like a ball during the day, and coming out at night in search of food. It can remain under water seven or eight minutes at a time. In one particular it is unlike any other animal known; the mother emits her milk in the water, and this rises to the surface, where it is sucked up by the young ones.

6. Its activities are as paradoxical as its structure. It can crawl like a tortoise, run like a badger, swim like a fish, dive like a duck, dig like a mole, and climb like a squirrel. In both structure and habit it is clearly a survival of forms which once existed all over the surface of the earth, but which are now elsewhere extinct; and it may justly be regarded as a living link connecting the present with the long past.

GRIZZLY.

1. Coward—of heroic size,
   In whose lazy muscles lies
   Strength we fear and yet despise;
   Savage—whose relentless tusks
   Are content with acorn-husks;
   Robber—whose exploits ne'er soared
   O'er the bee's or squirrel's hoard;
   Whiskered chin and feeble nose,
   Claws of steel on baby toes—
   Here, in solitude and shade,
   Shambling, shuffling plantigrade,
   Be thy courses undismayed.

2. Here, where Nature makes thy bed,
   Let thy rude, half-human tread
      Point to hidden Indian springs,
   Lost in ferns and fragrant grasses,
      Hovered o'er by timid wings,
   Where the wood-duck lightly passes,
   Where the wild bee holds her sweets—
   Epicurean retreats,
   Fit for thee, and better than
   Fearful sports of dangerous man.

3. In thy fat-jowled deviltry
   Friar Tuck shall live with thee.
   Thou mayst levy tithe and dole;
      Thou shalt spread the woodland cheer,
   From the pilgrim taking toll;
      Match thy cunning with his fear;
   Eat and drink, and have thy fill,
   Yet remain an outlaw still!

Bret Harte.

PART XIV.

FOUR-HANDED FOLKS.

HOUSEHOLD PETS IN TRINIDAD.

1. The queen of all the pets is a black and gray spider-monkey from Guiana, consisting of a tail which has developed, at one end, a body about twice as big as a hare's; four arms (call them not legs), of which the front ones have no thumbs, nor rudiments of thumbs; a head of black hair, brushed forward over the foolish, kindly, greedy, sad face with its wide, suspicious, beseeching eyes; and a mouth which, as in all these American monkeys, as far as we have seen, can have no expression, not even that of sensuality, because it had no lips. Others have described the spider-monkey as four legs and a tail, tied in a knot in the middle; but the tail is, without doubt, the most important of the five limbs.

2. Wherever the monkey goes, whatever she does, the tail is the standing-point, or rather hanging-point. It takes one turn at least round something or other provisionally, and in case it should be wanted; often, as she swings, every other limb hangs in the most ridiculous repose, and the tail alone supports. Sometimes it carries, by way of ornament, a bunch of flowers or a live kitten. Sometimes it is curled round the neck, or carried over the head in the hands, out of harm's way; or, when she comes silently up

behind you, puts her cold hand in yours, and walks by your side like a child, she steadies herself by taking a half turn of her tail round your wrist. Her relative Jack, of whom hereafter, walks about, carrying his chain to ease his neck.

3. The spider-monkey's easiest attitude in walking, and in running also, is strangely upright, like a human being; but as for her antics, nothing could represent them to you save a series of photographs, and those instantaneous ones; for they change every moment, not by starts, but with a deliberate ease which would be grace in anything less horribly ugly, into postures such as Callot or Breughel never fancied for the ugliest imps who ever tormented St. Anthony. All absurd efforts of agility which you ever saw at a *séance* of the Hylobates Lar Club, at Cambridge, are quiet and clumsy compared to the rope-dancing which goes on in the boughs of the pine-tree.

4. But, with all this, Spider is the gentlest, most obedient, and most domestic of beasts. Her creed is, that yellow bananas are the *summum bonum;* and that she must not come into the dining-room, or even into the veranda, whither, nevertheless, she slips, in fear and trembling, every morning, to steal the little green parrot's breakfast out of his cage, or the baby's milk, or fruit off the sideboard, in which case she makes her appearance suddenly and silently, sitting on the threshold like a distorted fiend, and begins scratching herself, looking at everything except the fruit, and pretending total absence of mind till the proper moment comes for unwinding her lengthy ugliness and making a snatch at the table. Poor, weak-headed thing, full of foolish cunning; always doing wrong, and knowing that it is wrong, but quite unable to resist temptation; and then profuse in futile explanations, gesticulations, mouthings of an "Oh! oh! oh!" so pitiably human that you can only punish her by laughing at her,

which she does not at all like. One can not resist the fancy, while watching her, either that she was once a human being, or that she is trying to become one.

5. Her friends are every human being who will take notice of her, and a beautiful little Guazupita, or native deer, a little larger than a roe, with great, black, melting eyes, and a heart as soft as its eyes, who comes to lick one's hand, believes in bananas as firmly as the monkey, and, when she can get no hand to lick, licks the hairy monkey for mere love's sake, and lets it ride on her back, and kicks it off, and lets it get on again and take a half turn of its tail round her neck, and throttle her with its arms, and pull her nose out of the way when a banana is coming, and all out of pure love, for the two have never been introduced to each other by man, and the intimacy between them, like that famous one between the horse and the hen, is of Nature's own making up.

6. Very different from the spider-monkey in temper is her cousin Jack, who sits, sullen and unrepentant, at the end of a long chain, having an ugly liking for the calves of passers-by, and ugly teeth to employ them. Sad at heart he is, and testifies his sadness sometimes by standing bolt upright, with his long arms in postures oratoric, almost prophetic, or, when duly pitied and moaned to, lying down on his side, covering his hairy eyes with one hairy arm, and weeping and sobbing bitterly.

7. He seems, speaking scientifically, to be some sort of Mycetes or Howler, from the flat, globular throat, which indicates the great development of the hyoid bone ; but, happily for the sleep of the neighborhood, he never utters in captivity any sound beyond a chuckle ; and he is supposed, by some here, from his burly, thick-set figure, vast breadth between the ears, short neck, and general cast of countenance, to have been, in a prior state of existence, a man and a brother—and that by no means of negro blood

—who has gained in this, his purgatorial stage of existence, nothing save a well-earned tail. At all events, more than one of us was impressed, at the first sight, with the conviction that we had seen him before.

8. Poor Jack! and it is come to this; and all from the indulgence of his five senses plus "the sixth sense of vanity." His only recreation save eating is being led about by the mulatto turnkey, the one human being with whom he, dimly understanding what is fit for him, will at all consort; and having wild pines thrown down to him from the pine-tree above by the spider-monkey, whose gambols he watches with pardonable envy. Like the great Mr. Barry Lyndon, he can not understand why the world is so unjust and foolish as to have taken a prejudice against him. After all, he is nothing but a strong, nasty brute; and his only reason for being here is that he is a new and undescribed species, never seen before, and, it is to be hoped, never to be seen again. *Charles Kingsley.*

THE LIVING BRIDGE.

1. The noise that we heard we now ascertained proceeded from an army of monkeys on their march through the forest. As they approached the stream we could very clearly see all their movements. "They are coming toward the bridge; they will most likely cross by the rocks yonder," observed Raoul. "How—swim it?" I asked. "It is a torrent there." "Oh, no!" answered the Frenchman; "monkeys would rather go into the fire than water. If they can not leap the stream, they will bridge it." "Bridge it! and how?" "Stop a moment, Captain; you shall see." The half-human voices now sounded nearer, and we could perceive that the animals were approaching the spot

where we lay. Presently they appeared on the opposite bank, headed by an old gray chieftain, and officered like so many soldiers. They were, as Raoul had stated, of the ring-tailed tribe. One—an aide-de-camp, or chief pioneer, perhaps—ran out upon a projecting rock, and, after looking across the stream, as if calculating the distance, scampered back, and appeared to communicate with the leader. This produced a movement in the troop. Commands were issued, and fatigue parties were detailed and marched to the front. Meanwhile, several of them—engineers, no doubt—ran along the bank, examining the trees on both sides of the stream.

2. At length they all collected round a tall cotton-wood that grew over the narrowest part of the stream, and twenty or thirty of them scampered up its trunk. On reaching a high point, the foremost—a strong fellow—ran out upon a limb, and, taking several turns of his tail around it, slipped off and hung head downward. The next on the limb, also a stout one, climbed down the body of the first, and, whipping his tail tightly round the neck and forearm of the latter, dropped off in his turn and hung head down. The third repeated the manœuvre upon the second, and the fourth upon the third, and so on, until the last upon the string rested his fore paws on the ground.

3. The living chain now commenced swinging backward and forward, like the pendulum of a clock. The motion was slight at first, but gradually increased, the lowermost monkey striking his hands violently on the earth as he passed the tangent of the oscillating curve. Several others upon the limbs above aided the movement. This continued until the monkey at the end of the chain was thrown among the branches of a tree on the opposite bank. Here, after two or three vibrations, he clutched a limb and held fast. This movement was executed adroitly, just at the culminating point of the oscillation, in order to save

the intermediate links from the violence of a too sudden jerk.

4. The chain was now fast at both ends, forming a complete suspension bridge, over which the whole troop, to the number of four or five hundred, passed with the rapidity of thought. It was one of the most comical sights I ever beheld to witness the quizzical expression of countenances along that living chain! The troop was now on the other side, but how were the animals forming the bridge to get themselves over? This was the question that suggested itself. Manifestly, by number one letting go his tail. But then the point of support on the other side was much lower down, and number one, with half a dozen of his neighbors, would be dashed against the opposite bank, or soused into the water.

5. Here, then, was a problem, and we waited with some curiosity for its solution. It was soon solved. A monkey was now seen attaching his tail to the lowest on the bridge, another girdled him in a similar manner, and another, and so on, until a dozen more were added to the string. These last were all powerful fellows; and, running up to a high limb, they lifted the bridge into a position almost horizontal. Then a scream from the last monkey of the new formation warned the tail end that all was ready, and the next moment the whole chain was swung over and landed safely on the opposite bank. The lowermost links now dropped off like a melting candle, while the higher ones leaped to the branches and came down by the trunk. The whole troop then scampered off into the chaparral and disappeared.

Adventures in the Tropics.

JACKO.

1. WHILE examining the tropical birds in an old museum at Havre de Grace my ears were assailed by a harsh and unearthly noise, as of a duel between two rabid cats, which brought in the proprietor, breathless, to ascertain the cause. He finds that the tailless, green-coated African monkey, who hangs suspended from an old parrot's cage outside the window, has seized the incautiously protruded tail of his prettier and, therefore, more favored brother, the monkey from South America; he, unfortunate creature, has crossed the "herring-pond" in a hen-coop, which is much too small to contain himself, tail and all. This appendage, which in his present condition is neither useful nor ornamental, is perpetually getting him into scrapes, which the honorable representative of Africa, being tailless, escapes.

2. Conscious of his condition, the poor American monkey pulls in his tail, coils it up as well as he can, and gives it a most malicious bite, as much as to say, "I wish you were off; you are of no use to me now, and you look terribly shabby." He then covers it up with straw, and looks miserable.

3. "How much for that monkey?" I say—"the one in the hen-coop." The monkey looks up as though he understood what was said, and with a face which evidently says, "Please buy me." The merchant's price is too high. The African rascal he will sell for half the sum; but this gentleman grins so maliciously at the customer that the bargain is off.

4. A few months later, business called me to a neighboring French village, and when I was ready to depart I went into the stable to find the coachee, and there, what was my delight to see my old friend of the hen-coop

perched on the manger, looking as happy as a monkey could look. He really was a pretty fellow: his bright eyes sparkled like two diamonds from beneath his deep-set eyebrows; his teeth were of the most pearly whiteness, and of these, through pride or a wish to intimidate, he made a formidable display on the entrance of visitors. His hands were certainly not similar to those of fair Rosamond of Woodstock renown, but more like the shriveled and dried-up palms of the old monks of St. Bernard, whose mortal remains are made an exhibition of in that far-famed convent. A more wicked pair of pickers and stealers, however, never graced the body of man or monkey.

5. His tail, which had now recovered its good looks, gave additional charms to his personal appearance, and, moreover, was most useful, inasmuch as it performed the office of a hand, giving to the owner three or five of these useful members. With this he could cling on to the bar of the rack above the manger and swing himself about, a perfect living pendulum. Well, too, he knew the use of it. If a nut or apple thrown to him lodged just out of reach of his hands or feet, he would run to the full length of his chain, turn his face so as to get as much length as possible, stretch out this member, and pull toward him the coveted delicacy. If pursued, moreover, and the chain, dangling after him, got in his way, he would invariably coil his tail around the links and carry it high over his head, out of the way of his spider-like legs.

6. After a considerable amount of bargaining, Jacko was bought, and transferred—chain, tail, and all—to his new English master. At the hotel Jacko was secured by being chained in a little closet adjoining the bedroom, and when I returned, after a half-hour's absence, the paper was all torn from the walls. The pegs were all loosened, and the individual peg to which his chain had been fastened torn completely from its socket. An unfortunate garment

which happened to be hung up in the closet was torn into a thousand shreds; and if he had tied the torn strips together and made his escape from the window, I could scarcely have been more surprised.

7. After such misdeeds it was quite evident that Jacko must no longer be allowed full liberty, and a lawyer's blue bag, with a little hay at the bottom for a bed, was provided for him. It was a movable home, and therein lay the advantage, for, when the strings were tied, there was no mode of escape. He could not get his hands out to unfasten them; the bag was too strong for him to bite his way through, and his efforts to get out only had the effect of making the bag roll on the floor or jump into the air, much to the amusement, and sometimes the consternation, of the spectators.

8. While getting tickets at the Southampton railway station, Jacko, who must needs see everything that was going on, suddenly poked his head out of the bag and gave a malicious grin at the ticket-seller. This much frightened the poor man, but, with great presence of mind, quite astonishing under the circumstances, he retaliated the insult. "Sir, that's a dog; you must pay for it accordingly." In vain was the monkey made to come out of the bag and exhibit his whole person; in vain were arguments used to prove the animal in question was not a dog but a monkey. A dog it was in the views of the official, and three and sixpence was paid, as demanded.

9. Thinking to carry the joke further, I took out from my pocket a live tortoise I happened to have with me, and, showing it, said: "What must I pay for this, as you charge for all animals?" The employé adjusted his specs, withdrew from the desk to consult with his superior, then, returning, gave the verdict, with a grave but determined manner, "No charge for them, sir; them be insects."

10. When Jacko arrived at his destination, he was pro-

vided with a comfortable home in the stall of a stable, where he could ascend through an aperture to the hay-loft. While sitting in the manger, he had one amusement, and that was catching mice. These unsuspecting little animals would come out to pick up the corn left by the horses in the next stall. To get at their feeding-ground they had to run the gantlet of Jacko's premises. He was up to this, and would pretend to be asleep, keeping, however, one eye half open. The trick answered; the mouse made a rush, in vain; Jacko, as quick as lightning, had his paw upon him, and with a tight squeeze crippled the poor brute. He would then play with him for some minutes, every now and then giving him a pat to make him go faster. When the poor victim thought he had got away, Jacko caught him again, and then—O carnivorous representative of the class *Quadrumana!*—ate him up like a sugar-plum.

11. The servants, having observed Jacko's talent in this line, bethought themselves that they could turn it to some good account; and, as the cat of the house was ill, and not having undergone a severe training in the logical school of Aristotle, they reasoned to themselves as follows: "Cats catch mice in the dark; monkeys catch mice in the dark; therefore monkeys are cats." Acting upon this misleading syllogism, they one evening took Jacko out of his comfortable bed of hay in the loft and chained him up in the larder, having previously removed every eatable or drinkable thing, except some jam-pots, which were put seemingly out of reach, and, moreover, were well secured with bladder stretched over their tops.

12. The night passed long and miserably to poor Jacko, who was evidently much astonished at this unwonted treatment. All night long the mice scampered about the place, regardless of their enemy, while he, most uncatlike, was coiled up in a soup-tureen, fast asleep. The morning

dawned, and the mice retired to their holes; Jacko awoke, scratched his shivering hide, and, having pushed the tureen, his bed, from the shelf to its utter demolition, looked around for something to eat. The jam-pots attracted his notice. "There is something good here," thought he as he smelled the coverings. "I'll see." His sharp teeth soon made an aperture: he was not disappointed. The treasured jams — raspberry, strawberry, plum — the vaunted Scotch marmalade, the candied apricots, the pride and care of the cook, disappeared in an unaccountably short time down into the seemingly small gullet of the sweet-toothed Jacko.

13. Not if I had a hundred mouths and a hundred tongues could I describe the imprecations hurled at the devoted head of the now sick and overgorged gourmand by the disappointed and illogical cook, the owner of the jams, as she opened the door of the larder at breakfast-time to see how many mice the monkey had caught. Great was the anger of the female jailer; great were the malicious grins of the captive.

14. Some few days after this affair Jacko, having been restored to health and favor, was warming himself before the kitchen fire. A cricket that had been singing merrily came a little too far out on the hearth-stone. His fate was sealed; the next jump was down the throat of Jacko, who munched him as an epicure does the leg of a woodcock. The next tidbit was a black beetle, who ran out to secure a crumb dropped from the servants' supper-table; he, too, became a victim to his rashness. Having ascertained that these beetles were nuts to Jacko, I one day gave him a great treat by upsetting the kitchen beetle-trap in his presence. Both paws instantly went to work; whole bunches of the unfortunate insects he crammed into his cheek-pouches, which served him for pockets, munching away as hard as he could at the same time. His paws could not catch the

prey fast enough, so he set his feet to work, and grasped with them as many as he could hold. This was not enough. He swept a lot together with his tail, and kept them there close prisoners till his mouth was a little empty, and he had time to catch and devour them.

15. Jacko's insectivorous propensities were not confined to black beetles alone. Spiders formed a pleasant variety. Not a spider was left alive in the stable where he was confined or outside of it; the most enormous stones would he pick out of the wall with his little fingers, in search of a runaway web-spinner. He was really of great use in clearing the house of this housemaid's pest. I often used to put a bit of string to the end of his chain and let him run up the curtains. He would then completely rummage out and devour the spiders, who, having had their webs so frequently knocked down by the relentless broom, had thought to spin in security on the top of the cornices and among the curtain-rods.

16. A great treat it was to Jacko to have a large bowl of warm water given him. He would, first of all, cunningly test the temperature with his hand, and then gradually step into the bath, first one foot, then the other, finally completely sitting down in it. Comfortably placed, he would then take the soap in his hands or feet, as the case might be, and rub himself all over. Having made a dreadful mess on the table, and finding the water becoming cold, the next part of the play was to get out and run as quickly as he could to the fire, where his coat soon became dry. If anybody laughed at him during this performance, he would chatter and grin at them, and frequently even splash water out of the bath at them.

17. Poor fellow! his love for a bath one day got him literally "into hot water." The large kitchen-kettle, filled with water, was left on the fire to boil; Jacko took the lid off, and, finding it warm, sat down, his head only ap-

pearing above the water. This was very comfortable for some time, but the water, heated by the flames beneath, began to get hot; Jacko raised his body a little, but, finding the air very cold by contrast, immediately sat down again. This he continued to do for some time, never being able to sum up the courage to face the cold air. The consequence was that the poor little wretch was nearly scalded, and if it had not been for the timely interference of one of the servants, who took his parboiled carcass out by main force, he would have become a martyr to his own want of pluck and firmness in action.

18. Jacko's organ of imitation appears to have been very great. On one occasion he tried his hand at knife-cleaning; but it was the handles which he attempted to polish, while he held the blade in his hand, as a cut attested the next day. He next set to work to polish shoes as he had seen William do, but he covered the soles all over with the blacking, and emptied what was left of a bottle of Day & Martin into the shoe, nearly filling it. When the servants entered he retreated to his basket in the corner, and tried to look as though nothing had happened. After several years of mischief and torment, Jacko got an attack of bronchitis. He was wrapped in flannel and placed before the fire, and great care was taken of him, but all in vain; he died. Not wishing to lose sight of him altogether, I had his bones made into a skeleton, and now,

> In a cabinet high on a shelf,
> He lies as a monument raised to himself.

Frank Buckland.

PART XV.

ADVENTURES AND INCIDENTS.

OUR HUNTING-LODGE AND NEIGHBORS.

1. THE scene of the following description is in the Scottish Highlands, where the writer and his brother passed several years in the enjoyment of the scenery and wild sports of the region. Their temporary quarters were fixed at a little hamlet, and to reach the deer-forests they were obliged to cross the Findhorn River, a small stream in the very heart of the Highlands. Here follows the story:

2. The Findhorn, however, which was so calm and bright and sunny when the otters floated down its current in a still summer's morning, was a fierce and terrible enemy in its anger; and, for a great part of the year, the dread of its uncertainty and danger was a formidable cause for the preservation of that profound solitude of the forest which so long made it the sanctuary of deer, roe, and every kind of wild game. The rapidity with which the river comes down, the impassable height to which it rises in an incredibly short time, its incertitude and fury, would render it an object of care to bold forders and boatmen; but with the peasants, unaccustomed, like the Highlanders, to wrestle with a mountain-torrent, and, excepting in rare instances, unable to swim, it inspires a dread almost amounting to awe. Pent within a channel of rocks from fifty to a hun-

dred and eighty feet in height, the rise of the water is rapidly exaggerated by the incapability of diffusion; and the length of its course sometimes concealing beyond the horizon the storms by which it is swelled at its source, its floods then descend with unexpected violence.

3. Frequently, when the sun is shining in a cloudless sky, and the water scarce ripples over the glittering ford, a deep, hollow sound, a dull, approaching roar, may be heard in the gorges of the river; and almost before the wading fisherman can gain the shore, a bank of water, loaded with trees and rocks and wreck, will come down three, four, five feet abreast, sweeping all before it in a thunder of foam and ruin. In ordinary cases, after two days of rain, the stream will rise twenty or thirty feet—it has risen nearly ten fathoms in its rocky gulf; and once, upon this occasion, it mounted fifteen feet in a quarter of an hour. When the day broke, it appeared sweeping through the trees, which the evening before hung fifty feet above its brink, a black, roaring tempest, loaded with ruins and *débris*, from which were seen at times the white skeletons of trees, peeled of their bark, beams and fragments of houses —a cart, a door, a cradle—hurrying and tilting through the foam and spray, like the scattered flotsam of a wreck.

4. Often have we gone out in a clear, sapphire morning, when there was scarce a ripple on the pools, and the water on the ford was not over our boots; and when we returned at evening, and approached through the dark veil of pines which descended toward the river, have heard a roar as if the world were rolling together down the black trough before us, and, as we came out on the bank, found a furious tempest of water tumbling and plunging and leaping, over stock and rock, twenty feet upon the rocks where we had left it whimpering among the pebbles in the morning; while in the far, deep, birch-embowered channel, where the stream was then so still and placid that you

could only guess its course by the bright, glistening eye which here and there blinked between the trees and stones —now it came yelling and skirling and clamoring down the rocks and falls, as if all the air was full of gibbering, babbling, laughing demons, who were muttering and yammering and prophesying and hooting at what you were going to do if you attempted to cross.

5. As the bridge was two miles below, and there was this continual uncertainty at the ford, I determined to build a hunter's hut, where we might lodge for the night when it was impossible to cross the water. There is a high and beautiful crag at the crook of the river, near the "Little Eas"—a precipice eighty feet in height, and then, like a vast stone helmet, crowned with a feathery plume of wood, which nodded over its brow. From its top you might drop a bullet into the pool below, but on the south side there is an accessible woody bank, down which, by planting your heels firmly in the soil and among the roots of the trees, there is a descent to a deep but smooth and sandy ford. Upon the summit of the rock there is, or there was—my blessing upon it!—a thick and beautiful bird-cherry, which hung over the crag, and whose pendent branches, taking root on the edge of the steep, shot up again like the banyan, and formed a natural arbor and close trellis along the margin of the precipice.

6. Behind its little gallery there is a mighty holly, under which the snow rarely lies in winter, or the rain drops in summer. Beneath the shelter of this tree, and within the bank at its foot, I dug a little cell, large enough to hold two beds, a bench, a hearth, a table, and a "kistie." The sides were lined with deals well calked with moss, and the roof was constructed in the same manner, but covered with a tarpaulin, which, lying in the slope of the surrounding bank, carried off any water which might descend from thaw or rain, and, when the autumn trees shook off

their leaves, could not be distinguished from the adjoining bank.

7. Its door was on the brink of the crag, veiled by the thick bird-cherries on the edge of the precipice; and the entrance to the little path, which ascended from either side upon the brow of the rock, was concealed by a screen of birch and hazel, beneath which the banks were covered with primroses, wood-anemones, and forget-me-not. Bowers of honeysuckle and wild roses twined among the lower trees; and even in the tall pines above, the rose sometimes climbed to the very top, where all its blossoms, clustering to the sun, hung in white tassels out of the dark-blue foliage. There the thrush and the blackbird sang at morning and evening, and the owl cried at night, and the buck belled upon the Torr. Blessed, wild, free, joyous dwelling, which we shall never see again!

8. When in our little bothy, we had companions on every side; from the passenger which came from Norway, to the little native guest—the robin which roosted in the holly-bush above us. "*The* robin?" you smile and say. Yes, there was but one. He lived in the bush, as we lived in the bothy, and we were his neighbors too long not to be very well acquainted. His species, as well as all the small tribes, are very local in their range and habits, and may be found all the year in, or near, the same place; and those who feed them will rarely wait many minutes for their appearance. There were many robins which lived about the bothy, and all were continually in its vicinity, and very tame, but none so gentle and grateful as our little neighbor of the holly.

9. They would, however, enter the hut, sit on the bed or the table, and hop about the floor, and, when I went out, follow me to the brae. They liked very much to see me turn up the soil, which always provided them with a little feast; accordingly, they were never absent at the planting

of a shrub or a flower; and when I brought home, in my shooting-bag, a tuft of primroses, pyrolas, or lilies of the valley, they were always in attendance to see them put into the bank. For watching my occupation, they preferred something more elevated than the ground, but not so high as the branches of the trees, which were too far from the earth to give them a clear sight of what I turned up; for their accommodation, therefore, I made little crosses and crotchets, and, when I was planting, set them up beside me, moving them as I proceeded from place to place. Each was immediately occupied by an attentive observer; and, whenever an insect or a worm was discovered, one of the nearest darted down and caught it, even from between my fingers, and disappeared for a few moments under the rock or between the great holly, to enjoy his success undisturbed. At his disappearance his place was immediately occupied by another, but at the return of the first it was amiably resigned by his successor.

10. The blue-bonnets were almost as numerous as the robins, but they never arrived at the same intimacy and confidence. They never entered the bothy in my presence, and even when I fed them they would not approach as long as I remained outside the door; but as soon as I went in they descended four or five together, chattering and fluttering about the entrance, peeping in at the little window, and stretching their necks as far as they could to see where I was, and if all was right. Then they would begin their breakfast on what I had left for them, talking a great deal about it, but occasionally ogling the door, in a manner from which I concluded that there was but small esteem or gratitude in their conversation.

11. Far different was the friendship of our little neighbor in the holly. In the morning he used to come down and perch on the arm of the bird-cherry, which stretched over the precipice before the door, waiting for its opening

and the preparation of the breakfast, which he always shared; and when we were seated he would venture over the sill and gather the crumbs about the table at our feet. Often, when the first blood-red streaks of the autumn morning shone like lurid fire through the little window, we were awakened by his sad and solitary whistle, as he sat on his usual branch, his jet-black eye cast toward the door, impatient for our appearance. Many of his little cousins there were in the wood, with whom we were also well acquainted, and between us happened many an incident which increased our interest and familiarity.

12. I remember a day—one of those deep, still, blue days, so solemn in the forest; the ground was covered with a foot of snow, and all the trees were hanging like gigantic ostrich-feathers; but all the world was blue; the sky was a sleeping mass of those heavy indigo clouds which forbode a "feeding storm"; not a tempest, but a fall of snow; for in Scotland snow is called *storm*, however light and still it falls; thus, in tracking the deer, we say he "has just brushed the storm from the heather"; and a feeding storm is when the clouds are continually feeding the earth with its velvet pall. The reflection of those deep-blue clouds cast a delicate tint of the same color over the whitened world. I was standing with my back against a huge pine, waiting for the hunters and dogs.

13. As I had been through all the swamps and stripes and wet hollows on that side of the forest, and waded through two and three feet of snow-wreaths, my kilt and hose, and, as it seemed, my flesh, was saturated to the bones with "snawbree," and I began to beat, first one foot, and then the other, to quicken the blood, which was warm enough in my trunk. I had scarce commenced this exercise when I heard a little "tic!" close to my ear, and the soft, low voice of a bird—a sound, neither a whistle nor a chirp, but which I knew very well before I turned and saw

the robin, who sat on a dry branch within a yard of my cheek. I guessed what had brought him: he was very cold, his ruffled back humped as round as a ball, and his tail drooping almost perpendicular with his legs, as if it was a little brown peg to lean on, like that on which the traveling Tyrolean merchant rests his pack.

14. He looked at me with his large, black eye; then, with a flirt of his tail and a bow with his head, indicated that, if I had no objection, he should like to descend to the place which I occupied, the object of which he expressed by turning his head sidelong, and directing one eye into the black earth which my foot had beaten bare in the snow. I immediately drew back a couple of feet, and he instantly dropped into the spot of mold, peeped and picked under every leaf and clod of earth, and, when there was nothing more, hopped up on the guard of my rifle, on which I was leaning, and, turning his head, looked at me with his upper eye. I again stepped forward, and recommenced my foot-exercise, during which he returned to his branch, examining my progress with some impatience. As soon as my foot was removed he again dropped into the hollow, and busily collected all the little grubs and chrysales which, though too small for me to see as I stood, I knew abounded beneath the sere leaves and thatch of moss and sticks.

15. In this manner I repeated his supply several times, on one of which, when I was too long, or he too impatient, he dropped from his perch and hovered over the space in which my foot was at work, and, as I continued, lighted on the point of the other shoe, and remained there, peeping into the hollow, until I withdrew my foot, and then descended to finish his repast. When he was satisfied, he ruffed his feathers, looked up sidelong to me, and, after a shake of satisfaction, resumed his perch close to my head, and, after pruning and oiling his feathers, mounted another branch higher, and opened his little throat with that most sad,

sweet, and intermitting warble which gives such a melancholy charm to a still winter's day.

Charles Edward Stuart.

THE-SLOTH.

1. This singular animal is destined by nature to be produced, to live, and to die in the trees; and, to do justice to him, naturalists must examine him in this upper element. He is a scarce and solitary animal, and, being good food, he is never allowed to escape. He inhabits remote and gloomy forests, where snakes take up their abode, and where cruelly stinging ants and scorpions, and swamps, and innumerable thorny shrubs and bushes, obstruct the steps of civilized man. Were you to draw your own conclusions from the descriptions which have been given of the sloth, you would probably suspect that no naturalist has actually gone into the wilds with the fixed determination to find him out, and examine his haunts, and see whether nature has committed any blunder in the formation of this extraordinary creature, which appears to us so forlorn and miserable, so ill put together, and so totally unfit to enjoy the blessings which have been so bountifully given to the rest of animated nature; for he has no soles to his feet, and he is evidently ill at ease when he tries to move on the ground, and it is then that he looks up in your face with a countenance that says, "Have pity on me, for I am in pain and sorrow."

2. However, we are now in his own domain. Man but little frequents these thick and noble forests, which extend far and wide on every side of us. This, then, is the proper place to go in quest of the sloth. We will first take a near view of him. By obtaining a knowledge of his anatomy, we shall be enabled to account for his movements

hereafter, when we see him in his proper haunts. His fore legs, or, more correctly speaking, his arms, are apparently much too long, while his hind legs are very short, and look as if they could be bent almost to the shape of a corkscrew. Both the fore and hind legs, by their form, and by the manner in which they are joined to the body, are quite incapacitated from acting in a perpendicular direction, or in supporting it on the earth, as the bodies of other quadrupeds are supported by their legs. Hence, when you place him on the floor, his belly touches the ground. Now, granted that he supported himself on his legs like other animals, nevertheless he would be in pain, for he has no soles to his feet, and his claws are very sharp and long and curved; so that, were his body supported by his feet, it would be by their extremities, just as your body would be were you to throw yourself on all fours, and try to support it on the ends of your toes and fingers— a trying position. Were the floor of glass, or of a polished surface, the sloth would actually be quite stationary; but, as the ground is generally rough, with little protuberances upon it, such as stones, or roots of grass, etc., this just suits the sloth, and he moves his fore legs in all directions, in order to find something to lay hold of; and when he has succeeded, he pulls himself forward, and is thus enabled to travel onward, but at the same time in so tardy and awkward a manner as to acquire the name of sloth.

3. Indeed, his looks and his gestures evidently betray his uncomfortable situation; and, as a sigh every now and then escapes him, we may be entitled to conclude that he is actually in pain.

4. Some years ago I kept a sloth in my room for several months. I often took him out of the house and placed him upon the ground, in order to have an opportunity of observing his motions. If the ground was rough, he would pull himself forward, by means of his fore legs, at a pretty

good pace; and he invariably immediately shaped his course toward the nearest tree. But, if I put him upon a smooth and well-trodden part of the road, he appeared to be in trouble and distress. His favorite abode was the back of a chair; and, after getting all his legs in a line upon the topmost part of it, he would hang there for hours together, and often, with a low and inward cry, would seem to invite me to take notice of him.

5. The sloth, in its wild state, spends its whole life in trees, and never leaves them but through force, or by accident; and, what is more extraordinary, not *upon* the branches, like the squirrel and the monkey, but *under* them. He moves suspended from the branch, he rests suspended from it, and he sleeps suspended from it. To enable him to do this, he must have a very different formation from that of any other known quadruped.

6. It must be observed that the sloth does not hang head downward like the vampire. When asleep, he supports himself from a branch parallel to the earth. He first seizes the branch with one arm, and then with the other; and, after that, brings up both his legs, one by one, to the same branch, so that all four are in line. He seems perfectly at rest in this position. Now, had he a tail, he would be at a loss to know what to do with it in this position; were he to draw it up within his legs, it would interfere with them; and were he to let it hang down, it would become the sport of the winds. Thus his deficiency of tail is a benefit to him; it is merely an apology for a tail, scarcely exceeding an inch and a half in length.

7. I observed, when he was climbing, he never used his arms both together, but first one, and then the other, and so on alternately. There is a singularity in his hair, different from that of all other animals, and, I believe, hitherto unnoticed by naturalists; his hair is thick and coarse at the extremity, and gradually tapers to the root, where it

becomes fine as a spider's web. His fur has so much the hue of the moss which grows on the branches of the trees that it is very difficult to make him out when he is at rest.

8. The male of the three-toed sloth has a longitudinal bar of very fine black hair on his back, rather lower than the shoulder-blades; on each side of this black bar there is a space of yellow hair, equally fine; it has the appearance of being pressed into the body, and looks exactly as if it had been singed. If we examine the anatomy of his fore legs, we shall immediately perceive, by their firm and muscular texture, how very capable they are of supporting the pendent weight of his body, both in climbing and at rest; and, instead of pronouncing them a bungled composition, as a celebrated naturalist has done, we shall consider them as remarkably well calculated to perform their extraordinary functions.

9. As the sloth is an inhabitant of forests within the tropics, where the trees touch each other in the greatest profusion, there seems to be no reason why he should confine himself to one tree alone for food, and entirely strip it of its leaves. During the many years I have ranged the forests, I have never seen a tree in such a state of nudity; indeed, I would hazard a conjecture that, by the time the animal had finished the last of the old leaves, there would be a new crop on the part of the tree he had stripped first, ready for him to begin again, so quick is the process of vegetation in these countries.

10. There is a saying among the Indians that when the wind blows the sloth begins to travel. In calm weather he remains tranquil, probably not liking to cling to the brittle extremity of the branches, lest they should break with him in passing from one tree to another; but, as soon as the wind rises, the branches of the neighboring trees become interwoven, and then the sloth seizes hold of them, and pursues his journey in safety. There is seldom an

entire day of calm in these forests. The trade-wind generally sets in about ten o'clock in the morning, and thus the sloth may set off after breakfast, and get a considerable way before dinner. He travels at a good round pace; and were you to see him pass from tree to tree, as I have done, you would never think of calling him a sloth.

11. Thus it would appear that the different histories we have of this quadruped are erroneous on two accounts: first, that the writers of them, deterred by difficulties and local annoyances, have not paid sufficient attention to him in his native haunts; and, secondly, they have described him in a situation in which he was never intended by nature to cut a figure—I mean on the ground. The sloth is as much at a loss to proceed on his journey upon a smooth and level floor as a man would be who had to walk a mile on stilts upon a line of feather-beds.

12. One day, as we were crossing the Essequibo, I saw a large two-toed sloth on the ground upon the bank; how he had got there nobody could tell. The Indian said he had never surprised a sloth in such a situation before; he would hardly have come there to drink, for both above and below the place the branches of the trees touched the water, and afforded him an easy and safe access to it. Be this as it may, though the trees were not above twenty yards from him, he could not make his way through the sand time enough to escape before we landed. As soon as we got up to him he threw himself upon his back, and defended himself in gallant style with his fore legs. "Come, poor fellow!" said I to him; "if thou hast got into a hobble to-day, thou shalt not suffer for it. I'll take no advantage of thee in misfortune; the forest is large enough both for thee and me to rove in; go thy ways up above, and enjoy thyself in these endless wilds. It is more than probable thou wilt never have another interview with man. So fare thee well."

13. On saying this, I took a long stick which was lying there, held it for him to hook on, and then conveyed him to a high and stately mora. He ascended with wonderful rapidity, and in about a minute he was almost at the top of the tree. He now went off in a side direction and caught hold of the branch of a neighboring tree; he then proceeded toward the heart of the forest. I stood looking on, lost in amazement at his singular mode of progress. I followed him with my eye till the intervening branches closed in betwixt us; and then I lost sight for ever of the two-toed sloth. I was going to add that I never saw a sloth take to his heels in such earnest; but the expression will not do, for the sloth has no heels. That which naturalists have advanced of his being so tenacious of life is perfectly true. I saw the heart of one beat for half an hour after it was taken out of the body.

14. So much for this harmless, unoffending animal. He holds a conspicuous place in the catalogue of the animals of the New World. Though naturalists have made no mention of what follows, still it is not less true on that account. The sloth is the only quadruped known which spends its whole life from the branch of a tree suspended by its feet. I have paid uncommon attention to him in his native haunts. The monkey and squirrel will seize a branch with their forefeet, and pull themselves up, and rest or run upon it; but the sloth, after seizing it, still remains suspended, and, suspended, moves along under the branch till he can lay hold of another. Whenever I have seen him in his native woods, whether at rest or asleep, or on his travels, I have always observed that he was suspended from the branch of a tree. When his form and anatomy are attentively considered, it will appear evident that the sloth can not be at ease in any situation where his body is higher or above his feet.

Charles Waterton.

ILLUSTRATIVE STORIES.

1. **The Arab's Horse.**—The Arab's pride in the purity of breed and speed of his horse is well illustrated in the following story: A young Arab eloped with the daughter of a sheik, and effected his escape upon a mare stolen from the bride's father. The sheik was incensed at the loss of his daughter, but his pride was gratified that his favorite mare had distanced all the horses which he had sent in pursuit. The latter sentiment was so strong that he suppressed his wrath, and easily became reconciled to his son-in-law.

2. **The Horse's Docility.**—An Eastern traveler relates that the Arab horse seems to know when he is about to be sold, or when his master is bargaining for him. He becomes restless, gives a side-glance from his beautiful eye to the bargainers, and shows his discontent by scraping the ground with his foot; neither the buyer nor any one else then dare come near him. But when the bargain is concluded, and the old master delivers the halter, with a slice of bread and some salt, to the new owner, and then turns and walks away, the horse immediately becomes tractable, and in a short time seems to transfer his regard to the one who is henceforth to be his companion and friend.

3. **A Trained Horse.**—A few years ago a horse in one of the London theatres officiated as waiter in the performances. He brought in the tea-table, set the requisite number of chairs, and finished his achievements by taking a kettle of boiling water from a blazing fire. He would also ungirth his own saddle, and wash his feet in a pail of water.

4. **A Helpful Horse.**—A gentleman of Leeds had a horse of unusual sagacity and powers of observation. He was

accustomed to drink from a trough supplied by a pump. Upon being turned into a field by himself, he made his way to the trough as usual, but finding no water, he seized the handle of the pump in his mouth and worked it until he had obtained water enough. This he continued to do as long as he remained in the field.

5. A FAITHFUL HORSE.—The affection and intelligence of the horse are well shown in the following story, related by Professor Kruger. of Halle : " A friend of mine, who was riding home one dark night through a wood, struck his head against the branch of a tree and fell from his horse, stunned by the blow. The horse immediately returned to the house they had left, a mile distant. Finding the door closed, he pawed upon it with his hoof until the inmates were aroused, and when the door opened he turned, and seemed to beckon them to follow. This they did, and the master was found and saved."

6. HORSE FRIENDSHIP.—Horses sometimes show great attachment to their own kind. An incident illustrative of this is related by a captain of French cavalry. An old horse belonging to the company became disabled by age from eating his hay and grinding his oats. His companions on the right and left seemed to appreciate his condition, and for two months they chewed up the food and laid it before their aged companion, thus preserving his life.

7. A TRAINED DONKEY.—In the sixteenth century a trained donkey at Cairo attracted much attention. He would dance in an exceedingly diverting manner, and apparently in high glee; but in the midst of his caperings his master would say that the soldan intended to employ all donkeys to carry bricks and mortar to a new palace he was building, when the donkey would fall upon the floor,

with closed eyes and heels upward, as though dead. No efforts or commands would make him stir, until his master proclaimed that the soldan had issued an edict that the best and comeliest donkeys were to be invited to the feast to-morrow, when he would start up and prance for joy. When his master informed him that he had been selected to carry an ugly and deformed woman through the city, he lowered his ears and limped as though he could scarcely stand.

8. SAGACITY OF A SHEEP.—A gentleman, while passing through a lonely district in the highlands of Scotland, observed a sheep hurrying toward the road before him, and bleating most piteously. On approaching nearer, it redoubled its cries, and seemed to implore assistance. The gentleman alighted, and followed the sheep to a field at no great distance, where he found a lamb completely wedged in between two stones, and feebly struggling with its feet uppermost. He set the lamb at liberty, and the grateful mother gave her thanks in a series of joyful bleats, very different in tone from those she used to first attract his attention.

9. COURAGE OF THE HOG.—In the early settlement of this country hogs were allowed to run in the woods, where they became exceedingly wild. A gentleman traveling through the forest in a hilly region saw a herd of swine acting in a very curious manner. They had formed into a kind of sharp-pointed triangle, the pigs in the center, and the heads of the old hogs all pointing outward. At the apex of the triangle was an old boar, who seemed to be in supreme command. He now saw the cause of the commotion. A half-famished wolf was endeavoring to seize one of the lesser hogs, but the old boar constantly fronted him, and the whole triangle shifted its position, but retained its

shape. There was a sharp skirmish and the hogs dispersed, and the traveler found the wolf dead on the field.

10. COURAGE OF THE CAT.—A cat was one day playing with her kittens before the door of a stable where she lived, when a large hawk darted down and seized one of the kittens. The old cat at once sprang upon the enemy, and obliged him to let the kitten go. A terrific battle then ensued between the two. The hawk, from the power of his wings, the sharpness of his talons, and the strength of his beak, for a while had the advantage, and cruelly lacerated the cat and tore out one of her eyes. Nothing daunted, puss continued the fight, and succeeded in breaking one of the hawk's wings. She had him then at her mercy, and, after a few more vigorous scratches, she tore off his head. Satisfied with her victory, and unheeding her own condition, she ran to the bleeding kitten, licked its wounds, and purred in great contentment over her rescued offspring.

11. A DOG'S SENSIBILITY.—A few years since, a nobleman, who had an estate upon the famous Loch Erne, in the north of Ireland, had a spaniel which on many occasions exhibited an uncommon intelligence. It seemed to have an instinct to fetch and carry, and would often exhibit this propensity without special training. Observing the gardener laying down his hatchet to adjust his stakes, the dog took the hatchet in his mouth, and, at the proper moment, presented it handle first. This he continued to do until the job was finished. One day a frightened sheep broke away from the flock, plunged into the loch, and swam directly away from the shore. The dog followed and caught the sheep a mile and a half out, just as it was sinking from the weight of its water-soaked fleece, and held it up by the horns until a boat arrived which had been sent in pursuit.

This dog was a general favorite for the kindness of his disposition and great intelligence. One day, when about two years old, he came to his old friend the gardener, gave two or three short yelps, and went away without paying any heed to the efforts of his friend to engage him in his customary plays. He went to each member of the household and saluted them in the same manner, reserving his last visit to his mistress, the lady of the house. From her presence he went immediately to the kitchen and laid down and died. The poor fellow, feeling his approaching end, had bid good-by to each of his friends, and then, alone by himself, had yielded up his breath. He was mourned almost as a human being.

12. THE DOG AS A DETECTIVE. — At St. German an Englishman visited the public gardens, but was obliged to leave his dog, a fine mastiff, outside in care of the guard. During his visit he was robbed of his watch, and, upon informing the guard, he was permitted to take in his dog to help discover the thief. He then carefully informed the dog of his loss, and told him to seek the watch. The dog seemed to comprehend at once, and set out on a tour through the crowd. He ran in and out in all directions, and at last seized hold of a man. The guard, upon searching him, found not only the Englishman's watch, but six others which the industrious pickpocket had secured.

13. AN INTELLIGENT MONKEY.—The chimpanzee, of all the monkey tribes, exhibits the most intelligence. Upon the authority of a French traveler we have the following story: "A chimpanzee, captured on the coast of Africa, became quite domesticated upon a vessel, and rendered herself very useful. She learned to heat the oven, taking care that none of the coals fell out, and, when sufficiently heated, she apprised the baker, who came to rely with perfect con-

fidence upon her judgment. She learned to splice ropes and to assist in furling sails. The brutal mate assaulted her one day, and beat her severely without provocation. She made no resistance, but in a piteous manner held out her hands to break the force of the blows. After this she seemed to take no interest in anything, refused all food, and on the fifth day died."

14. THE ELEPHANT AS NURSE.—A military officer in the East India service says: "I have seen the wife of a mahout give a baby in charge to an elephant while she went on some business, and have been highly amused in observing the manœuvres of the unwieldy nurse. The child began crawling about, and would soon get under the feet of the elephant or entangled in the branches of the tree on which he was feeding. The elephant, in the most tender manner, would lift it out of the way, or remove the obstacle to his progress. If the child reached the limits of the elephant's chain, he would pull it back as gently as possible. When the child fell asleep, he broke off a branch and kept away the flies, although he was himself greatly annoyed by the same pests."

15. A COURAGEOUS HEN.—In an inn-yard a favorite hen hatched out a brood of chickens, but lost all but one. One day, as she was scratching about, a large rat seized her only remaining offspring. The old hen heard the cry of distress, and with the greatest fury flew at the rat, seizing him by the neck. The rat, however, contrived to get free, and in turn attacked the hen. The fight lasted twelve minutes, when, with a violent blow, she laid the rat lifeless at her feet. She then turned to the frightened chicken, folded it under her wings, and clucked soothingly and triumphantly.

16. THE RAVEN'S STRATAGEM.—A gentleman in Perthshire had a tame raven named Jacob, which he kept in a stable. The bird proved of great use in destroying rats, and the methods which he took showed almost human intelligence. In the forenoon, while the servants were out airing the horses, Jacob took care to provide himself with a bone on which was some meat. This he placed near the rat's hole in front of the crib, and then perched himself above, watching the bone with a keen and steady look. When a rat, attracted by the smell, made his appearance, Jacob pounced upon it at once, and dispatched it in an instant. He would then take his place as before and wait for another victim. After the horses returned, and there was no further opportunity for sport, he would leisurely feed upon the game he had captured.

17. TAME CROWS.—When a crow is tamed, he soon learns to distinguish all the members of the family; flies toward the gate, screaming, at the approach of a stranger; learns to open the door by alighting on the latch; attends to meals at regular hours; is extremely noisy and loquacious; imitates the sounds of various words pretty distinctly; and is a great thief and hoarder of curiosities, hiding in holes, corners, and crevices every loose article he can carry off, particularly small pieces of metal, corn, bread, and food of all kinds. He becomes very fond of the one who takes care of him, and will recognize him, after a long absence, with many marks of affection.

18. THE JACKDAW IN LIQUOR.—A tame jackdaw one day found some whisky left upon the kitchen-table, and drank it with great gusto. In a few moments symptoms of intoxication began to appear: his wings drooped, his eyes half closed, he staggered in his walk in the most ludicrous manner, and he seemed to have lost the use of his wings.

He stood upon the edge of the table for a moment, as if meditating flight, when his eyes finally closed, and he fell upon his back with his legs in the air, apparently dead. He was wrapped in a flannel and laid away on the shelf. The next morning his owner expected to find Jackie dead, but he soon emerged from the blanket, took a prodigious draught of water, and, apparently, was no worse for his potations. N. B.—He would never touch whisky again.

19. THE FRIENDLY ROBIN.—Some years ago, in Edinburgh, during a severe storm, a gentleman perceived a robin pecking at the glass. Upon opening the window, the bird hopped into the room and commenced picking up crumbs from the floor. The window was kept closed until the storm was over, by which time the robin had become so tame and pleased with its new quarters that it refused to leave. After a little time it would sit on the table where the gentleman was writing, and, when the day was very cold, it would perch on the fender before the fire. When a stranger came in, it flew to the top of the door, where it perched during the night. It remained a favored inmate of the household until spring, when it took its departure for the summer. In the autumn it came back to its old quarters, and it passed three winters in its comfortable home. The next spring it disappeared, and never came back, much to the regret of the family.

20. THE BOBOLINK.—
"June's bridesman, poet of the year,
  Gladness on wings, the bobolink is here;
  Half-hid in tip-top apple-blooms he swings,
  Or climbs against the breeze with quivering wings,
  Or, giving way to it in a mock despair,
  Runs down, a brook of laughter, through the air."

APPLETONS' READERS.

SOME DISTINGUISHING FEATURES.

Modern Methods made easy.—Education is a progressive science. Methods of the last century must be discarded. The question "How shall we teach reading?" is fully answered in these books, and teachers who have adopted and followed this method have greatly improved their schools.

Word and Phonic Method.—By taking at first words with which the child is quite familiar, and which contain sounds easily distinguished and continually recurring, both teacher and pupil will find the sounds a great help in reading new words as well as in acquiring a distinct articulation.

Spelling.—Words selected from the lessons are given for spelling with each piece, thus affording the best opportunity for oral and written spelling-lessons as well as for definitions. In the Third, Fourth, and Fifth Readers, graded exercises in spelling analysis, together with daily lessons of words often misspelled or mispronounced, are placed in the Appendix for constant study. With these Readers no "Speller" will be needed.

Illustrations.—The illustrations are beautiful and attractive, and are well adapted to serve as a basis for the language and thought lessons that are so prominent in these books.

Helps for Teachers.—Teachers will find in these books a simple plan that will greatly aid them; while the notes, questions, and suggestions will help the teacher to impart the most instruction and the best culture, which makes the reading-lesson something more than a mere naming of words.

Oral Reading.—Proper oral expression depends on the sense. Get the sense of each extract and the correct oral expression will be an easy matter. This is the key-note to Professor Bailey's excellent lessons on accent, emphasis, inflection, and general vocal expression, that are placed as reading-lessons in the Third, Fourth, and Fifth Readers.

Selections.—The selections embrace gems of literature from leading authors. No other readers include such a wide range of thought, showing from the simple stories for children in the earlier books, to the extracts from the best authors in the Fourth and Fifth, unity of design and a just appreciation of the needs of our schools.

Great Success.—Since the publication of these Readers, their sale has averaged nearly a million a year, which is unprecedented in the sale of school-books.

Endorsements.—These Readers have received the endorsement of nearly every educator of note in the United States, but the best proof of their merits is found in the great improvement manifested everywhere they are used.

D. APPLETON & CO., Publishers,
New York, Boston, Chicago, and San Francisco.

APPLETONS'
ELEMENTARY READING CHARTS.

Forty-seven Numbers.

Prepared by REBECCA D. RICKOFF.

WITH PATENT SUPPORTER.

Designed to make learning to read a pleasant pastime.

Designed to cultivate the observing powers of children.

Designed to teach the first steps of reading in the *right* way.

Designed to train the mind of the child by philosophical methods.

Designed to furnish the primary classes with a variety of interesting occupations in school-hours.

Every step in advance is in a logical order of progression and development.

The beautiful and significant illustrations are an especially noticeable and attractive feature of these charts.

Every chart in the series has in view a definite object, which is thoroughly and systematically developed.

Pictures, objects, and things are employed, rather than abstract rules and naked type.

They are in accord with the educational spirit of the day, and with the methods followed by the best instructors.

They are the only charts planned with special reference to the *cultivation of language* and the *power of expression*.

They follow the natural method of teaching, appealing to those faculties of the child that are most easily awakened, and inciting correct mental processes at the outset.

These charts introduce a new and improved mode of suspension while in use, a feature of much practical value.

These charts should be in every primary-school room in the country.

D. APPLETON & CO., Publishers,
New York, Boston, Chicago, and San Francisco.

AN HISTORICAL READER

FOR THE USE OF

CLASSES IN ACADEMIES, HIGH SCHOOLS, AND GRAMMAR SCHOOLS.

By HENRY E. SHEPHERD, M. A.,

SUPERINTENDENT OF PUBLIC INSTRUCTION, BALTIMORE, MARYLAND.

12mo. Cloth, $1.25.

This work consists of a collection of extracts representing the purest historical literature that has been produced in the different stages of our literary development, from the time of Clarendon to the era of Macaulay and Prescott, its design being to present to the minds of young pupils typical illustrations of classic historical style, gathered mainly from English and American writers, and to create and develop a fondness for historical study.

The book is totally devoid of sectarian or partisan tendencies. The biographical and critical notes are just sufficient to stimulate inquiry and independent research. The intention of notes and comments is to suggest new lines of thought, and to develop a taste for more extended investigation.

"This book is one of the most important text-books issued within our recollection. The preface is a powerful attack upon the common method of teaching history by means of compendiums and abridgments. Professor Shepherd has 'long advocated the beginning of history teaching by the use of graphic and lively sketches of those illustrious characters around whom the historic interest of each age is concentrated.' This volume is an attempt to embody this idea in a form for practical use. Irving, Motley, Macaulay, Prescott, Greene, Froude, Mommsen, Guizot, and Gibbon are among the authors represented; and the subjects treated cover nearly all the greatest events and greatest characters of time. The book is one of indescribable interest. The boy or girl who is not fascinated by it must be dull indeed. Blessed be the day when it shall be introduced into our high schools, in the place of the dry and wearisome 'facts and figures' of the 'general history'!"—*Iowa Normal Monthly.*

"The most vivid of historical studies from the hands of the greatest masters of historical description. It is a school-book which deserves a decided success."—*Baltimore Sun.*

"The idea of the book is excellent—to teach history by a sound method; not by abridgments or compendiums, but by taking the student at once to the best historical works and selecting with judgment the masterpieces of the greatest writers. Among the selections we note many of the finest passages of the most eminent historians."—*Wilmington (N. C.) Morning Star.*

For sale by all booksellers; or sent by mail, post-paid, on receipt of price.

New York: D. APPLETON & CO., 1, 3, & 5 Bond Street.

A GEOGRAPHICAL READER,

A COLLECTION OF

Geographical Descriptions and Explanations, from the best Writers in English Literature.

Classified and arranged to meet the wants of Geographical Students.

By JAMES JOHONNOT.

12mo, cloth - - - - - - - $1.25.

It is **original and unique** in conception and execution.

It is varied in style, and treats of **every variety** of geographical topic.

It **supplements** the geographical text-books, and, by giving **additional interest** to the study, it leads the pupil to more extensive geographical **reading and research.**

It is not simply a collection of dry statistics and outline descriptions, but **vivid narrations** of great literary merit, that convey **useful information** and promote **general culture.**

It conforms to the **philosophic ideas** upon which the new education is based.

Its selections are from well-known **writers and standard authorities.**

It is **handsomely bound,** and embellished with numerous illustrations, giving views of many interesting **objects and noted scenery.**

It is an attractive and instructive book for the **home libraries** of both young and old readers.

"Mr. Johonnot has made a good book, which, if judiciously used, will stop the immense waste of time now spent in most schools in the study of geography to little purpose. The volume has a good number of appropriate illustrations, and is printed and bound in almost faultless style and taste."—*National Journal of Education.*

A sample copy, for examination, will be forwarded, post-paid, to any teacher or school-officer, on receipt of 75 *cents.*

New York: D. APPLETON & CO., 1, 3, & 5 Bond Street.

APPLETONS' STUDENTS' LIBRARY.

Consisting of Thirty-four Volumes on Subjects in SCIENCE, HISTORY, LITERATURE, *and* BIOGRAPHY. *In neat 18mo volumes, bound in cloth. Each set put up in a box.*

SOLD IN SETS ONLY.   **PRICE, PER SET, $20.00.**

CONTAINING:

Homer. By W. E. GLADSTONE. Shakespeare. By E. DOWDEN.	1 vol.	The Apostolic Fathers and the Apologists. By the Rev. G. A. JACKSON.
English Literature. By S. A. BROOKE. Greek Literature. By R. C. JEBB.	"	The Fathers of the Third Century. By the Rev. G. A. JACKSON.
Philology. By J. PEILE. English Composition. By J. NICHOL.	"	Thomas Carlyle: His Life—his Books—his Theories. By A. H. GUERNSEY.
Geography. By G. GROVE. Classical Geography. By H. F. TOZER.	"	Ralph Waldo Emerson. By A. H. GUERNSEY. Macaulay: His Life—his Writings. By C. H. JONES.
Introduction to Science Primers. By T. H. HUXLEY. Physiology. By M. FOSTER.	"	Short Life of Charles Dickens. By C. H. JONES.
Chemistry. By H. E. ROSCOE. Physics. By BALFOUR STEWART.	"	Short Life of Gladstone. By C. H. JONES.
Geology. By A. GEIKIE. Botany. By J. D. HOOKER.	"	Ruskin on Painting. The World's Paradises. By S. G. W. BENJAMIN.
Astronomy. By J. N. LOCKYER. Physical Geography. By A. GEIKIE.	"	Town Geology. By CHARLES KINGSLEY.
Political Economy. By W. S. JEVONS. Logic. By W. S. JEVONS.	"	The Childhood of Religions. By E. CLODD.
History of Europe. By E. A. FREEMAN. History of France. By C. YONGE.	"	History of the Early Church. By E. M. SEWELL. The Art of Speech. Poetry and Prose. By L. P. TOWNSEND.
History of Rome. By M. CREIGHTON. History of Greece. By C. A. FYFFE.	"	The Art of Speech. Eloquence and Logic. By L. P. TOWNSEND. The Great German Composers. By G. T. FERRIS.
Old Greek Life. By J. P. MAHAFFY. Roman Antiquities. By A. S. WILKINS.	"	The Great Italian and French Composers. By G. T. FERRIS.
Sophocles. By LEWIS CAMPBELL. Euripides. By J. P. MAHAFFY.	"	Great Singers. First Series. By G. T. FERRIS.
Vergil. By Prof. H. NETTLESHIP. Livy. By W. W. CAPES.	"	Great Singers. Second Series. By G. T. FERRIS.
Milton. By STOPFORD A. BROOKE. Demosthenes. By S. H. BUTCHER.	"	Great Violinists and Pianists. By G. T. FERRIS.

New York: D. APPLETON & CO., 1, 3, & 5 Bond Street.

APPLETONS'
Standard American Geographies.

Based on the Principles of the Science of Education, and giving Special Prominence to the Industrial, Commercial, and Practical Features.

A Comprehensive Course, in Two Books, for Graded Schools.

The remarkable success which Appletons' Readers have attained, both commercially and educationally, is due to the fact that no effort or expense was spared to make them not only mechanically but practically and distinctively superior, in their embodiment of modern experiences in teaching, and of the methods followed by the most successful and intelligent educators of the day.

We now offer a new series of Geographies, in two books, which as far excel all geographical text-books hitherto published as our Readers are in advance of the old text-books in Reading.

BRIEF MENTION OF NOTICEABLE FEATURES.

PREPARED in accordance with the views of the *best teachers and educators.*

The subject is treated first objectively; then subjectively.

No formal definitions; new and necessary *ideas* are imparted in reading-lessons.

Geographical facts are linked with striking facts of *history, natural history, commercial* and *social life.*

Illustrations are furnished on which to base questions leading up from things familiar.

The pupil is taught to appreciate *distance* and to *apply the scale of the map.*

The *system of reviews,* the *written exercises,* the *paragraphs in heavy-faced type,* and the *occasional references to standard works,* are worthy of special attention.

Great prominence is given to *commerce* and to the *leading industries,* which are illustrated with graphic designs.

SUGGESTIVE QUESTIONS, requiring independent thought, are introduced.

Pronunciation of difficult proper names is given where they occur, as well as in the Reference-Tables.

THE STUDY MAPS challenge comparison in point of *correctness, distinctness,* and *artistic finish.* By the use of both *black* and *brown lettering* a convenient study-map is combined with a Reference Map, with marginal indexes.

THE PHYSICAL MAPS are unequaled in usefulness, comprehensiveness, and beauty; the *Commercial Map of the World,* the *Historical Maps,* and the *Map of the Arctic Regions,* will be found of great value for reference.

THE ILLUSTRATIONS are *fresh, graphic,* and *instructive works of art.*

The results of recent discovery, including the last census, have been embodied, and the most trustworthy statistics and authorities have been consulted to insure correctness.

Liberal terms made to schools for introduction and exchange. For prices and full information, address

D. APPLETON & CO., New York, Boston, Chicago, San Francisco.

www.ingramcontent.com/pod-product-compliance
Lightning Source LLC
Chambersburg PA
CBHW051722300426

44115CB00007B/423